T'UNG SHU

T'UNG SHU

THE ANCIENT CHINESE ALMANAC

Edited and translated by
Martin Palmer
with Mak Hin Chung,
Kwok Man Ho and Angela Smith

SHAMBHALA

Boston   1986

SHAMBHALA PUBLICATIONS, INC.
314 Dartmouth Street
Boston, Massachusetts 02116

First Edition
Printed in the United States of America
Distributed in the United States by Random House
and in Canada by Random House of Canada Ltd.

Library of Congress Cataloging in Publication Data
Main entry under title:
T'ung shu, the ancient Chinese almanac.
1. Almanacs, Chinese. I. Palmer, Martin.
AY1148.A8T66   1986   059'.951   85-2520
ISBN 0-87773-346-5 (pbk.)
ISBN 0-394-74221-4 (Random House : pbk.)

CONTENTS

THE SECTIONS OF THE ALMANAC

ACKNOWLEDGEMENTS

As editor I wish to express my thanks to my colleagues in the Chinese section team of the International Consultancy on Religion, Education and Culture (ICOREC). My partners in this endeavour were Barbara Cousins, Kwok Man Ho, Mak Hin Chung and Angela Smith. Together we have spent many months poring over the texts, arguing, researching, discussing and thoroughly enjoying ourselves. The following is the fruit of our labours.

We also owe an enormous amount to others within ICOREC, especially Liz Breuilly, Mr Chan and Ann Gibson. The facilities provided for us by Didsbury Faculty of Manchester Polytechnic, Manchester, and the School of Oriental and African Studies, University of London, were invaluable.

We should also like to thank the many Chinese friends and relations who gave time, trouble, food and advice. To them in particular we owe a great debt of gratitude.

Two Westerners also need mentioning. To Sandra Palmer and Carl Stefan Copley, our thanks. Without their comments we would have finished in half the time and have produced a book of much less value!

Finally to Oliver Caldecott and Sue Hogg – thanks. No team could ask for better, more enjoyable company. If only all publishers were such fun.

MARTIN PALMER

The 16th day of the fifth moon, the Yi Ch'ou year of the Ox
The feast day of Heaven and Earth's union. Birthday of
   Tathagatha Buddha
The 3rd day of July in the Year of Our Lord 1985
The feast day of St Thomas the Doubter (Thomarist)

PREFACE

A book, parts of which have a legendary history stretching back over 2250 years before Christ, which was commonly available in a printed form in the ninth century CE, and which is acknowledged by both Chinese and non-Chinese scholars to have exerted more influence over the lives of ordinary Chinese to the present day than the Confucian Classics, is obviously of considerable importance. Furthermore, any ancient book which has been extensively worked upon by shamans, Taoists, Buddhists, Moslems and Christians at various stages over the last 3000 years has a significance within the study of the history of religion. When you add to this the belief that the book is itself a powerful charm and a guide to everyday life and your personal fortune for every day – which is why just one of the current editions of the book sells over a million copies a year – then it is plain that the Chinese Almanac is no ordinary book. It is thus even more surprising that this is the first time a detailed examination of the book in any language other than Chinese has been published.

The Almanac is known amongst the Cantonese-speaking Chinese as the T'ung Shu – The Book of Myriad Things. (It is often referred to as the T'ung Sing. This is a pun in which the word for 'book' – Shu – is replaced by the word for 'good luck' – Sing. This turns the title into 'Good Luck in Everything', a truly auspicious title.) It is also sometimes referred to as the Calendar – the Li Shu. And these two titles give us the essence of the T'ung Shu. At its heart is the calendar, a careful attempt to give details of the lunar calendar and the seasons. This core of the book has a legendary history of over 4200 years, symbolizing and confirming the rulers' power in China for thousands of years. The annual compilation of the astronomical calendar was the duty of one of the most senior officials and his department within Chinese bureaucracy and the Court. The annual construction of the calendar still continues under the aegis of powerful astrologers in Hong Kong and Taiwan.

Around this calendar core has grown a unique and fascinating collection of other material. From extraordinarily diverse sources has come fortune-telling, divination, geomancy, herbal medicine, physiognomy, palmistry, charms and talismans, moral codes, dictionaries, predictions, legends, planets, auspicious and inauspicious days, numerology, astronomical details, telegram and telex charts, pregnancy charts and stories. Many of these sections have been published annually with the calendar for over 2000 years, whilst others have appeared in the last few decades. The Chinese Almanac therefore constitutes one of the most comprehensive and traditional collections of Chinese belief and practice in existence, and the fact that it still shapes and informs the lives of millions of Chinese today makes it a religio-cultural book of outstanding importance.

Nor is it a fossilized collection of folk wisdom, for the T'ung Shu is still changing and adapting today. Its origins lie, as we have noted, in the calendar, the Imperial Calendar. This was designed to aid agriculture. For many centuries the T'ung Shu was commonly known as the Farmers' Almanac, and most of its practical information was geared to weather, crops, sowing, harvesting and so on. While this still underpins the current T'ung Shu, which is issued each year, the explicitly agricultural side has been diminishing. For instance, the 1984 and 1985 editions from Hong Kong differ. In 1984 there was a two-page section on the proper times for planting and harvesting certain crops. In the 1985 edition this has been removed. Similarly, the abridged editions which have appeared in recent years carry material concerned with the calendar, divination, charms, geomancy and fortune-telling, but very little agricultural material, as they are designed largely for urban overseas Chinese.

Much of the Almanac remains the same each year. The basic processes of divination, horoscopes, fortune-telling, physiognomy, dreams, etc., continue from edition to edition. The roots of some of these sections lie over a thousand years in the past. They are proven, ancient methods. By a process of historical and literary criticism it is possible to detect hints as to the age of other aspects. Readers will find this with regard to the predictions in Section 7 – the Biscuit Poem of Liu Po Wen – which are remarkably accurate up to about the mid-1910s, but which then become very vague, indicating the approximate date of the main composition of the prediction. Another example is that of the scientific explanation of eclipses (Section 39). From study of nineteenth-century editions of the Almanac, it seems likely that this was inserted during the twentieth century as an attempt to respond to the impact of Western science and the resulting criticism of traditional ways.

As regards the rest of the book – those sections which are altered each year – the framework always stays the same while the details change. These parts – for instance Sections 3, 5, 16, 24 and most of 46 – are worked out each year by professional astrologers and astronomers such as Choi Pak Lai of Hong Kong, using methods taken from the last makers of the

Imperial Almanac – the Bureau of Astronomy of the Ch'ing dynasty (1644–1911). It is to these sections, particularly Section 46, the detailed day-by-day account of the year, that people turn to see whether such and such a day is 'lucky' for whatever they are planning to do.

While the T'ung Shu has often been mentioned by both Chinese and non-Chinese writers and scholars, strangely no one has previously translated it or sought to explore this unique storehouse of protoscience, religion, folk wisdom and practice. In presenting this, the first attempt ever to open up the Almanac to the non-Chinese world, we have had to bear a number of issues in mind.

First, there is the persistent difficulty of translating phrases and concepts of a philosophical and religious nature from one language and culture into another. This is not helped in this instance in that over the centuries various errors have crept into the Chinese text which have sometimes caused us great confusion. Added to this is the problem of finding apposite English terms to express complex Chinese traditions and beliefs. It is worth noting here that we have chosen to use the word 'he' in the translations although the Chinese text is often nonspecific. It was felt that although we might be accused of sexism, the use of 'he' accurately reflects the patriarchal presuppositions which are so evident in traditional Chinese life and thought.

Secondly, much of the material is well nigh incomprehensible to ordinary Chinese readers as it is esoteric in nature and requires the skills of a practitioner to reveal the coded meaning. In this we have been aided by two such Chinese colleagues. However, the difficulty of how to give a translation which is worth reading while simultaneously explaining and unravelling very intricate meanings and nuances was constantly with us.

In translating this book we worked in Cantonese, this being the dialect we had in common. Certain parts have been left in Cantonese phonetics where the names are not too important. However, elsewhere we have rendered the characters into the standard Wade-Giles system. We have not used pinyin as this is still largely unfamiliar. However, there are a few examples of pinyin in quoted passages.

The result is that this book is not a word-for-word translation of the Almanac of a particular year. There would be little point in doing this even if it were feasible as it would thus be, in part, out of date before it came off the press. Rather, what we have sought to provide is a mixture of part translation, part description, part explanation. In most cases, it is as much the method, say, of fortune-telling or divination, or the purpose, as in charms and 'Child Talk', as the actual text that is important. For this book will open up the doors into traditional Chinese folk beliefs and practice in a unique way. What it is not capable of doing, nor is it intended to do, is to provide a handbook by which non-Chinese readers can use the Almanac as a guide to daily living. For Chinese readers who have always found the Almanac fascinating but obscure the book will unlock large sections. But for the Western reader it will reveal a whole world of Chinese belief which has been largely ignored or scorned by Westerners. In a sense, it is the last great major Classic to be translated – not a Confucian or a scholarly Classic, but a folk Classic.

The reader will find that some sections contain full or substantial part translations, for example Sections 7, 18 and 26. Other sections contain only those parts in translation which are necessary in order to comprehend the function and use of that section, for example Sections 3, 27 and 34. Finally, a number of sections are of little importance in themselves and, although we have provided a description of them, no translation is given, for example Sections 30 and 39.

May we just remind readers that Chinese books of traditional style are read from what Westerners see as the back to the front. As far as the Chinese are concerned, of course, it is from the front to the back – and therein lies a good illustration! We have also adopted the use of the terms BCE and CE to replace the normal BC and AD. BC stands for 'Before Christ', whilst AD stands for *Anno Domini* – the Year of our Lord. Both these are overtly Christian terms giving specific acknowledgement to the figure of Jesus Christ. In the context of this book it is not appropriate to use these terms, so we have used instead the non-confessional format of BCE – Before the Common Era – and CE – Common Era. The terms BCE and CE simply replace those of BC and AD, hence this year is 1986 CE. In one instance we have used AD, but this is a personal context and relates to the various beliefs of the authors; it is also accompanied by the Chinese date and Buddhist festivals (see p. 8). We would also like to draw the reader's attention to the fact that, in the sections of translation, which are printed in italic, squared brackets contain editorial comment, whilst rounded brackets represent original material thus set apart in the Chinese text.

The Almanac, still in mass publication and used today, has a history of quite astonishing variety and it is to this that we now turn to gain a clearer understanding of The Book of Myriad Things.

INTRODUCTION

There is a scene very early on in the great eighteenth-century Chinese novel *The Dream of the Red Chamber*, by Cao Xueqin, in which two men, a gentleman called Zhen Shi-yin and a poor but ultimately successful scholar, Yu-cun, are discussing the scholar's journey to the capital city. When they have packed money and other such material needs, the following comment is made: 'The almanac gives the nineteenth as a good day for travelling.'[1]

This automatic reference to the Almanac gives some hint at the power and pervasiveness of this extraordinary book. Long commented upon, the Almanac has, however, never been translated in any detail or been regarded as having any great significance because it was termed 'superstitious'. Both Western and Chinese scholars have acknowledged its authority and role in Chinese life. For instance, C. K. Yang comments: 'It is generally recognised that, even in the modern period, the highly religious Almanac (Li-shu) enjoys a much wider sale in China than the "rationalistic" Confucian classics.'[2]

Yang's comments reflect the fact that in the Chinese communities in Southeast Asia, Hong Kong and Taiwan, and in Europe, North America and Australasia, the Almanac continues to exercise much if not all its former power. A visit to any Chinese bookshop in the months just before or just after Chinese New Year will show how popular the Almanac still is – for it enjoys pride of place in the shops and sells very well.

Yet it would be a mistake to think that it is understood fully by ordinary Chinese. The comment made by Mrs J. G. Cormack in 1922 still holds true today. 'It is not used or understood by ordinary people otherwise than as a calendar and recorder of days; but it is indispensable to the diviner.'[3] For most Chinese it is a closed book, opened for them by specialists when the need arises, such as for marriage, funerals, travel, opening new premises, choosing a house and so on. However, there are few homes which do not have a copy of the Almanac, for it is more than just a complicated book with a useful calendar. It is a force, a charm or talisman of great power. It is also so much part of virtually every Chinese person's background and home life that to be without this year's Almanac would be like forgetting to get dressed. Throughout our work on this book we only needed to be seen reading the Almanac, or even just carrying it in our hands, for Chinese people of all ages immediately to start up a conversation about it. This is no dead book, of interest only in a historical sense, such as the Classics. Its power is as great today as it ever was. Wolfram Eberhard writing of Taiwan in 1970 says: '. . . one book which has the widest distribution of all books: the folk almanacs. The almanacs, which have a venerable history of far more than a thousand years. . . . We are told that every Chinese would consult them before he started out on some trip, initiated an important business transaction, or thought of marrying.'[4]

The Almanac, filled as it is with a vast treasury of details, stories, tables, charms, predictions, divination and so on, is also popular as a basic source of knowledge and as a home tutor. Many Chinese children first learn to read or write Chinese from the Almanac. The advice and tables concerning such everyday matters as rearing children or sending telegrams in Chinese are still used in many households, while its dictionary function, in homes where few if any other dictionaries exist, is not to be ignored.

We shall return later to the theme of its role, place and ritual within the home, but it is important first to look at the strong and ancient history of the Almanac.

HISTORY

If tradition and the records of the classic *Shu Ching – The Book of Historical Documents* – parts of which go back to at least the tenth century BCE, are to be believed, then the Almanac, or rather the calendrical part of the Almanac, has been in constant publication for over 4200 years. The traditional first date for publication is 2256 BCE. The event is recorded in the *Shu Ching*, which states that, during the reign of the Emperor Yao, the Emperor commanded two officials or groups of officials to correlate the lunar and solar dates and to advise the ordinary people. 'He commanded Hsis and Ho, in reverent accordance with (their observation of) the wide heavens, to calculate and delineate (the movements and appearances of) the sun, the moon, the stars and the zodiacal spaces and so to deliver respectfully the seasons to be observed by the people.'[5]

It is this event which is traditionally seen as the first formal construction of the calendar – at least so far as Chinese concepts of recorded history go. There is great debate about the value and authenticity of those sections of the *Shu Ching* which deal with the period of the last two of the Five August Emperors (of which Yao was the fourth) and their successors, the Hsia dynasty (*c.* 2000–1523 BCE). Suffice it to say that, within traditional historical thought, Emperor Yao in 2256 BCE instituted a regular publication of the coming year's calendar, expressly for the sake of guiding the people. We know that it was a regular publication because later in the *Shu Ching*, Part 3 Book 4, Hsis and Ho are upbraided for failing, through drunkenness, properly to observe and record the sun, moon, stars and zodiacal spaces. This, according to the *Shu Ching*, has led to chaos: 'They have been the first to allow the regulations of heaven to get into disorder, putting far from them their proper business.'

There is, according to certain Taoist traditions, an even earlier date for the invention of the calendar. Before the Five August Emperors lived semi-human, semi-divine figures, sometimes called the Three August Ones. Credited with living for thousands of years, they taught humans the basic skills of civilization. It is to the first of these Three August Ones, Fu-hsi, that the invention of the calendar is ascribed. Fu-hsi is also credited with inventing marriage, writing, the civil administrative system and the Eight Trigrams. It is only with the later Five August Emperors such as Yao and Shu that specifics are added to these supposed general discoveries.

So we can see that legend at least places the first edition of what has become the fuller Almanac in 2256 BCE. Nor should it be lightly set aside. One of the constant major marks of Imperial authority and power was the right and ability to produce an accurate yearly calendar. By ordering and assisting agriculture, by giving warning of eclipses and movements in the heavens, the Emperor showed he was a true 'son of Heaven', ruling by and with the supreme authority of Heaven. In Chinese political thought, dynasties fell because Heaven had removed its approval and placed the mantle of responsibility on a more worthy line. Part of this mantle was the calendar. To be in control of the heavens and the seasons was to be part of the balance of forces – the yin and yang – of creation. To lose control was a sign of dangerous failure. One of the signs of territorial authority which the emperors gave to vassal kingdoms was the presentation of a copy of the calendar each year. With such deep symbolism inherent within the role of calendrical science, plus its totally agricultural basis, it is quite valid to believe that the calendar goes very far back into Chinese history.

The crucial role of the calendar as a sign of the ruler's right to govern echoes down through the records from the earliest times to today. When the last August Emperor, Shun, took over from Yao, the *Shu Ching* recalls that: 'He gave audience to the nobles of the East, putting in accord their seasons and

, and rectifying the days.'[6] The historian Ssu-ma
writing *c.* 100 BCE, records that T'ang, the over-
.... r of the Hsia dynasty and founder of the Shang dynasty,
'changed the initial month and the first day' of the calendar.[7]
This idea of altering the calendar as a sign both of a new
dynasty and of taking on the mantle of authority continues
throughout Chinese history to our own century, as we shall
see.

Similarly, the *Shu Ching* records that, at the fall of the
Shang, Emperor Wu, the founder of the Chou dynasty (*c.* 1028
BCE), sought advice on how to rule and was informed of the
importance of the regulation of the year through the calendar.[8]

When the Chou dynasty fell in 221 BCE to Cheng of the new
Ch'in dynasty, Ssu-ma Ch'ien again records that there were
many changes, amongst them that 'the start of the year was
changed to the first day of the tenth moon'.[9]

With the appearance of Cheng, the first Emperor of what we
would think of as China proper, we come to one of the most
complete and interesting documents in this long history. For
preserved virtually intact in the Five Classics, in the *Li Chi*
(*The Record of Rites*), is a copy of the Imperial Almanac. It is
difficult to date this copy, but it is thought to have been
compiled by Lu Pu-wei (the famous Prime Minister of the
Ch'in) around 250 BCE. Legend places it in the twelfth century
BCE, but we can be fairly sure that a date between 300 and 250
BCE is more appropriate. The section of the *Li Chi* containing
this detailed calendar is known as the *Yueh Ling*. Although its
date of formal compilation is post-Confucian, it is very likely
that contained within it are traditions and details which go
back to pre-Confucian times. So much of the symbolism of
direction, heaven, earth and colour is found in Chou- and
Shang-dynasty material that it seems probable that much of
the ritual associated with the *Yueh Ling* is of considerable
antiquity. To give the reader some feel of the earliest extant
copy of the Imperial Almanac, here are some of the details for
the first month of spring. Readers may like to compare these
with the translation and notes concerning the calendar and
festivals section of the present Almanac (Section 46).

In the first month of spring, the sun is in Shih, the star culminating at
dusk being Zhan, and that culminating at dawn, Wei. Its days are
Chia and Yi [the first two Heavenly Stems; see p. 34 below]. Its divine
ruler is Thai Hao, and the spirit is Kau-mang. . . . The east winds
resolve the cold. Creatures that have been torpid during the winter
begin to move. The fish rise up to the ice. Otters sacrifice fish. The
wild geese make their appearance. . . . In this month there takes place
the inauguration of spring. Three days before this ceremony, the
Grand Recorder informs the Son of Heaven, saying, 'On such and

such a day is the inauguration of the spring. The energies of the season are fully seen in wood'. . . . He also orders the Grand Recorder to guard the statutes and maintain the laws, and (especially) to observe the motions in the heavens of the sun and moon, and of the zodiacal stars in which the conjunction of these bodies take place, so that there should be no error as to where they rest and what they pass over; that there should be no failure in the record of all these things, according to the regular practice of early times.[10]

Throughout its detailed prescription for the twelve moons, many of the features of our present Almanac are to be found, such as the Five Elements, the Ten Heavenly Stems and Twelve Earthly Branches, eclipses, the Twenty-Four Joints and Breaths (see p. 30), festivals and agricultural hints. As we have seen, the *Yueh Ling* sees itself as being heir to age-old traditions 'according to the regular practice of early times'. Here, in our earliest copy of the Almanac, over 250 years before Christ, the Almanac sees itself as merely the most recent in a long line.

In the writings of the historian Ssu-ma Ch'ien, the calendar appears very clearly as the powerbroker of Imperial politics as well as the centre of the best intellectual minds of the Han dynasty. Ssu-ma Ch'ien himself worked on the calendar and assisted in its thorough revision.[11] The following picture is found in his *Shih Chi – The Records of the Historian*. It relates to the early years of the Han.

When Chang Ts'ang became minister of calculation, however, he set to work arranging and rectifying the calendar and the pitch-pipes which had been neglected up to this time. Since Kan-tsu had first reached Pa-shang in the 10th month, he continued the old Ch'in practice of beginning the new year with the 10th month and made no change. Calculating the cycle of the Five Elements Chang Ts'ang decided that the Han corresponded to a period dominated by the element Water and should therefore honour black, the colour of water. . . .

When Chang Ts'ang became chancellor he brought his labours to completion and for this reason all who expound the pitch-pipes and the calendar for the House of Han base themselves upon Chang Ts'ang's work. Chang Ts'ang always loved books. There were none he did not examine and none he did not understand, but what he loved most were matters pertaining to the pitch-pipes and the calendar.[12]

Chang Ts'ang, however, was ousted by Kung-sun Ch'en who said the Han was dominated by the element Earth. As proof he predicted that a yellow dragon would appear in the next few years. Chang Ts'ang refuted this before the Emperor. A few years later just such a dragon was reported. Chang Ts'ang was dismissed, Kung-sun Ch'en appointed and he immediately installed a new calendar.

This small incident gives a sense of the status of the calendar and the authority it carried.

It is also recorded that during the decline of the Chou and rise of the Ch'in the concept of auspicious and inauspicious days arose. With the very sudden collapse of the Ch'in empire, this trend towards the inclusion of lucky days, evil stars and so on gained ground. The idea of order and harmony was now even more important, as the brutal Ch'in empire seemed to show that force and terror are not the ways of Heaven.

Even the normally stoic Confucians were beginning to be drawn into speculation about fortunes and prediction. We find the great Confucianist thinker Hsun Tzu in the early years of the Han dynasty (c. 250 BCE) writing thus: 'Heaven has its seasons, Earth its resources and man his government. Thus is man able to form a triad with Heaven and Earth. If man neglects his own role in the triad, and puts all his trust in Heaven and Earth with which he is part of the triad, he is making a terrible mistake.'[13] If man played his part and was in accord with Heaven and Earth, then all was well. Should this fail, then calamity.

But Hsun Tzu found it necessary to criticize sternly the drift away from bold principles towards the study of auspicious and inauspicious days, omens and divination. His protests were in vain. By the time of the T'ang dynasty (618–906 CE) the selection of auspicious and inauspicious days had come to dominate the calendar in the way that it still does today.

The invention of block printing in the early seventh century CE proved a massive boost to the use of the calendar and its development as an almanac. It seems likely that the Almanac was one of the first books published by printing and soon came to dominate the printed world. In 835 CE the writer Feng Su commented:

In all the provinces of Szechwan and Huai-nan, printed calendars are on sale in the markets. Every year, before the Imperial Observatory has submitted the new calendars for approval and had it officially promulgated, these printed calendars have flooded the empire. This violates the principle that (the Calendar) is a gift of His Majesty.[14]

This evidence means that the Almanac has the longest continuous printed history of any book in the world: the British Museum has a printed edition of 877.

Having seen the development of the Calendar–Almanac in its first three thousand years as recorded by the Chinese, we obtain our next important piece of information not from a Chinese writer but from a Westerner, Marco Polo. In his *Travels* Polo, who visited and worked in China from 1275 to 1293 CE, describes on two occasions the role and function of the Almanac. Early on in the journey to the city of Kublai Khan, the modern-day Peking, Polo arrives at the city of Campichu in the province of Tanguth (in present-day Inner Mongolia). He reports that 'They employ an almanac, in many respects like our own, according to the rules of which, during five, four or three days of the month, they do not shed blood, nor eat flesh or fowl; as is our usage in regard to Friday, the Sabbath and the vigils of the saints.'[15]

Later on he describes the role of the astrologers at the Khan's court in Kambalu (Peking).

There are in the city of Kambalu, amongst Christians, Saracens and Cathaians, about five thousand astrologers and soothsayers. . . . They have their astrolabes upon which are described the planetary signs, the hours and their several aspects for the whole year. The astrologers of each distinct sect annually proceed to the examination of their respective tables, in order to ascertain the course of the heavenly bodies, and their relative positions. They discover therein what the state of the weather shall be, from the paths of the planets in the different signs, and from this foretell the peculiar phenomena of each month. For instance, they predict that there shall be thunder and storms in a certain month, earthquakes; in another, strokes of lightning and violent rains; in another, diseases, mortality, wars, discords, conspiracies.

As they find the matter in their astrolabes, so they declare it will come to pass; adding, however, that God, according to his good pleasure, may do more or less than they have set down. They write their predictions for the year upon certain small squares, which are called Tacuin, and these they sell, for a groat apiece, to all persons who are desirous of peeping into the future.

Those whose predictions are found to be the more generally correct are esteemed the most perfect masters of their art, and are consequently the most honoured.

When any person forms the design of executing some great work, of performing a distant journey in the way of commerce, or of commencing any other undertaking, and is desirous of knowing what success may be likely to attend it, he has recourse to one of these astrologers, and, informing him that he is about to proceed on such an expedition, inquires in what disposition the heavens appear to be at the time. The latter thereupon tells him, that before he can answer, it is necessary he should be informed of the year, the month, and the hour in which he was born; and that, having learned these particulars, he will then proceed to ascertain in what respect his horoscope corresponds with the aspect of the celestial bodies at the time of making the inquiry. Upon this comparison he grounds his prediction of the favourable or unfavourable termination of the adventure.

The importance of the Almanac, which Polo draws out, in deciding major events and auspicious days reflects exactly its current use. By now not only was there the Imperial Calendar – still very much in the style of the *Yueh Ling* – but there were also other versions, which were based upon the Imperial one but reflected the specific interests of particular groups. For instance, the Almanac Polo encountered in Campichu was almost certainly a Lamaist Buddhist one – hence the prohibition on meat. In Kambalu Polo records Christians, Moslems (Saracens) and Taoists/Confucians (Cathaians) at work. Each group produced its own Almanac, and particular lords and powerful religious centres also produced their own.

While Polo was in China, one of the most eminent mathematicians of the Yuan dynasty (1260–1368), Kuo Shou-ching (*c.* 1290), gathered together all the almanacs he could find and produced the first ever attempt at an overall system. This he published under the title *A System of Divination – Sou-shi-shuh*. With this publication, the pattern of the Almanac was set. Calendar, divination, advice, tales, charts, feng-shui (geomancy) and so on, side by side – one of the most important collections of official and unofficial Chinese religious beliefs available.

Under the Yuan dynasty, the Calendar was extensively reformed, but not by Taoists, Buddhists or Confucians. Into the complex history of the Almanac comes another faith – Islam.

As Polo records, the Mongols filled the main official posts with non-Chinese, as they did not trust the Chinese. Into positions of power came Mongols, Nestorian Christians and most particularly Moslems. With an empire stretching from Russia to Peking and taking in Persia en route, the influence of Islam was extensive and came to colour the later stages of the Mongol empire. It is recorded that in 1267 a Persian Moslem astronomer arrived in Peking with a collection of astronomical instruments. A major debate then took place between Islamic calendrical science – which only observes the lunar year – and the Chinese lunar/solar year (see pp. 29–31) – which was defended by the mathematician and inventor Kuo Shou-ching. The end result was a compromise. Keeping the old-style mixed calendar, the Yuan emperors appointed Moslems to run it and asked them to develop more sophisticated astronomical instruments. These beautiful instruments were made around 1300 CE – one set for Peking and one for Pingyang. The Peking set is still in situ, although some pieces were looted by the Germans after the Boxer Uprising in 1901 and only restored after the defeat of Germany in the First World War. Of the Pingyang set, more later.

Moslems continued to play an important role in the Bureau of Astronomy and the Department of Calendrical Studies until well into the seventeenth century. Indeed, for many people in the seventeenth century Islam and the calendar were so interconnected that legends placed the arrival of Moslem astronomers back at the very start of Islam. In 1657 CE, Wu Ming-hsuen, a Moslem astronomer of considerable power, stated that, '1058 years ago, eighteen men from the Western area' had come to China bringing Islamic calendrical science.[16]

Under Islamic guidance one might have expected that the 'magical' and auspicious aspects of the Almanac would have diminished. Not a bit of it. The pattern was too well set, and with the coming of the Ming dynasty (1368–1644 CE) it was further consolidated. The collection of almanacs published by Kuo Shou-ching was further expanded and published under Imperial edict with the title *Ta-t'ung – Official Almanac*. It is from this Ming title that the popular mass-produced almanacs (now, of course, lacking any Imperial model) derive their title *T'ung Shu*.

It must not be thought, however, that the criticisms of superstitious elements of the Almanac, voiced originally by Hsun Tzu, had ceased. During the T'ang period many attacks were made on it, particularly by Lu-ts'ai, the Minister of Rites under Emperor T'ai-tsung (627–50 CE). He sought to persuade the people to give up the habit of lucky days, etc., and return to the 'ancient ways'. In the Yuan period, Hsieh Ying-fang (*c.* 1350) included a penetrating critique of astrology, divination, feng-shui, physiognomy and lucky and unlucky days in his study *Pien Huo Pien – Disputes on Doubtful Matters*. Under the Ming, this was carried further by Ts'ao-tuan (*c.* 1400) and Wang Ch'uan-shan (*c.* 1650). In all cases it was Confucians who ridiculed the superstitious aspects of the Almanac, and Taoists and Buddhists who defended it.

Into this history now steps perhaps the strangest contributors to the Almanac – none other than Renaissance-inspired Christians from Europe in the guise of the Order of the Society of Jesus, better known as the Jesuits. For nearly two hundred years the Jesuits were to exercise immense power over the Bureau of Astronomy and the Department of Calendrical Studies. For two periods – 1629–64 and 1669–87 – Jesuits held the most senior post of Director of the Bureau of Astronomy, responsible not only for predicting eclipses, recording dates and such like, but also for determining auspicious days, lucky stars, Taoist, Buddhist and Confucian festivals, and so on. The very system by which the dates of the present Almanac are computed was devised by Jesuits. How did this come about?

The story begins with Matteo Ricci who pioneered Jesuit work in China. Although Nestorian Christianity (a heretical form common throughout Central Asia) had arrived in the seventh century and survived into the fourteenth century,

Christianity had virtually no impact on the mainstream of Chinese thought. In the 1570s, as contact became possible through Portuguese traders, the Roman Catholic Church turned its attention to China and Japan. Foremost amongst the missionaries were the Jesuits. Highly trained and learned, they sought to draw into Christianity the best of each culture and faith they encountered. Matteo Ricci, for instance, spent twenty years studying the Chinese language and Classics, until he was more learned and skilled than many of the scholars. Into the somewhat arid world of Chinese scholarship he introduced not only Christianity but also the intellectual, astronomical and mechanical knowledge of the Renaissance. The Chinese scholars showed great interest in this knowledge and in Christianity, and by stages Ricci was allowed to draw closer and closer to Peking and the Imperial Court. In 1599, fifteen years after arriving in China, he was in Nanking, the capital of Southern China. He was invited to visit the astronomical observatory in the Imperial University. Here he found an extraordinary sight – beautiful astrolabes and gnomon wrought in delicate ironwork. Impressed, he sought details from his escort, who began to get agitated. Then Ricci made a discovery which began the extraordinary climb of the Jesuits to the directorship of the Bureau. The instruments were a complete mystery to the officials. They could not work them. Ricci soon discovered why. The instruments were aligned for use on the 36-degree line. Nanking stands on 32. These were none other than the Pingyang Islamic instruments of the Yuan dynasty, which had been brought south but never realigned.

When Ricci eventually succeeded in being allowed to work in Peking in 1602, he translated astronomical works and presented them to the Court, sure that if he were permitted to reform the calendar he could strike a blow at the superstitious practices which surrounded it and thus discredit Taoism and Buddhism. He died in 1610 without achieving this, but in 1613 one of the Chinese converts, and an important member of the Court, Leo Li, was able to get a revision of the calendar undertaken by Ricci's assistant, Sabatino de Ursis, owing to the failure by the Bureau in 1610 to predict accurately an eclipse. However, opposition within the Bureau prevented any use being made of it. In 1629 a Christian convert, Hsu Kuang-ch'i, was made Director of the Bureau, but opposition continued.

It was not until 1644 that the Jesuits consolidated their hold. Adam Schall, another Jesuit, had arrived in Peking in 1623 to carry on Ricci's work. By 1644 he was respected by the authorities. On 29 July he issued a challenge to the Bureau and Department. Could they accurately predict the exact time of an eclipse due to fall on 1 September? The Emperor allowed this challenge to take place and Schall's predictions, based on Western astronomy, were correct. Those of the Bureau and Department were not. Schall was appointed Director of the Bureau, and the calendar passed firmly into Christian control. Schall ran the Bureau, along reformed lines, until 1664, two years before his death. He was ousted by the traditionalists who returned to the old methods, but in 1669 a worthy successor, Ferdinand Verbiest, again challenged the traditional interpretation. He won against both Yang Kuang-hsien, a Taoist astronomer, and Wu Ming-hsuen, a Moslem. The Bureau returned to Jesuit hands.

Although Schall and Verbiest stand out both as individuals and as Directors, Jesuits continued to service the Bureau and Department from Verbiest's death in 1687 until the Society of Jesus was suppressed worldwide by the Pope in 1773.

How did the Jesuits cope with responsibility for lucky days, etc.? Ricci's dream had been to reform the calendar and its associated material. This did not happen. One Dominican writer (the Dominicans were never great fans of the Jesuits) recorded in his diary: 'Father Adam being president of the College of Mathematics, had the charge of, as well in Political as Religious respects, assigning lucky and unlucky days for everything they are to do (tho some excused the said Father as to this particular).' His duties, reported the monk, were to choose 'days and hours for everything except eating, drinking and sinning'.[17]

In other words, the Almanac, as it approached its reputed 4000th year of publication, had easily absorbed both Moslem and Christian assistance, but remained itself. However, serious challenges were beginning to appear on the horizon.

In 1644 the Ming dynasty fell to the Manchu horsemen who swept over the Great Wall and captured China. They founded the Ch'ing dynasty – the last Imperial dynasty of China. In the early days, particularly under K'ang Hsi (1661–1722), the Ch'ing brought prosperity to China. But soon the incursions of British imperialism moving out from India were felt. By the middle of the nineteenth century China was being 'opened up' by a mixture of missionaries, adventurers and gunboats. Vast peasant revolts took place, of which the T'ai-ping ('Great Peace') rebellion of 1848–64 is the most significant. This revolt, which came close to toppling the Ch'ing dynasty, and which at its peak controlled almost half of China, had a crude form of Protestant Christianity as its basis. Apart from its leader, Hung Hsiu-chuan, believing himself to be the younger brother of Jesus Christ, the movement showed its evangelical Christian roots in attacks on all 'idols' and 'superstition'.

Although it was a largely peasant-based revolution, this did not spare the Almanac. One of the constant planks of the T'ai-ping programme was the abolition of the old calendar and its replacement by the Western Julian-style calendar and the seven-day week. As at any other time when there was a change of dynasty, the calendar was altered. Unlike previous success-ful and unsuccessful claimants to the mantle of Heaven, the T'ai-ping threw out the collected wisdom and details of the old Almanac and produced instead Westernized versions without the details. When the revolution was finally suppressed, with terrible loss of life, the Almanac reappeared in the T'ai-ping areas without opposition.

The Protestant mission to China started within the first decade of the nineteenth century. By the end of the century there were more Protestant missionaries in China than in the rest of the world. Their impact was enormous, not least in terms of education and science. And they saw the Almanac, along with much else of Chinese religious life, as simply superstition or, at worst, the work of the Devil. With the impetus for reform and Westernization, the Almanac began to be challenged more seriously than ever before. The voices of Confucians, modernists, republicans and Christians were raised against much of China's traditional past.

Then, in 1911, the Ch'ing dynasty fell, to be replaced by a shaky republicanism headed – in theory – by Sun Yat-sen. With the end of Imperial rule (apart from an abortive attempt to found a new dynasty in 1915 and an attempted Ch'ing restoration in 1917) the Imperial Calendar ended. The new Republican government introduced the Western Gregorian-style calendar, and it appeared that the days of the Almanac were numbered. Yet, despite for the first time in its history the lack of an emperor, the Almanac continued to appear. Indeed, the astrologers continued to be employed by the various warlords who controlled Peking, and publication continued unabated. An attempt was made by the National-ist government, in 1927, to ban the Almanac but this was not pursued with much enthusiasm, and soon the government were endorsing what they now termed the Nang Li – the Farmers' Calendar – thus distinguishing it from the official Western calendar. Now, instead of being Imperial and issued in the such and such year of Kuang Hsu, or whoever was the Emperor, the Almanac came out in the such and such year of the Republic. The Taiwanese-authorized Almanacs continue this, 1986–87 being the seventy-sixth year of the Republic.

In 1923 Mrs J. G. Cormack recorded that: 'The Almanac is prepared annually by the astrologers appointed by the ruler of the land, who have their offices near the east wall of the city of Peking in close proximity to the astronomical instruments set up by the Jesuit Fathers.'[18]

While all seemed relatively smooth, the most serious threat ever to the continuity and role of the Almanac was being set in motion. In March 1927 a young man published his first serious political and revolutionary analysis. The work was called *Report on an Investigation of the Peasant Movement in Hunan*. It was written for the fledgling Chinese Communist Party by one Mao Tse-tung. In chapter 7, entitled 'Overthrowing the Clan Authority of the Ancestral Temples and Clan Elders, the Religious Authority of Town and Village Gods, and the Masculine Authority of Husbands', the first hint of what lay in store for traditional Chinese beliefs was spelled out.

While I was in the countryside, I did some propaganda against superstition among the peasants. I said:

'If you believe in the Eight Characters, you hope for good luck; if you believe in geomancy, you hope to benefit from the location of your ancestral graves. This year within the space of a few months the local tyrants, evil gentry and corrupt officials have all toppled from their pedestals. Is it possible that until a few months ago they all had good luck and enjoyed the benefit of well-sited ancestral graves, while suddenly in the last few months their luck has turned and their ancestral graves have ceased to exert a beneficial influence? The local tyrants and evil gentry jeer at your peasant association and say "How odd! Today the world is a world of committeemen. Look, you can't even go to pass water without bumping into a committeeman!" Quite true, the towns and the villages, the trade unions and the peasant associations, the Kuomintang and the Communist Party, all without exception have their executive committee members – it is indeed a world of committeemen. But is this due to the Eight Characters and the location of the ancestral graves? How strange! The Eight Characters of all the poor wretches in the countryside have suddenly turned auspicious! And their ancestral graves have suddenly started exerting beneficial influences! The Gods? Worship them by all means. But if you had only Lord Kuan and the Goddess of Mercy and no peasant association, could you have overthrown the local tyrants and evil gentry? The gods and goddesses are indeed miserable objects. You have worshipped them for centuries, and they have not overthrown a single one of the local tyrants or evil gentry for you! Now you want to have your rent reduced. Let me ask how you will go about it? Will you believe in the gods or in the peasant association?'[19]

During the 1930s and 1940s the Almanac's influence as well as production declined rapidly. War, Communism, Christian-style education, republicanism, science and the upsurge of rationalism cast heavy shadows of doubt over the book. The attraction of all things modern and/or Western meant it was a lean time for traditional beliefs. Many peasants still followed the old ways and used the Almanac, but increasingly they were criticized and urged to look to more modern forms of agricultural planning and production. Under both Chiang Kai-shek and Mao Tse-tung there was little space for the old-style calendar and its various functions.

In 1949 the Communist Party won the Civil War and established the People's Republic of China. While religious freedom was guaranteed, so was the right to propagate against religion. This, combined with a scientific materialist approach to agriculture, led to major attempts to eradicate the Almanac. Dr Joseph Needham records that in the early 1950s the Academia Sinica joined in: 'Until very recently, calendars produced in country towns always marked lucky and unlucky days, and not many years ago the Academia Sinica itself began to publish rural calendars in order to attack the superstition and to impart elementary astronomical information.'[20]

It is difficult to tell exactly when, if ever, production of the Almanac ceased in mainland China. Given the extent to which traditional religious practices have re-emerged in the recent softening of attitudes since the fall of the Gang of Four in 1976, it is perhaps unwise to assume that production of the Almanac ever ceased in China. At certain points we catch a glimpse of a peasantry who are far from abandoning the older practices. In an article published in the *People's Daily* in 1963, Ya Han-chang commented:

Among the people of our country, especially people of the Han nationality [of pure Chinese ethnic background] such superstitious activities as fortune telling, physiognomy, and geomancy were quite prevalent in the past. While these, of course, are superstitions, they are not religious, being neither the activities of any religion nor any religions in themselves. Among the people of the Han nationality in our country, those who really believe in any religion and are the followers of any religion are numerically in the minority. But, among the peasants especially, those who believe in the existence of spirits and gods, in fate, and in such superstitions as fortune telling, physiognomy, and geomancy are still quite numerous. In view of this, we must be good not only at struggling against religious superstitions but also at struggling against all other kinds of ordinary superstitious activities.[21]

In 1977 an attempt was made to abolish the giving of the old calendar dates alongside the Western calendar in mainland Chinese newspapers. This has failed and in the mid-1980s the old dates and calendar reappeared.

The only apparent reference to the Almanac in the media of mainland China in recent years appears in the newspaper *Red Flag* on 16 February 1981. The following report is taken from the *Religion in the People's Republic of China*.

Red Flag on 16.2.81 carried an article by Zhong Chuping entitled 'It is the glorious duty of publishing workers to publish more good books for the broad masses of peasants', in which the author discussed the necessity of publishing good reading material for the peasants who constitute eighty per cent of China's population. More good books are needed to meet the demand and also to strengthen ideological and political work in the rural areas. It is important, the article claims, to propagate the ideology of socialism and communism and to clear away the influence of feudal and bourgeois ideas. The author notes: 'We should also see that feudal and superstitious activities are quite common and absurd books and magazines and harmful novels are found everywhere. . . .'[22]

It seems highly probable that amongst the 'absurd books' is the Almanac. This is strengthened by the list given over and over again in the Chinese press of what it calls 'superstitious' practices. For most of those listed, the Almanac would be a basic source, without which they could not function. The *Guangming Daily* on 20 April 1981 gave a typical list:

When we talk about feudal superstition, we usually mean telling fortunes by using the eight diagrams [*sic*], feeling a person's bones and looking at his appearance to forecast his future, practising geomancy, reading horoscopes in search of an elixir of life, exorcising spirits to cure illness, planchette-writing, offering sacrifices to the gods, beseeching gods to bestow children on people, offering prayers to gods to ward off calamities and to ask for rain and so on.[23]

The present Almanacs, published largely in Hong Kong and Taiwan, are enormously popular. The Hong Kong edition sells well over a million copies each year and the numbers are rising. Despite all that has happened in the last eighty-odd years, the Almanac has survived and its influence has spread beyond the confines of China itself to the many overseas communities. This very book itself testifies to the continuing significance of the Almanac, being the first book not in Chinese to deal exclusively with the Almanac.

Opposition to the Almanac, as we have seen, has long been in existence. The Confucian scholars from Hsun Tzu to this century have attacked its 'superstitious' role and its authority. Modern doctrines have now entered the fray but still the Almanac continues. Perhaps the despisal of the Communist authorities can be put into a succinct historical perspective. This chapter opened with the scene from *The Dream of the Red Chamber* in which the gentleman Zhen Shi-yin automatically referred to the Almanac for an auspicious day to travel. Lower down the same page comes this – the other side of the Chinese relationship with this most ancient book. A servant reports back to Zhen Shi-yin.

'The monk says that Mr Jia set out for the capital at five o'clock this morning, sir. He says he left a message to pass on to you. He said to tell you, "A scholar should not concern himself with almanacs, but should act as the situation demands", and he says there was not time to say goodbye.'[24]

THE ALMANAC AND ITS RITUAL

As we have seen, the Almanac, or rather its calendrical section in particular, is no ordinary book. Invested with, as well as investor of, Imperial authority, it was a symbol of the current ruler's right of office. As such, it became in certain circumstances the very embodiment of the Emperor. This passage from the *Ta Tai Li Chi* (*Records of Rites of the Older Tai*), *c*. second century BCE, reminds us succinctly of the authority of the calendar:

Thereby the sage can be the master of Heaven and Earth, the master of the mountains and rivers, the master of the gods and spirits and the master of the sacrifices in the ancestral temple. The sage marks carefully the numbers of the sun and moon, so he can observe the motions of the stars and constellations, and thence arrange the four seasons in order according to their progressions and retrogradations. This is called the 'calendar'.[25]

The calendar was prepared annually by the Bureau and Department, and its construction was a highly formalized procedure. Once the Emperor had inspected it and declared it good, copies were made. These were then presented formally to all high-ranking officials and to vassal states when they rendered their annual tribute. Copies bound for the provinces were treated as though they were the Emperor himself. They were carried in sedan chairs and upon arrival they were placed upon a special chair while proclamations of loyalty were made before them, ending in later years with the ceremonial prostration and banging of the head upon the ground three times – the kowtow.

Although all the Imperial traditions have now gone, certain remnants of this attitude can still be found where the Almanac is still freely published. For instance, each New Year, Choi Pak Lai, the calendar maker of Hong Kong, presents a copy of his tables to the Governor of Hong Kong. The Almanac is received with due solemnity. While this is in fact a reversal of the Imperial pattern, it reflects the authority and status of the Almanac, even when the recipient is a foreigner.

In the homes of Chinese around the world, traditions as old as the Imperial ones still continue. As we saw earlier, the Almanac is one of the most common books, if not the most common book, to be found in Chinese homes since the Diaspora. Nor is it simply yet another book. It is a manifestation, a representative of that other world, Heaven, of which this world is but a poor reflection.

It is customary to buy the new Almanac about a month before New Year itself. The book is kept, carefully wrapped and placed upon a high shelf. To put the Almanac under a table, on the floor or in any other disrespectful position is to court trouble. On New Year's Eve, after supper when all the family are gathered (see Section 46, Major Festivals), the old Almanac is taken down from its hook by the main door. The new copy is then hung up by the red cord loop at the top of the book. Many people will wash their hands before doing so as a sign of respect. From then on until the next New Year's Eve, the Almanac will function as charm and talisman, calendar and dictionary, medical guide and planner. The old Almanac, so highly charged with spiritual power, is not just cast aside. Where possible, it is taken to a temple and presented to the monks or priests who will then burn it in one of the large incinerators kept in the temple grounds. These incinerators are used for burning Bank of Hell notes and other paper offerings used at funerals (see Ch'ing Ming in Section 46, Major Festivals). Thus the powers of the Almanac are released back to Heaven. Where no temple exists nearby, the Almanac will be carefully burned by the father of the family, in the back courtyard or garden – again just as happens at Ch'ing Ming or funerals when the family cannot use a temple.

We have already mentioned the use to which the Almanac is put for cures, in pregnancy and in physical distress. It is also used to prevent nightmares and other 'terrors of the night'. In all these situations, those handling the book will do so with clean hands and with a degree of reverence. This is no ordinary tome.

THE CONSTRUCTION OF THE CALENDRICAL CHARTS

For Christians BC and AD denote the central historical importance of Jesus. For Moslems, the dates start with Mohammed's journey to Medina in 622 CE. For Jews, the start of dating time commences with the traditional date of the Creation. For the Chinese, the traditional starting point for reckoning time is 2637 BCE. In this year the Prime Minister of the first of the Five August Emperors, Huang-ti, according to legend, worked out the cycle of sixty years which lies at the centre of calendrical study. For all calendrical study the major problem is the same. How can the solar year be reconciled with the lunar cycle?

The Chinese solution comprises the introduction, every two to three years, of an extra month. The reason for this is quite simple. The lunar year consists of the twelve moons. These periods last just over 29½ days each. In order to keep the days in each moon as full days, the year is made up of six 'small' months, each being 29 days long, and six 'big' months, each being 30 days long. This gives a grand total of 354. Some years will have seven 'big' months = 355 days, and every so often there will be seven 'small' months = 353. Thus, on average, each lunar year falls short of the solar year by 10, 11 or occasionally 12 days, per year. To bring the calendar in line again it is necessary to put in an extra month at roughly three-year intervals. These extra months (see Section 4 for examples from 1801 to 1885 CE) come after the month they are equated with. Hence, in 1984 the extra month was month 10, and thus it came after the normal month 10, and had 29 days. In 1987 the extra month is month 6, hence it comes after the normal month 6. Early on in Chinese astronomy it was noted that over a period of nineteen years the sun and moon move through a cycle, returning to their relative positions at the end of every nineteen years. It seems that this principle was discovered possibly as early as the Shang dynasty. From this, the astronomers were able to evolve a regular number of extra months. It was found that during each nineteen-year cycle, seven years needed an extra month. This principle was also discovered, later than the Chinese, by the Athenian Meton. His discovery was considered to be so important that the details of the Metonic Cycle were carved in the Temple of Athena on the Acropolis.

As for the solar year – the months being the province of the lunar cycle – it is subdivided in twenty-four two-week periods known collectively as the Twenty-Four Joints and Breaths. They start on the days when the sun is in the 1st or the 15th degree of each of the animal signs (see below, pp. 34–6). Those on the 1st are called 'principal terms'; those on the 15th 'divisional terms'. This set of twenty-four starts almost always on 4 February, with the Li Ch'un – the Beginning of Spring (see Section 5).

So far as the Almanac is concerned, Li Ch'un is the real start of the year – the agricultural year – and for this reason the very first page of the Almanac is concerned with the Li Ch'un festival (see Section 1). As the Twenty-Four Joints and Breaths never alter, barring one day or so, they are a very good grid reference for the year. Moreover, their names – Beginning of Spring, Coming of Rain, or Great Cold – are usually very precise forecasts of the type of weather to be expected. The terms originated in northern China, the original homeland of the Han people. As such they reflect the weather conditions of that area best. However, even if 'Great Snow' does not precisely describe the weather conditions in Hong Kong on and after 7 December, the spirit of the statement is certainly accurate!

The lunar year begins, of course, with New Year. Because of the fluctuation of a month in the calendar, New Year falls between 21 January and 20 February. Thus, Li Ch'un, the start of the solar year, can often fall before New Year and on occasion can fall twice within the same year. For instance, 1984–85 – the year of the Rat – had an extra month 10. New Year fell on 2 February 1984 with Li Ch'un coming as usual on 4 February. New Year 1985 did not come until 20 February; hence on 4 February, the 15th day of the twelfth moon of the year of the Rat, Li Ch'un came again. As Chinese astrology usually takes the start of a year from Li Chun, this means that anyone born on or after the 15th day of the twelfth moon in the year of the Rat (1984–85) is counted as having been born under the sign of the next year, the year of the Ox. Thus it is important when calculating Chinese year signs from English birthdates for anyone born between 4 and 20 February to check whether New Year fell after 4 February that year. Most of the Chinese festivals follow the lunar year, with two major festivals, Ch'ing Ming and the Winter Festival, following the solar year.

THE SIXTY-YEAR CYCLE

Apart from the nineteen-year cycle – the Metonic Cycle – the Chinese calendar has the sixty-year or Sexagenary Cycle. The same cycle is also used to construct a pattern of sixty days. The cycle is formed by the interaction of the two tables of the Ten Heavenly Stems and the Twelve Earthly Branches. In Appendix 1 there is a complete list of the cycle of sixty. This is achieved by taking the Ten Heavenly Stems and repeating them six times. The Twelve Earthly Branches are paired off with them and repeated five times – giving in each case the number 60. The first Heavenly Stem is Chia (甲). The first Earthly Branch is Tzu (子). The cycle of sixty thus always starts with Chia Tzu.

In counting the years the sixty-year cycle is of greater importance, both in fortune-telling and in recording the year, than the animal name of the year. This is shown, for instance, in the fact that the only really major celebration of a person's birthday comes when he is sixty, for he has thus completed one full cycle.

The Heavenly Stems are associated in pairs with the Five Elements. The Five Elements in turn are the primary and most essential expression of yin and yang. We shall thus need to make a short detour to look into these forces as they underpin so much within the Almanac.

YIN AND YANG AND THE FIVE ELEMENTS

The yin and yang are the basic opposing forces, negative and positive, dark and light, cold and hot, which keep the world and all life spinning. One of the most powerful descriptions of yin and yang appears in the *Huai Nan Tzu*. This was written down *c.* 120 BCE for the Prince of Huai Nan – hence its title, *The Book of Huai Nan*. It is a study of natural philosophy in twenty-one volumes.

Before heaven and earth had taken form all was vague and amorphous. Therefore it was called the Great Beginning. The Great Beginning produced emptiness and emptiness produced the universe. The universe produced material-force which had limits. That which was clear and light drifted up to become heaven, while that which was heavy and turbid solidified to become earth. It was very easy for the pure, fine material to come together but extremely difficult for the heavy, turbid material to solidify. Therefore heaven was completed first and earth assumed shape after. The combined essences of heaven and earth became the yin and yang, the concentrated essences of the yin and yang became the four seasons, and the scattered essence of the four seasons became the myriad creatures of the world. After a long time the hot force of the accumulated yang produced fire and the essence of the fire force became the sun; the cold force of accumulated yin became water and the essence of the water force became the moon. The essence of the excess force of the sun and moon became the stars and planets. Heaven received the sun, moon and stars while earth received water and soil.[26]

Because they are opposites, they need each other to make the whole. Out of the tension (rather than the idea of harmony) which arises from this attraction of opposites comes the dynamic of life. Quite how old is the theory of yin and yang is very hard to determine. Certain writers see a foreshadowing in the sun and moon imagery of the ancient poems of the *Shu Ching* such as this one:

O Sun, O Moon,
From the East which come forth.
O father, O mother,

There is no sequel to your nourishing of me.
How can he get his mind settled?
Would he then respond to me, contrary to all reason?[27]

Similarly, the male–female divide, hinted at above, is also seen as a precursor of yin and yang. Whatever their roots, by the third to fourth centuries BCE the terms had developed their current meaning. It is important to stress that yin and yang are not gods or any form of divine power. Yin and yang are purely natural forces. As such they have been equated at times with the forces operating at the subatomic level in modern physics, for instance.[28]

From yin and yang came forth, and come forth, the Five Elements. This is succinctly captured by the Sung dynasty Confucian philosopher Chou Tun-yi (1017–73 CE), who wrote:

The Non-Ultimate! And also the Great Ultimate (T'ai-chi). The Great Ultimate through movement generates the yang. When its activity reaches its limit, it becomes tranquil. Through tranquility the Great Ultimate generates the yin. When tranquility reaches its limit, activity begins again. Thus movement and tranquility alternate and become the root of each other, giving rise to the distinction of yin and yang, and these two modes are thus established.

By the transformation of yang and its union with yin, the five agents of water, fire, wood, metal, and earth arise. When these five material-forces (ch'i) are distributed in harmonious order, the four seasons run their course.[29]

Again, the origins of the highly systematized relationships between the Five Elements cannot be easily traced. There is detailed mention of them in the *Shu Ching*. In the section known as *The Great Plan* (supposedly set in the changeover from the Shang to the Chou dynasty, *c.* 1025 BCE), the ruler inquires how Heaven wishes the world ordered. The reply quotes 'the great Plan with its nine Divisions' given to Emperor Yu.

First of all the divisions, the principles of order, come the Five Elements:

First, of the Five Elements – The first is named water; the second, fire; the third, wood; the fourth, metal; the fifth, earth. (The nature of) water is to soak and descend; of fire, to blaze and ascend; of wood, to be crooked and to be straight; of metal, to obey and to change; while the virtue of earth is seen in seed-sowing and ingathering. That which soaks and descends becomes salt; that which blazes and ascends becomes bitter; that which is crooked and straight becomes sour; that which obeys and changes becomes arid; and from seed-sowing and ingathering comes sweetness.[30]

The earliest chart of their relationships is credited by Needham to Tsou Yen, who is believed to have lived between 350 and 270 BCE. However, the ancient nature of these elements is not doubted. The Five Elements are not linked to just the Ten Heavenly Stems. As we saw above in the quotation from the *Shu Ching*, they are also linked to tastes and characteristics. Below is a table of some of the main relationships of the Five Elements.

Element	Heavenly Stems	Planet	Colour	Taste	Animal
Wood	Chia and Yi	Jupiter	Green	Sour	Tiger and Rabbit
Fire	Ping and Ting	Mars	Red	Bitter	Horse and Snake
Earth	Wu and Chi	Saturn	Yellow	Sweet	Dog and Ox
Metal	Keng and Hsin	Venus	White	Acrid	Cock and Monkey
Water	Jen and Kuei	Mercury	Black	Salt	Pig and Rat

To return to the sixty-year cycle: the Ten Heavenly Stems go thus:

Chia	甲	(Wood)	Chi	己	(Earth)
Yi	乙	(Wood)	Keng	庚	(Metal)
Ping	丙	(Fire)	Hsin	辛	(Metal)
Ting	丁	(Fire)	Jen	壬	(Water)
Wu	戊	(Earth)	Kuei	癸	(Water)

The Twelve Earthly Branches function on three important and separate levels. As regards the sixty-year cycle, they work with the Ten Heavenly Stems to form each year's horoscope pairing. They also tie in exactly with the Twelve Creatures of the calendar, the animal signs. However, it is important to stress that each Earthly Branch character does not *mean* the specific creature of the animal cycle with which it is linked. Below we give the animal and its character, and the Earthly Branch name with which it is linked and its character. We also show a third function, for this set of twelve characters is also used to denote the Chinese 'hours' of the day. The Chinese 'hour' covers two ordinary hours, as can be seen in the table. Throughout the book we have placed speech marks around the word 'hour' when we are referring to Chinese 'hours'. The importance of the 'hours' will become obvious as we begin to get into the area of astrology and various other parts of the Almanac.

Animal sign		Earthly Branch		'Hour'
Rat	鼠	Tzu	子	11 p.m.–1 a.m.
Ox	牛	Ch'ou	丑	1 a.m.–3 a.m.
Tiger	虎	Yin	寅	3 a.m.–5 a.m.
Hare	兔	Mao	卯	5 a.m.–7 a.m.

Dragon	龍	Ch'en	辰	7 a.m.–9 a.m.
Snake	蛇	Szu	巳	9 a.m.–11 a.m.
Horse	馬	Wu	午	11 a.m.–1 p.m.
Ram	羊	Wei	未	1 p.m.–3 p.m.
Monkey	猴	Shen	申	3 p.m.–5 p.m.
Cock	雞	Yu	酉	5 p.m.–7 p.m.
Dog	狗	Hsu	戌	7 p.m.–9 p.m.
Pig	豬	Hai	亥	9 p.m.–11 p.m.

By a combination of six rounds of the Heavenly Stems (6 × 10 = 60) and five rounds of the Earthly Branches (5 × 12 = 60), the full sixty-year cycle is completed.

The traditional way of giving dates in the past was to find the pairing for a particular year and whose reign it fell in. For instance, 1815 was the Yi Hai year in the reign of Ch'ing Emperor Chia-ch'ing. This system only broke down when emperors ruled for more than sixty years. In the past six hundred years only one Emperor, K'ang Hsi (1662–1723), exceeded this number. Taiwan, however, is beginning to run into difficulties. It still counts from 1912 as the start of the Republic. In the Hong Kong Almanacs political diplomacy shows itself thus. From 1912 to 1948 the Republic dates are shown, ending in 1948 with the thirty-seventh year. From 1949 to the present no year number is shown. This leaves open the question of to whom the 'mandate of Heaven' has descended.

THE TWELVE CREATURES

A great deal is made in the West of the 'Chinese zodiac' and of the Twelve Animals or Creatures. Whole books have been written on the 'meaning' behind each creature and the resulting personality of those born under its sign. This is rather a shame, as the Chinese themselves ascribe little significance to these twelve creatures and view any details about personalities related to each creature as of little if any value. Other than giving some colour to the New Year festivities and a general title to the year (of far less importance than its Heavenly and Earthly characters), the creature of the year has no real function. As regards astrology and horoscopes, the creature is of relatively minor significance. The following are the basic characteristics associated with each creature:

Rat	Very smart and quick-witted
Ox	Grumbles a lot but is nevertheless big-hearted and long-suffering

Tiger	Keeps promises and becomes very angry if others break theirs
Rabbit	Clever and talented
Dragon	Full of energy and very direct
Snake	Never lets slip an opportunity
Horse	Hardworking
Ram	Quiet, restful, patient and gentle
Monkey	Full of energy and plans
Cock	Keeps time well and is always punctual
Dog	Keeps things to himself. Does not want to lead; prefers to follow
Pig	Always comfortable and very home-loving

There are numerous legends about why these twelve creatures are together. A basic theme is that the Jade Emperor wanted to hold a banquet for all the creatures of the earth. In some accounts, invitations were sent out to all creatures but only the twelve named above turned up. They were therefore honoured by being given a year and a time each. The order always starts with the Rat and ends with the Pig.

THE TWENTY-EIGHT CONSTELLATIONS

The Twenty-Eight Constellations exert a mysterious authority over the calendar and over fortune-telling. They occupy a prominent place in the detailed listings for each day in the calendar and are essential for cup divination, one of the most solemn of all divination methods (see Section 21). They exercise either great benevolence or evil and never change. Their roots lie deep in antiquity and legend. Each constellation has three names (see Section 11). The first is the name of a former soldier. Legend tells that when the Shang dynasty was dying a terrible civil war broke out between the decaying dynasty and the feudal state of Chou. The leading military genius, so legend recalls, was a Taoist, T'ung-t'ien Chiao-chu. To his aid came twenty-eight great warriors (although some accounts see them as attacking T'ung-t'ien Chiao-chu). They were eventually defeated by a heavenly army in a vast and terrible battle. However, to honour the twenty-eight who had fought so well, their names and spirits were taken to be given to the Twenty-Eight Constellations. So each constellation has its soldier's or, as it is normally known, its general's name.

Secondly, each constellation is associated with a creature. The list is given in Section 11 with the associated auspicious or inauspicious term. The origin of the names is not known, nor their date.

Finally, each constellation has a single character which is usually used (as in the calendar and in cup divination) to denote the constellation in question.

The Twenty-Eight Constellations are divided into four blocks of seven. In the calendar, they mark out exactly the seven days of the week (see below). Quite when the idea of a seven-day week entered the calendar is difficult to say. Some writers see it as beginning in the seventh century CE and as being due to the influence of the Nestorian Christians who are first officially recorded on the famous Nestorian monument erected in 781 CE in Shensi province as having entered China in 635 CE. Whether this is so or not, it is an interesting area of speculation.[31] The constellations are linked with the five planets plus the sun and moon and these too are then associated with the days of the week. The pattern is as follows:

Sunday	Constellations 4, 11, 18, 25	Sun
Monday	Constellations 5, 12, 19, 26	Moon
Tuesday	Constellations 6, 13, 20, 27	Mars
Wednesday	Constellations 7, 14, 21, 28	Mercury
Thursday	Constellations 1, 8, 15, 22	Jupiter
Friday	Constellations 2, 9, 16, 23	Venus
Saturday	Constellations 3, 10, 17, 24	Saturn

DIVINATION AND THE ALMANAC

The Almanac contains the largest number of divination methods gathered within one popularly available book. This, of course, is partly the reason for its popularity. As the reader will find, the methods are enormously varied. Some are for everyday use, such as those mostly associated with the chronomancy of the calendar. Others can be understood only with the help of a profesional fortune-teller or diviner. A few are considered of such power that dire warnings about their misuse are contained in the Almanac. It was this mass of material which constantly brought forth the wrath of the Confucians, who saw in it a dulling of humanity's intellect and sense of propriety. Yet it is this part which is of greatest interest to those who buy the Almanac, even if to most it is and remains a closed book. In the following example of how to find a horoscope Chinese readers may turn to the Almanac; but for Western readers, however, it is not possible here to lay out the entire system so that they can work out their horoscopes for themselves.

Essential to much of the divination and chronomancy is the system of the Eight Characters. In Western astrology the horoscope depends upon knowledge of the person's time, date and place of birth. In Chinese astrology it is necessary to know the 'hour', the day, the month and the year. Each of these will be known by their combination of the Heavenly Stem and Earthly Branch, giving eight characters in all. Take the example of a child born at 6 a.m. on the 13th day of the seventh moon, 1984. As has been shown, each year has a combination of the Heavenly Stems and Earthly Branches. Thus a child born in 1984 will have Chia and Tzu (甲子) as the first two characters of his horoscope. For the month, one of the Twelve Earthly Branches relates to each month. However, each year the relationship changes. In 1984 the first moon month was under the character Yin (寅). Thus the seventh moon month will be the seventh character along the list from Yin (counting Yin as the first character). This gives Shen (申). To find the Heavenly Stem it is necessary to place the list of stems alongside the twelve months, repeating the first two in the list in order to complete the required twelve. Again the list moves each year. In 1984 it started with Ping (丙). Thus the seventh character down the list was Jen (壬). So the two characters for the seventh month are Shen and Jen. Next comes the day. Each day is also accorded a Heavenly and an Earthly character. The sixty-year cycle here becomes the sixty-day cycle following exactly the pattern of the yearly cycle. The calendar gives the details for each day (Section 46). The 13th day of the seventh month in 1984 was Yi (乙) Hai (亥). Finally the 'hour': as the child was born at 6 a.m., the Earthly Branch is Mao (卯). Because the Heavenly Stem for the day is Yi (乙), then the Heavenly Stem for the 'hour' of Mao is Chi (己). In finding the Heavenly/Earthly correlation for the 'hour' a special chart is used.

With the resulting eight characters, namely:

甲 Chia 子 Tzu } year 壬 Jen 申 Shen } month 乙 Yi 亥 Hai } day 己 Chi 卯 Mao } 'hour'

it is possible for the inquirer to make basic use of the calendar himself, plus certain other simple fortune-telling and divination charts in the Almanac. Even more important, he can consult a fortune-teller who can delve more deeply.

Instances of fortune-telling/divination will be found in Sections 3, 8, 13 and 23.

GEOMANCY AND THE ALMANAC

The ancient Chinese science of geomancy – called feng-shui, which means 'wind–water' – is a persistent thread which runs

戊、癸	丁、壬	丙、辛	乙、庚	甲、己	日干／時辰
壬子	庚子	戊子	丙子	甲子	子
癸丑	辛丑	己丑	丁丑	乙丑	丑
甲寅	壬寅	庚寅	戊寅	丙寅	寅
乙卯	癸卯	辛卯	己卯	丁卯	卯
丙辰	甲辰	壬辰	庚辰	戊辰	辰
丁巳	乙巳	癸巳	辛巳	己巳	巳
戊午	丙午	甲午	壬午	庚午	午
己未	丁未	乙未	癸未	辛未	未
庚申	戊申	丙申	甲申	壬申	申
辛酉	己酉	丁酉	乙酉	癸酉	酉
壬戌	庚戌	戊戌	丙戌	甲戌	戌
癸亥	辛亥	己亥	丁亥	乙亥	亥

右側注記：「應須注意」時柱天干之配加，是以日柱天干為依據（月柱天干配加是以年柱天干為依據，這個不同）時柱天干亦五相，稱「五鼠通日」兹例舉表於下，一查便明瞭：

左側注記：四柱排出以後便可使用神煞，依規定之使用法即可斷出一個人之初步大概贏幅之傾向。（此表與查月干表不可混用）

Mao

三四

The Heavenly/Earthly correlations for the 'hour' of birth

through Chinese communities worldwide. For instance, in one middle-class suburb of Manchester, England, a family opened a new restaurant. Ill health, bad luck and a general sense of dis-ease affected the family. They therefore called in a geomancer. He swiftly identified the problem. The restaurant (with living accommodation above) was on a slope. Hence the good fortune simply ran past the building. This was resolved by putting a small, low brick block on the pavement beside the door. But, most inauspicious of all, across the way from the front of the building are three trees standing stark and alone. In geomantic thought these resemble the three candles lit at death and are thus a malignant force. If the family had controlled the land the trees were on, the problem could have been overcome by planting many more trees, thus turning the existing three into part of a defensive barrier against evil forces. However, this was not possible, so instead, special symbols of a tiger spear and a mirror using the Eight Trigrams were placed on the front of the building to ward off the evil. The family and their business have improved ever since, but essentially they should never have bought such a property without checking its feng-shui attributes. This could have been done, at least at a simple level, by using the charts contained in the Almanac. Then they would have had to consult an expert, a master of feng-shui.

Details of geomancy will be found on pp. 46–50. It does not have a great deal of space devoted to it in the Almanac because it is a very complicated technique. However, its inclusion, even when largely incomprehensible to the general reader, testifies to its power and authority. The sections largely concern details of burial, travel and building, and can at least give the ordinary reader some idea as to fortunate and unfortunate directions. With regard to this, the geomancer's compass on the second page of the Almanac is the most significant element in the book.

THE ALMANAC AS A REFLECTION OF TRADITIONAL LIFE AND VALUES

One of the most important functions of the Almanac is as a set of principles – as certain people would put it, a 'role model'. Scattered through the book are homilies, exhortations, moral tales, details of behaviour, letter etiquette, and so on. As with most such things, be they Chinese or English, it is unlikely that anyone ever actually lived up to, or could ever live up to, the expectations set out. However, within the traditional hierarchical and structured life of China until the recent past, it was possible to find families organized and run along the lines outlined in the homilies or moral tales. As such, the collection in the Almanac throws a light on traditional Chinese values and patterns of behaviour which is unique. From the highly philosophical discussions of K'ung Fu-tzu (Confucius) the infant prodigy (Section 26) to the details of how to live properly (Section 36), facets of Chinese life and values appear before us in story or proverb form. In considering these reflections of a now almost totally destroyed way of life, it is perhaps significant that in the abridged editions of the Almanacs which are now appearing it is these moralistic parts which have been dropped whilst the fortune-telling and divining parts have been largely retained.

Apart from the specific tales and homilies mentioned above, traditional patterns and values appear as a subcurrent throughout. In Section 18, on dreams, for instance, they form the normative matrix within which the dreams occur and are interpreted. In the calendar (Section 46) actions allowed and forbidden, plus details of certain of the festivals, reflect the type of society which was Imperial China. A fascinatingly intimate door is thus found in the Almanac, which leads us back to the style and format of traditional Chinese life.

T'UNG SHU

THE ANCIENT
CHINESE ALMANAC

Section 1

THE SPRING FESTIVAL COW (LI CH'UN) AND THE GEOMANCER'S COMPASS

The first page of the Almanac often confuses those who have only a passing knowledge of Chinese language and culture. For there at the top of the page is a picture of a cow being led by a young boy. Many take this to mean that this year is the year of the Cow! This is not the case, for this picture appears every year. It is in fact the Spring Festival Cow, the main figure associated with Li Ch'un – the Beginning of Spring. Each year some small detail of the picture changes, for this picture reflects the type of weather which the year will have.

For instance, if Meng Shan, the cowherd, wears shoes, then there will be plenty of rain. If he has bare feet, then it will be a dry year. If he is wearing his hat, then it will be a very sunny year. If his hat is on his back, then it will be cool.

The symbol of the cow harks back to the original ritual of spring when, during the Shang dynasty, cows were sacrificed. In many areas of China until recent years, paper models of the cow were burned, and up to the last century Fukien province still sacrificed a real cow or buffalo. The Almanac gives detailed instructions for making such a paper model including the length and the colour. In 1985 the cow had a light green head – meaning sickness in the spring.

Around the picture and below it are the details of crops and health for the year. Ancient deities such as the Mother or Queen of Earth are invoked, for in this section we reach back to the earliest religious traditions of China.

At the very end of the calendar comes next year's Spring Cow (Section 47), with very brief details of the predictions for that year.

On the second page of the Almanac is the geomancer's compass and details concerning burial direction (see p. 48). These two, the cow and the compass, introduce the reader to the fascinating world of Chinese tradition and belief preserved in the Almanac. Below is a translation of the main blocks of Section 1. Following this, the roles of geomancy and the feng-shui compass are explained.

乙丑年春牛圖

乙丑春來瘟成禍　魏燕受損傷魯楚
時見牛羊蟄災起　陌路流郎侍巡趨

早種高田勤工效　晚者收成八分禾
撫憑育桑半竹斗　惟是種蒔滿箕籮

地母經

歲為乙丑年　春溫害萬民
偏傷於魯楚　多損魏燕入
高田宜早種　晚承成八分
蠶娘爭關走　枝葉亂紛紜
濾父浴山釣　流郎陌上巡
牛羊多瘴死

春夏米如珍

地母曰

本年太歲姓陳名泰
天干屬木地支屬土
納音屬金歲德在庚
乙危月燕

值年鬼宿未日張宿遇
歲德合在乙

為暗金伏斷二日得
辛三龍治水十二牛
耕地三姑把畫食
一葉行雷鄧元帥

水猫田頭臥
犢子水中眼
有三伏不生蠶
桑葉不成賞
種植倍收牧全

春社　正月廿九日
秋社　八月十二日
冬至　十一月十二日
大寒　十二月十一日

小滿　五月初五日
初伏　六月初三日
中伏　六月十三日
末伏　六月廿三日

上用田事
二月廿八日
六月初三日
九月初七日
十二月初八日

春牛身高四尺長八尺尾長一
尺二寸頭青身黃腹白角耳尾
青脛黃蹄紅尾右撖口合籠頭
索用白色絲繩構子桑柘木
踏板縣門右扇芒神身高三尺牛
六寸五分童子像青衣白腰帶
平梳兩鬢右在耳後
罨耳用柳枝長二尺四寸五色
鞭杖用柳枝長二尺四寸五色
絲結芒神早忙立於牛前右邊

YI CH'OU [1985] SPRING COW CHART

During this Yi Ch'ou year, in the springtime, things will not go well. This is the season for crop farming and rearing livestock. If the family is not well behaved during spring, then the people of the country will not have good yields. You will frequently see sickness amongst the livestock. Because of this you will have to work even harder to rear your livestock.

If you plant early and work hard, you will still only get 80 per cent of the fruits of your labour. The most you will collect this year is half your grain harvest. You will have more containers empty than full.

THE MOTHER OR QUEEN OF EARTH'S BOOK

During the spring there will be epidemics. This will bring ill fortune to many people. During this year it is wise to start farming earlier. Even the silkworms will leave because there will be no mulberry leaves. The fishermen will sit idly beside the mountains trying to fish. The strong men will all be unemployed and will hang around the fields. Most of the cows and sheep will die because of the epidemics. Therefore during spring and summer rice will be more precious, even though it too is scarce.

THE MOTHER OR QUEEN OF EARTH'S DAY

Even cows do not have work to do and are just standing around the fields. The cowherders have no work and sit around. You cannot even grow mulberry leaves. What you need is someone with knowledge to advise you, or you will not have a good harvest.

INSTRUCTIONS FOR BUILDING A SPRING COW MODEL

The Spring Cow is 4 feet tall, 8 feet long. The tail is 1 foot 2 inches long. The colour of the head is light green; the body, yellow; belly, white; horns, ears and tail light green; lower leg yellow and hooves red. The tail is facing right and pointing upwards. The mouth is closed. There is a silk thread tied through its nose. Meng Shen is guarding the field, 3 feet $6\frac{1}{2}$ inches tall. The cowherdsman is wearing a light green coat of which the belt is white. The boy's hair is combed in two bunches. The right bunch is in front of the ear; the left is behind the ear. He uses his right hand to cover his ear. The boy's stick is 2 feet $4\frac{1}{2}$ inches long. Meng Shen is standing in front of the cow, on the right-hand side.

FENG-SHUI
IN THE ALMANAC

(Sections 1, 16 and 24)

Of all the ancient and distinctive arts or sciences of traditional China, feng-shui (literally, wind–water) is one of the most complex and, to the Western mind, both mystifying and mysterious. It has provoked Western commentators to condemn it – 'it retards progress, forbids railways, closes coal mines, prevents enterprise, checks new efforts at advancement, interrupts the free thought of the people, and keeps them wrapped in the mummy folds of ancient prejudices'[1] – while others have become euphoric – 'I say would God that our own men of science had preserved in their observatories, laboratories and lecture-rooms that same child-like reverence for the living powers of nature, that sacred awe and trembling fear of the mysteries of the unseen, that firm belief in the reality of the invisible world, and its constant intercommunication with the seen and the temporal. . . .'[2]

So what is this 'feng-shui' which causes such strong reactions? As we saw in the Introduction, Chinese thought posits the existence of two opposite but equal forces – yin and yang. These maintain a balance of opposition which keeps the world active. Yin and yang are within everything, even what Westerners would see as inert matter such as land. Furthermore, this world is seen as reflecting, less gloriously, the pattern of Heaven. Hills and valleys, rivers and lakes are where they are for good reasons. When humans come to live in or 'develop' an area, they must do so in balance with the forces already within the area, and with due regard for the heavenly influences which operate upon the landscape. To do other than this is to disrupt the balance, to disturb adversely the yin–yang equation and ultimately to bring some form of disaster upon the heads of those who have disregarded feng-shui. The art or science of divining the land is thus of great importance and it is this which has become known as feng-shui (wind and water being two symbols for yin and yang) or geomancy.

Nor is geomancy a thing of the past. It is found in all Chinese overseas communities and affects things as diverse as the construction and siting of the Hyatt Hotel in Singapore, the healing of a man in Taiwan (where currently some 20,000–30,000 geomancers work) and the positioning of new restaurants in England.

While buildings, roads and so on have been the main focus of geomancy, its most important role for most Chinese has been in the choice of a grave site for the family dead. If the fortunes of the living are adversely affected by dwelling in or creating bad feng-shui, then imagine the distress this causes the spirits of the dead. Furthermore, if the ancestors are unhappy because of bad feng-shui, then it is the living descendants who will suffer through the ancestors' withholding blessings. So it is vital that tombs have good feng-shui.

Bad feng-shui can be created by others not planning properly around you. This can be rectified by use of Eight Trigram mirrors. These small mirrors, often with a painting of a deity below, are circled by the Eight Trigrams – sets of three lines – which form the basis of the celebrated *I Ching*. These mirrors will reflect back the adverse properties of bad planning. For instance, across the road a building goes up with hard, straight lines aimed at your building. This is bad feng-shui, so you reflect it back. Recently in Hong Kong one government office had a large bank built opposite with dark mirror-glass in its windows. The day after it opened, the government office windows each had an Eight Trigram mirror defiantly reflecting the bad feng-shui back at the bank.

Although feng-shui has not been without its enemies in Chinese society (as reflected in the proverb: 'If you invite a geomancer to inspect your house, you might as well start packing to move now!'), it still exerts a fascination and a power. There is much common sense within it and its philosophical basis is an intriguing antidote to Western concepts. Yet it is a highly complex art and understood by very few Chinese. Hence, the pages devoted to it in the Almanac (Sections 1, 16 and 24) are few, although it is featured as the sole subject of the second page. Like physiognomy, the details given in the Almanac are sparse and very general. As with physiognomy, it is expected that those needing to apply it will seek an expert. Yet the basic ideas of feng-shui flow through the Almanac in terms of lucky directions, the stars, and so on, like an undercurrent.

The history of organized feng-shui is not as old as might be expected. Its first appearance is in the time of Confucius and just after. The *Li Chi* records that the dead were always buried pointing to the north because the north is seen as the female point of the compass and death and decay are the province of the female – yin – aspect of creation. Needham sees an early philosophical root of feng-shui in the words of Kuan Chung, a philosopher of the fifth century BCE. In his *Kuan Tzu* he writes thus:

太歲壓癸
六生人

甲戌壬辰庚戌
癸未辛丑己未

本年三殺在東五黃占巽歲破在未九辰
巽巳寅甲卯乙未八山忌用餘各山俱利

九宮

一白
六白
坎北 二黑
大利 小利 小退

乙丑年山向月利圖

壬山	子山	癸山	丑山	艮山	寅山	甲山	卯山	乙山	辰山	巽山	巳山
八遨葬宜二三四七	八遨葬宜二三四七	八遨葬宜二三四七	十遨葬宜二三七八	八九十十二月利 遨葬宜二三五七	本年犯三煞不利	本年犯三煞不利	本年犯三煞不利	本年坐三煞不利	本年坐三煞不利	本年坐傍黃不利	由丙兼線無妨

丙山	午山	丁山	未山	坤山	申山	庚山	酉山	辛山	戌山	乾山	亥山
遨葬宜正二四月八	遨葬宜正二四月八	九十十二月利	本年值歲破不利	八九十月利 遨葬宜正二三四五	八九十二月利 遨葬宜正三四五	八九十二月利 遨葬宜正四五七	八九十二月利 遨葬宜正四五七	八九十二月利 遨葬宜正四五七	八九十十二月利 遨葬宜正四五七	八九十二月利 遨葬宜三七八十	十十二月利 遨葬宜三七八十

The earth is the origin of all things, the root and garden of all life; and the place where all things, the beautiful, the ugly, the good, the bad, the foolish and the clever, come into being. Now water is the blood and breath of the earth, flowing and communicating (within its body) as if in sinews and veins.[3]

Throughout the Han dynasty, books on feng-shui began to emerge for the first time, such as the *Chia Ching (The Book of Dwellings)*. The philosopher Wang Ch'ung attacked the system in his writings *c*. 80 CE and various books on the siting of dwellings and tombs appear in catalogues of the time.

However, the consolidation and establishment of feng-shui seems to date from the Three Kingdoms period (221 CE) to the end of the Sung (1279 CE). Various 'classics' were written then which are still consulted today, such as the *Kuan Shih Ti Li Chih Meng (Master Kuan's Geomancer Indicator)* and the *Tsang Shu (Song of Geomancy)*, credited to the semi-legendary poet and philosopher Kuo P'u in the fourth century CE. By the end of the Sung dynasty the shape and format of contemporary feng-shui had been cast.

Of the sections concerning feng-shui in the Almanac, the most important is on the second page. Here is the geomancer's compass – vital for the geomancer's art – and a fundamental outline of the philosophy behind feng-shui (note: north is down). The centre of the compass contains the five directions (the four points plus the centre, known as 'colour white'). Next come subdivisions of the compass, i.e. southeast, etc., based upon the Eight Trigrams. The third ring is the colours of the nine directions (the Eight Trigrams and centre) and the Five Elements. The fourth ring is the characters for each 'hour' of the day (Heavenly and Earthly combined). The fifth ring contains details of where good and bad spirits are currently dwelling. Finally, outside the ring are the four ancient compass bearings to tell you which way to set the compass.

Around the compass runs this inscription:

T'ai Sui [the Minister of Time in Heaven, equivalent to the planet Jupiter] is in charge. If you are born under year characters Chia Hsu, Jen Ch'en, Keng Hsu, Kuei Wei, Hsin Ch'ou, Chi Wei, then you should avoid anything to do with burial ceremonies this year.

This year the positioning of disaster is in the east. Southeast has five yellow [meaning death and burial]. Southwest direction will shorten your life. Szu, Yin, Chia, Mao, Yi, Wei mountain directions cannot be used for burial this year.

The general details given here are further elaborated and expounded in the other charts in the Almanac. Section 16 covers the relationships, day by day, between the sixty-day cycle and the auspicious and inauspicious directions. The chart has ten categories of activities related to feng-shui influences. They are:

1. A list of incompatible signs
2. Direction of happiness
3. Direction from which assistance will come
4. Direction for money
5. Direction of the good-luck star which can bless your door
6. Direction of long life
7. Direction for a business to be facing when opened on a particular day
8. Dangerous direction
9. Direction of the evil influence of the Five Ghosts
10. Direction through which death will enter your gates

Section 24 contains details of the feng-shui directions associated with each day in the sixty-day cycle, plus the good and bad stars associated with that direction.

Finally, aspects of feng-shui also appear in Master T'ung's chart as an aid to general fortune-telling associated with the calendar (see Section 42).

Feng-shui, as we have said earlier, is highly complex. In the few insights given here only a fleeting glance is possible. The role of the geomancer is very considerable and what is contained in the Almanac is designed to illustrate feng-shui's importance but not to seek to go too deeply into this art. Nevertheless, it affords the outsider a chance to see a few of its ideas and to sense its underlying importance.

Section 2

YEARS AND ASTROLOGICAL
CHARACTERS OF THE MOST
RECENT 100 YEARS

In Chinese astrology it is vital to know the Eight Characters of your horoscope, these being the characters for the year, month, day and 'hour' of your birth. Central to this, and used in many of the simpler divination or fortune-telling sections of the Almanac, are the Heavenly Stem and Earthly Branch for the year of your birth. Hence this early in the Almanac comes a quick reference chart of years with their Heavenly and Earthly signs and the year creature. The very structure of this section is revealing. The first line of each part carries an age – e.g., 33 years old. At the base of each part comes the date according to the Western calendar – in this instance 1953. Some Chinese are better able to recall their age than the Western year it equates to. However, two further points must be made. It may come as a surprise to some Westerners to discover that their age does not seem to correspond to the year given. Thus someone born in 1953 and reading this in 1986 would expect to find the number 33 as being his age. Instead he finds he is reckoned to be 34! The explanation is quite simple. According to Chinese practice you are already one year old at your birth. The second point worth noting is that on the seventh day of New Year everyone is automatically counted as being one year older. It is not common to celebrate individual birthdays in traditional families, with the exception of the sixtieth birthday, which marks the completion of the sixty-year cycle of Heavenly Stems (HS) and Earthly Branches (EB). (The chart overleaf starts with 1985.)

乙丑年百歲圖

歲數	干支年	生肖	西元
一歲	乙丑年	肖牛	一九八五
二歲	甲子年	肖鼠	一九八四
三歲	癸亥年	肖猪	一九八三
四歲	壬戌年	肖犬	一九八二
五歲	辛酉年	肖雞	一九八一
六歲	庚申年	肖猴	一九八○
七歲	己未年	肖羊	一九七九
八歲	戊午年	肖馬	一九七八
九歲	丁巳年	肖蛇	一九七七
十歲	丙辰年	肖龍	一九七六
十一歲	乙卯年	肖兔	一九七五
十二歲	甲寅年	肖虎	一九七四
十三歲	癸丑年	肖牛	一九七三
十四歲	壬子年	肖鼠	一九七二
十五歲	辛亥年	肖猪	一九七一
十六歲	庚戌年	肖犬	一九七○
十七歲	己酉年	肖雞	一九六九
十八歲	戊申年	肖猴	一九六八
十九歲	丁未年	肖羊	一九六七
二十歲	丙午年	肖馬	一九六六
廿一歲	乙巳年	肖蛇	一九六五
廿二歲	甲辰年	肖龍	一九六四
廿三歲	癸卯年	肖兔	一九六三
廿四歲	壬寅年	肖虎	一九六二
廿五歲	辛丑年	肖牛	一九六一
廿六歲	庚子年	肖鼠	一九六○
廿七歲	己亥年	肖猪	一九五九
廿八歲	戊戌年	肖犬	一九五八
廿九歲	丁酉年	肖雞	一九五七
三十歲	丙申年	肖猴	一九五六
卅一歲	乙未年	肖羊	一九五五
卅二歲	甲午年	肖馬	一九五四
卅三歲	癸巳年	肖蛇	一九五三
卅四歲	壬辰年	肖龍	一九五二
卅五歲	辛卯年	肖兔	一九五一
卅六歲	庚寅年	肖虎	一九五○
卅七歲	己丑年	肖牛	一九四九
卅八歲	戊子年	肖鼠	一九四八
卅九歲	丁亥年	肖猪	一九四七
四十歲	丙戌年	肖犬	一九四六
四一歲	乙酉年	肖雞	一九四五
四二歲	甲申年	肖猴	一九四四
四三歲	癸未年	肖羊	一九四三
四四歲	壬午年	肖馬	一九四二
四五歲	辛巳年	肖蛇	一九四一
四六歲	庚辰年	肖龍	一九四○
四七歲	己卯年	肖兔	一九三九
四八歲	戊寅年	肖虎	一九三八
四九歲	丁丑年	肖牛	一九三七
五十歲	丙子年	肖鼠	一九三六
五一歲	乙亥年	肖猪	一九三五
五二歲	甲戌年	肖犬	一九三四
五三歲	癸酉年	肖雞	一九三三
五四歲	壬申年	肖猴	一九三二
五五歲	辛未年	肖羊	一九三一
五六歲	庚午年	肖馬	一九三○
五七歲	己巳年	肖蛇	一九二九
五八歲	戊辰年	肖龍	一九二八
五九歲	丁卯年	肖兔	一九二七
六十歲	丙寅年	肖虎	一九二六
六一歲	乙丑年	肖牛	一九二五
六二歲	甲子年	肖鼠	一九二四
六三歲	癸亥年	肖猪	一九二三
六四歲	壬戌年	肖犬	一九二二
六五歲	辛酉年	肖雞	一九二一
六六歲	庚申年	肖猴	一九二○
六七歲	己未年	肖羊	一九一九
六八歲	戊午年	肖馬	一九一八
六九歲	丁巳年	肖蛇	一九一七
七十歲	丙辰年	肖龍	一九一六
七一歲	乙卯年	肖兔	一九一五
七二歲	甲寅年	肖虎	一九一四
七三歲	癸丑年	肖牛	一九一三
七四歲	壬子年	肖鼠	一九一二
七五歲	辛亥年	肖猪	一九一一
七六歲	庚戌年	肖犬	一九一○
七七歲	己酉年	肖雞	一九○九
七八歲	戊申年	肖猴	一九○八
七九歲	丁未年	肖羊	一九○七
八十歲	丙午年	肖馬	一九○六
八一歲	乙巳年	肖蛇	一九○五
八二歲	甲辰年	肖龍	一九○四
八三歲	癸卯年	肖兔	一九○三
八四歲	壬寅年	肖虎	一九○二
八五歲	辛丑年	肖牛	一九○一
八六歲	庚子年	肖鼠	一九○○
八七歲	己亥年	肖猪	一八九九
八八歲	戊戌年	肖犬	一八九八
八九歲	丁酉年	肖雞	一八九七
九十歲	丙申年	肖猴	一八九六
九一歲	乙未年	肖羊	一八九五
九二歲	甲午年	肖馬	一八九四
九三歲	癸巳年	肖蛇	一八九三
九四歲	壬辰年	肖龍	一八九二
九五歲	辛卯年	肖兔	一八九一
九六歲	庚寅年	肖虎	一八九○
九七歲	己丑年	肖牛	一八八九
九八歲	戊子年	肖鼠	一八八八
九九歲	丁亥年	肖猪	一八八七
一百歲	丙戌年	肖犬	一八八六

PING YIN [1986] DIAGRAM OF 100 YEARS OF AGES

Age	HS	EB	Animal	Western date
1 year old	Ping	Yin	Year of the Tiger	1986
2 years old	Yi	Ch'ou	Year of the Ox	1985
3 years old	Chia	Tzu	Year of the Rat	1984
4 years old	Kuei	Hai	Year of the Pig	1983
5 years old	Jen	Hsu	Year of the Dog	1982
6 years old	Hsin	Yu	Year of the Cock	1981
7 years old	Keng	Shen	Year of the Monkey	1980
8 years old	Chi	Wei	Year of the Ram	1979
9 years old	Wu	Wu	Year of the Horse	1978
10 years old	Ting	Szu	Year of the Snake	1977
11 years old	Ping	Ch'en	Year of the Dragon	1976
12 years old	Yi	Mao	Year of the Rabbit	1975
13 years old	Chia	Yin	Year of the Tiger	1974
14 years old	Kuei	Ch'ou	Year of the Ox	1973
15 years old	Jen	Tzu	Year of the Rat	1972
16 years old	Hsin	Hai	Year of the Pig	1971
17 years old	Keng	Hsu	Year of the Dog	1970
18 years old	Chi	Yu	Year of the Cock	1969
19 years old	Wu	Shen	Year of the Monkey	1968
20 years old	Ting	Wei	Year of the Ram	1967
21 years old	Ping	Wu	Year of the Horse	1966
22 years old	Yi	Szu	Year of the Snake	1965
23 years old	Chia	Ch'en	Year of the Dragon	1964
24 years old	Kuei	Mao	Year of the Rabbit	1963
25 years old	Jen	Yin	Year of the Tiger	1962
26 years old	Hsin	Ch'ou	Year of the Ox	1961
27 years old	Keng	Tzu	Year of the Rat	1960
28 years old	Chi	Hai	Year of the Pig	1959
29 years old	Wu	Hsu	Year of the Dog	1958
30 years old	Ting	Yu	Year of the Cock	1957
31 years old	Ping	Shen	Year of the Monkey	1956
32 years old	Yi	Wei	Year of the Ram	1955
33 years old	Chia	Wu	Year of the Horse	1954
34 years old	Kuei	Szu	Year of the Snake	1953
35 years old	Jen	Ch'en	Year of the Dragon	1952
36 years old	Hsin	Mao	Year of the Rabbit	1951
37 years old	Keng	Yin	Year of the Tiger	1950
38 years old	Chi	Ch'ou	Year of the Ox	1949
39 years old	Wu	Tzu	Year of the Rat	1948
40 years old	Ting	Hai	Year of the Pig	1947
41 years old	Ping	Hsu	Year of the Dog	1946
42 years old	Yi	Yu	Year of the Cock	1945
43 years old	Chia	Shen	Year of the Monkey	1944
44 years old	Kuei	Wei	Year of the Ram	1943
45 years old	Jen	Wu	Year of the Horse	1942
46 years old	Hsin	Szu	Year of the Snake	1941
47 years old	Keng	Ch'en	Year of the Dragon	1940
48 years old	Chi	Mao	Year of the Rabbit	1939
49 years old	Wu	Yin	Year of the Tiger	1938
50 years old	Ting	Ch'ou	Year of the Ox	1937

Age	HS	EB	Animal	Western date
51 years old	Ping	Tzu	Year of the Rat	1936
52 years old	Yi	Hai	Year of the Pig	1935
53 years old	Chia	Hsu	Year of the Dog	1934
54 years old	Kuei	Yu	Year of the Cock	1933
55 years old	Jen	Shen	Year of the Monkey	1932
56 years old	Hsin	Wei	Year of the Ram	1931
57 years old	Keng	Wu	Year of the Horse	1930
58 years old	Chi	Szu	Year of the Snake	1929
59 years old	Wu	Ch'en	Year of the Dragon	1928
60 years old	Ting	Mao	Year of the Rabbit	1927
61 years old	Ping	Yin	Year of the Tiger	1926
62 years old	Yi	Ch'ou	Year of the Ox	1925
63 years old	Chia	Tzu	Year of the Rat	1924
64 years old	Kuei	Hai	Year of the Pig	1923
65 years old	Jen	Hsu	Year of the Dog	1922
66 years old	Hsin	Yu	Year of the Cock	1921
67 years old	Keng	Shen	Year of the Monkey	1920
68 years old	Chi	Wei	Year of the Ram	1919
69 years old	Wu	Wu	Year of the Horse	1918
70 years old	Ting	Szu	Year of the Snake	1917
71 years old	Ping	Ch'en	Year of the Dragon	1916
72 years old	Yi	Mao	Year of the Rabbit	1915
73 years old	Chia	Yin	Year of the Tiger	1914
74 years old	Kuei	Ch'ou	Year of the Ox	1913
75 years old	Jen	Tzu	Year of the Rat	1912
76 years old	Hsin	Hai	Year of the Pig	1911
77 years old	Keng	Hsu	Year of the Dog	1910
78 years old	Chi	Yu	Year of the Cock	1909
79 years old	Wu	Shen	Year of the Monkey	1908
80 years old	Ting	Wei	Year of the Ram	1907
81 years old	Ping	Wu	Year of the Horse	1906
82 years old	Yi	Szu	Year of the Snake	1905
83 years old	Chia	Ch'en	Year of the Dragon	1904
84 years old	Kuei	Mao	Year of the Rabbit	1903
85 years old	Jen	Yin	Year of the Tiger	1902
86 years old	Hsin	Ch'ou	Year of the Ox	1901
87 years old	Keng	Tzu	Year of the Rat	1900
88 years old	Chi	Hai	Year of the Pig	1899
89 years old	Wu	Hsu	Year of the Dog	1898
90 years old	Ting	Yu	Year of the Cock	1897
91 years old	Ping	Shen	Year of the Monkey	1896
92 years old	Yi	Wei	Year of the Ram	1895
93 years old	Chia	Wu	Year of the Horse	1894
94 years old	Kuei	Szu	Year of the Snake	1893
95 years old	Jen	Ch'en	Year of the Dragon	1892
96 years old	Hsin	Mao	Year of the Rabbit	1891
97 years old	Keng	Yin	Year of the Tiger	1890
98 years old	Chi	Ch'ou	Year of the Ox	1889
99 years old	Wu	Tzu	Year of the Rat	1888
100 years old	Ting	Hai	Year of the Pig	1887

Section 3

CHARTS FOR FINDING YOUR PERSONAL FORTUNE FOR THE YEAR

This section contains the first fortune-telling procedure which, although quite difficult to use, is not regarded as being particularly accurate. It gives a feel for the coming year rather than precise details.

The first two pages consist of a chart of the Twelve Earthly Branches, which are known as 'houses'. The second page (see p. 57) carries the charts which enable the inquirer to find out which house he is in for the present year. Starting with the top half of the page, the inquirer finds the month of his birth: for example, month 10. This is in the top block. He then looks in the next block down. Here the inquirer finds his 'hour' of birth – say 12 midnight. He then traces across from right to left until he comes to the column below his month of birth. This then gives the 'house' he is in for this year. In the case of the example cited above, this is Wu (午). The inquirer looks back to the first page (see p. 56) and finds his house, Wu. This tells him which are his good stars and which are his bad stars for the year.

Turning back to the charts, he looks at the bottom set of blocks. In the top of these two he locates his house sign – in this case Wu. Then in the bottom right-hand block he finds the Earthly Branch for his year of birth – in this case Tzu (子). He traces across until he comes below his house sign. This then gives the key character for the fortune-telling. In the example cited above this is Szu (巳).

55

火星　天官　羅星　　乙丑　　　　　月將

　　　　　　　　　　　　　　　　　　　　　氣星

　　　　　　　天賜福官　　　　　　　　太陰

　　　　　　　　　　　　　　　　　　　　木星

土星　計星　孛星　　流年　　　　　　　總圖

亥戌酉申未午巳辰卯寅丑子午巳辰卯寅子
生生生生生生生生生生生生與與與與與與
肖肖肖肖肖肖肖肖肖肖肖肖未申酉戌亥丑
猪犬雞猴羊馬蛇龍兔虎牛鼠合合合合合合

立命定局寅　法橫直看

	子時生人	丑時生人	寅時生人	卯時生人	辰時生人	巳時生人	午時生人	未時生人	申時生人	酉時生人	戌時生人	亥時生人
大寒後生人作正月立命	卯	寅	丑	子	亥	戌	酉	申	未	午	巳	辰
雨水後生人作二月立命	寅	丑	子	亥	戌	酉	申	未	午	巳	辰	卯
春分後生人作三月立命	丑	子	亥	戌	酉	申	未	午	巳	辰	卯	寅
穀雨後生人作四月立命	子	亥	戌	酉	申	未	午	巳	辰	卯	寅	丑
小滿後生人作五月立命	亥	戌	酉	申	未	午	巳	辰	卯	寅	丑	子
夏至後生人作六月立命	戌	酉	申	未	午	巳	辰	卯	寅	丑	子	亥
大暑後生人作七月立命	酉	申	未	午	巳	辰	卯	寅	丑	子	亥	戌
處暑後生人作八月立命	申	未	午	巳	辰	卯	寅	丑	子	亥	戌	酉
秋分後生人作九月立命	未	午	巳	辰	卯	寅	丑	子	亥	戌	酉	申
霜降後生人作十月立命	午	巳	辰	卯	寅	丑	子	亥	戌	酉	申	未
小雪後生人作十一月立命	巳	辰	卯	寅	丑	子	亥	戌	酉	申	未	午
冬至後生人作十二月立命	辰	卯	寅	丑	子	亥	戌	酉	申	未	午	巳

乙丑年排　定小限局

	子生年人	丑生年人	寅生年人	卯生年人	辰生年人	巳生年人	午生年人	未生年人	申生年人	酉生年人	戌生年人	亥生年人
子宮立命小限排在	亥	子	丑	寅	卯	辰	巳	午	未	申	酉	戌
丑宮立命小限排在	子	丑	寅	卯	辰	巳	午	未	申	酉	戌	亥
寅宮立命小限排在	丑	寅	卯	辰	巳	午	未	申	酉	戌	亥	子
卯宮立命小限排在	寅	卯	辰	巳	午	未	申	酉	戌	亥	子	丑
辰宮立命小限排在	卯	辰	巳	午	未	申	酉	戌	亥	子	丑	寅
巳宮立命小限排在	辰	巳	午	未	申	酉	戌	亥	子	丑	寅	卯
午宮立命小限排在	巳	午	未	申	酉	戌	亥	子	丑	寅	卯	辰
未宮立命小限排在	午	未	申	酉	戌	亥	子	丑	寅	卯	辰	巳
申宮立命小限排在	未	申	酉	戌	亥	子	丑	寅	卯	辰	巳	午
酉宮立命小限排在	申	酉	戌	亥	子	丑	寅	卯	辰	巳	午	未
戌宮立命小限排在	酉	戌	亥	子	丑	寅	卯	辰	巳	午	未	申
亥宮立命小限排在	戌	亥	子	丑	寅	卯	辰	巳	午	未	申	酉

辰宮立命

詩云
辰宮屬金
內藏翌軫角三宿
角宿六度入卯宮
命裡賜來一太陰
天德福星四面臨
蜜賀新人
本年太陰守命外逢紫微龍德天
喜歲合拱照天德福星當頭
難內有賁索勾神天煞外有天厄
捲舌諸凶亦當制伏立命在此當有樂龍
跨馬弄璋弄瓦之慶可喜可賀
鼓瑟吹
作福隨意

巳宮立命

詩云
巳宮屬水
內藏星張翌三宿
翌宿六度入辰宮
本年五鬼官符守命外逢太歲白虎劍鋒星扶馬連天解
興旺宅龍官符招妖祟黃旛白虎舞劍鋒將星扶馬連天解急斯堪
天解拱照辟馬持朝或可化凶災於一二立命城隍太歲作福
之虞勿理閒事為要
五鬼官符守命外逢太歲白虎劍鋒血及相攻幸有將星
立命在此妨有雀角之爭及災耗

午宮立命

詩云
午宮屬太陽
內藏井鬼柳星四宿
井宿廿五度入午宮
本年月德守命外有太陽天德福星歲合朝拱似乎甚吉無奈三星在
戶謹慎平安本命寡宿蚨煞刑剋相侵
咸池小耗六害同宮寡宿蚨煞刑剋相侵
子否則難免耗剋也
惡煞危病無統應立命在此宜財神城隍天后作福
喪白暑紅飄異色孤解難

未宮立命

詩云
未宮屬太陰
內藏參井二宿
井宿廿五度入午宮
本年歲破大耗命外逢太歲拔頭黃旛天狗吊客及紅白大事
化地神過本宮周行盛耗災狗吠蘭庭吊客來
地解同垣誠恐獨力難持寡不敵求立命在此妨太歲華陀醫靈作福
修造等不宜多見

The inquirer now turns through the following pages until he finds the specific predictions associated with Szu and there he will find the broad outline of the coming year's fortune (see opposite). It starts with a poem followed by an explanation.

Five ghosts, law breaking and many demons trouble you.
All around is evil; the White Tiger prowls and cutthroats are
*   near.*
Two auspicious stars come to your aid.
Using feng-shui, check your home and this will bring better
*   fortune.*

This year be careful in all you do because of the five ghosts and law breakers. You will be attacked by T'ai Sui [the planet Jupiter], the White Tiger and swords. Fortunately two auspicious stars will come and provide a little help. So be patient. Do not quarrel with friends or neighbours. Beware of accidents this year and generally mind your own business.

The last page of Section 3 gives the best dates to commence certain undertakings, such as beginning your studies or opening a business, as well as giving thanks. Most are concerned with the first time something is done in the New Year, when it is especially important to choose an auspicious day as this influences the rest of the year.

Section 4

THE NEAREST 200 YEARS ARRANGED ACCORDING TO CHINESE AND WESTERN CALENDARS

[HS = Heavenly Stem; name in bracket = Element;
EB = Earthly Branch.]

1801 6th year of Ch'ing dynasty
Emperor Chia-ch'ing
HS Hsin (Metal) EB Yu
Year of the Cock

1802 7th year of Chia-ch'ing
HS Jen (Water) EB Hsu
Year of the Dog

1803 8th year of Chia-ch'ing
HS Kuei (Water) EB Hai
Year of the Pig
Extra month after 2nd month

1804 9th year of Chia-ch'ing
HS Chia (Wood) EB Tzu
Year of the Rat

1805 10th year of Chia-ch'ing
HS Yi (Wood) EB Ch'ou
Year of the Ox
Extra month after 6th month

1806 11th year of Chia-ch'ing
HS Ping (Fire) EB Yin
Year of the Tiger

1807 12th year of Chia-ch'ing
HS Ting (Fire) EB Mao
Year of the Rabbit

1808 13th year of Chia-ch'ing
HS Wu (Earth) EB Ch'en
Year of the Dragon
Extra month after 5th month

1809 14th year of Chia-ch'ing
HS Chi (Earth) EB Szu
Year of the Snake

1810 15th year of Chia-ch'ing
HS Keng (Metal) EB Wu
Year of the Horse

1811 16th year of Chia-ch'ing
HS Hsin (Metal) EB Wei
Year of the Ram
Extra month after 3rd month

1812 17th year of Chia-ch'ing
HS Jen (Water) EB Shen
Year of the Monkey

1813 18th year of Chia-ch'ing
HS Kuei (Water) EB Yu
Year of the Cock

1814 19th year of Chia-ch'ing
HS Chia (Wood) EB Hsu
Year of the Dog
Extra month after 2nd month

1815 20th year of Chia-ch'ing
HS Yi (Wood) EB Hai
Year of the Pig

1816 21st year of Chia-ch'ing
HS Ping (Fire) EB Tzu
Year of the Rat
Extra month after 6th month

1817 22nd year of Chia-ch'ing
HS Ting (Fire) EB Ch'ou
Year of the Ox

1818 23rd year of Chia-ch'ing
HS Wu (Earth) EB Yin
Year of the Tiger

1819 24th year of Chia-ch'ing
HS Chi (Earth) EB Mao
Year of the Rabbit
Extra month after 4th month

1820 25th year of Chia-ch'ing
HS Keng (Metal) EB Ch'en
Year of the Dragon

1821 1st year of the Ch'ing
dynasty Emperor Tao-kuang
HS Hsin (Metal) EB Szu
Year of the Snake

1822 2nd year of Tao-kuang
HS Jen (Water) EB Wu
Year of the Horse
Extra month after 3rd month

近二百年中西年紀對照表

西元	中國紀年		西元	中國紀年
1801	嘉六年辛酉肖雞		1851	咸元年辛亥肖豬 閏八月
1802	慶七年壬戌肖犬		1852	豐二年壬子肖鼠
1803	八年癸亥肖豬 閏二月		1853	三年癸丑肖牛
1804	九年甲子肖鼠		1854	四年甲寅肖虎 閏七月
1805	十年乙丑肖牛 閏六月		1855	五年乙卯肖兔
1806	十一丙寅肖虎		1856	六年丙辰肖龍
1807	十二丁卯肖兔		1857	七年丁巳肖蛇 閏五月
1808	十三戊辰肖龍 閏五月		1858	八年戊午肖馬
1809	十四己巳肖蛇		1859	九年己未肖羊
1810	十五庚午肖馬		1860	十年庚申肖猴 閏三月
1811	十六辛未肖羊 閏三月		1861	十一年辛酉肖雞
1812	十七壬申肖猴		1862	同元年壬戌肖犬 閏八月
1813	十八癸酉肖雞		1863	治二年癸亥肖豬
1814	十九甲戌肖犬 閏二月		1864	三年甲子肖鼠
1815	二十乙亥肖豬		1865	四年乙丑肖牛 閏五月
1816	廿一丙子肖鼠 閏六月		1866	五年丙寅肖虎
1817	廿二丁丑肖牛		1867	六年丁卯肖兔
1818	廿三戊寅肖虎		1868	七年戊辰肖龍 閏四月
1819	廿四己卯肖兔 閏四月		1869	八年己巳肖蛇
1820	廿五庚辰肖龍		1870	九年庚午肖馬 閏十月
1821	道元年辛巳肖蛇		1871	十年辛未肖羊
1822	光二年壬午肖馬 閏三月		1872	十一年壬申肖猴
1823	三年癸未肖羊		1873	十二年癸酉肖雞 閏六月
1824	四年甲申肖猴 閏七月		1874	十三年甲戌肖犬
1825	五年乙酉肖雞		1875	光元年乙亥肖豬
1826	六年丙戌肖犬		1876	緒二年丙子肖鼠 閏五月
1827	七年丁亥肖豬 閏五月		1877	三年丁丑肖牛
1828	八年戊子肖鼠		1878	四年戊寅肖虎
1829	九年己丑肖牛		1879	五年己卯肖兔 閏三月
1830	十年庚寅肖虎 閏四月		1880	六年庚辰肖龍
1831	十一年辛卯肖兔		1881	七年辛巳肖蛇 閏七月
1832	十二年壬辰肖龍 閏九月		1882	八年壬午肖馬
1833	十三年癸巳肖蛇		1883	九年癸未肖羊 閏五月
1834	十四年甲午肖馬		1884	十年甲申肖猴
1835	十五年乙未肖羊 閏六月		1885	十一年乙酉肖雞
1836	十六年丙申肖猴		1886	十二年丙戌肖犬
1837	十七年丁酉肖雞		1887	十三年丁亥肖豬 閏四月
1838	十八年戊戌肖犬 閏四月		1888	十四年戊子肖鼠
1839	十九年己亥肖豬		1889	十五年己丑肖牛
1840	二十年庚子肖鼠		1890	十六年庚寅肖虎 閏二月
1841	廿一年辛丑肖牛 閏三月		1891	十七年辛卯肖兔
1842	廿二年壬寅肖虎		1892	十八年壬辰肖龍 閏六月
1843	廿三年癸卯肖兔 閏七月		1893	十九年癸巳肖蛇
1844	廿四年甲辰肖龍		1894	二十年甲午肖馬
1845	廿五年乙巳肖蛇 閏五月		1895	廿一年乙未肖羊 閏五月
1846	廿六年丙午肖馬		1896	廿二年丙申肖猴
1847	廿七年丁未肖羊		1897	廿三年丁酉肖雞
1848	廿八年戊申肖猴 閏四月		1898	廿四年戊戌肖犬 閏三月
1849	廿九年己酉肖雞 閏四月		1899	廿五年己亥肖豬
1850	三十年庚戌肖犬		1900	廿六年庚子肖鼠 閏八月

1823	3rd year of Tao-kuang HS Kuei (Water) EB Wei Year of the Ram	1838	18th year of Tao-kuang HS Wu (Earth) EB Hsu Year of the Dog Extra month after 4th month
1824	4th year of Tao-kuang HS Chia (Wood) EB Shen Year of the Monkey Extra month after 7th month	1839	19th year of Tao-kuang HS Chi (Earth) EB Hai Year of the Pig
1825	5th year of Tao-kuang HS Yi (Wood) EB Yu Year of the Cock	1840	20th year of Tao-kuang HS Keng (Metal) EB Tzu Year of the Rat
1826	6th year of Tao-kuang HS Ping (Fire) EB Hsu Year of the Dog	1841	21st year of Tao-kuang HS Hsin (Metal) EB Ch'ou Year of the Ox Extra month after 3rd month
1827	7th year of Tao-kuang HS Ting (Fire) EB Hai Year of the Pig Extra month after 5th month	1842	22nd year of Tao-kuang HS Jen (Water) EB Yin Year of the Tiger
1828	8th year of Tao-kuang HS Wu (Earth) EB Tzu Year of the Rat	1843	23rd year of Tao-kuang HS Kuei (Water) EB Mao Year of the Rabbit Extra month after 7th month
1829	9th year of Tao-kuang HS Chi (Earth) EB Ch'ou Year of the Ox	1844	24th year of Tao-kuang HS Chia (Wood) EB Ch'en Year of the Dragon
1830	10th year of Tao-kuang HS Keng (Metal) EB Yin Year of the Tiger Extra month after 4th month	1845	25th year of Tao-kuang HS Yi (Wood) EB Szu Year of the Snake
1831	11th year of Tao-kuang HS Hsin (Metal) EB Mao Year of the Rabbit	1846	26th year of Tao-kuang HS Ping (Fire) EB Wu Year of the Horse Extra month after 5th month
1832	12th year of Tao-kuang HS Jen (Water) EB Ch'en Year of the Dragon Extra month after 9th month	1847	27th year of Tao-kuang HS Ting (Fire) EB Wei Year of the Ram
1833	13th year of Tao-kuang HS Kuei (Water) EB Szu Year of the Snake	1848	28th year of Tao-kuang HS Wu (Earth) EB Shen Year of the Monkey
1834	14th year of Tao-kuang HS Chia (Wood) EB Wu Year of the Horse	1849	29th year of Tao-kuang HS Chi (Earth) EB Yu Year of the Cock Extra month after 4th month
1835	15th year of Tao-kuang HS Yi (Wood) EB Wei Year of the Ram Extra month after 6th month	1850	30th year of Tao-kuang HS Keng (Metal) EB Hsu Year of the Dog
1836	16th year of Tao-kuang HS Ping (Fire) EB Shen Year of the Monkey	1851	1st year of Ch'ing dynasty Emperor Hsien-feng HS Hsin (Metal) EB Hai Year of the Pig Extra month after 8th month
1837	17th year of Tao-kuang HS Ting (Fire) EB Yu Year of the Cock		

1852	2nd year of Hsien-feng	1854	4th year of Hsien-feng
	HS Jen (Water) EB Tzu		HS Chia (Wood) EB Yin
	Year of the Rat		Year of the Tiger
1853	3rd year of Hsien-feng		Extra month after 7th month
	HS Kuei (Water) EB Ch'ou		
	Year of the Ox		

For details of the Heavenly Stems, Earthly Branches and 'Year of' from 1887 to 1986, see Section 2.

The dates of the emperors and Republic from 1886 to present day are as follows:

Hsien-feng ruled until 1861, that year being the 11th year of his reign.

In 1862 T'ung-chih ascended the throne and ruled until 1874, that year being the 13th year of his reign.

In 1875 Kuaug-hu ascended the throne and ruled until 1908, that year being the 34th year of his reign.

In 1908 Hsuan-t'ung ascended the throne and abdicated in 1911. 1911 is thus termed the 3rd year of Hsuan-t'ung.

From 1912 the Republic commences. The Almanac records the years from 1912 to 1948 as the years of the Republic. 1948 is thus the 37th year of the Republic.

From 1949 onwards the Almanac gives no details of year titles.

Section 5

THE TWENTY-FOUR JOINTS AND BREATHS OF THE SOLAR YEAR

The Twenty-Four Joints and Breaths of the year have already been mentioned in the Introduction (see p. 30). However, it is important to stress their significance as agricultural and climatic landmarks in the year. Below is a full list of the twenty-four with the meaning of their names. They start on 4 February with Li Ch'un and continue at regular fifteen-day intervals throughout the year.

As weather predictions they are generally very good and when the term 'peasant calendar' is used these days it is often the Twenty-Four Joints and Breaths that are being referred to.

Apart from featuring here and in two other, smaller charts, the details of the Joints and Breaths also appear with due prominence in the appropriate places in the calendar section of the Almanac (Section 46). Below them are details of the exact time when each particular Joint and Breath starts, for example, in 1985 Ku Yu fell on Day 1 of the Third Moon and started at 11.26 a.m.

Certain of the twenty-four have achieved fame as occasions for festivals or as marking the alternative New Year. Ch'ing Ming has become the day and name for one of the most important ancestor festivals. Li Ch'un, as we saw earlier in the book, is the astrologers' New Year and the date of the famous former festival of the Spring Cow. The four seasons are naturally marked by the Twenty-Four Joints and Breaths. The first, seventh, thirteenth and nineteenth are the starts of the seasons, with the tenth and twenty-second being the solstices and the fourth and sixteenth marking the equinoxes.

The role of the twenty-four as the basis of the calendar is clearly seen in the dynastic shifts of New Year over two thousand years ago. The *Yueh Ling* (see p. 16) starts its record of the year thus: 'In the first month of spring . . .'. In other words, here is evidence of why the astrologers have used Li Ch'un, the Beginning of Spring, as their New Year. Ssu-ma Ch'ien records in his epic *History* that, in 106 BCE, Emperor Wu opened a special 'House of the Calendar' on the first day of the New Year marking a new cycle of Heavenly and Earthly signs. This took place on the day of the winter solstice, and Ssu-ma Ch'ien records Wu as saying 'The period has revolved!

香港地區

立春	雨水	驚蟄	春分	清明	穀雨	立夏	小滿
日出	日入	日出	日入	日出	日入	日出	日入
上午	下午	上午	下午	上午	下午	上午	下午
七點	六點	六點	六點	六點	六點	五點	六點
零分	五分	二分	二分	四分	一分	四十六分	五十九分

芒種	夏至	小暑	大暑	立秋	處暑	白露	秋分
日出	日入	日出	日入	日出	日入	日出	日入
上午	下午	上午	下午	上午	下午	上午	下午
五點	七點	五點	七點	五點	七點	六點	六點
四十六分	十一分	五十分	八分	五分	零分	四分	三十九分

寒露	霜降	立冬	小雪	大雪	冬至	小寒	大寒
日出	日入	日出	日入	日出	日入	日出	日入
上午	下午	上午	下午	上午	下午	上午	下午
六點	五點	六點	五點	六點	五點	七點	六點
零分	四十一分	十三分	三十四分	四十五分	三十分	十四分	五十分

新加坡地區

立春	雨水	驚蟄	春分	清明	穀雨	立夏	小滿
日出	日入	日出	日入	日出	日入	日出	日入
上午	下午	上午	下午	上午	下午	上午	下午
六點	六點	六點	六點	六點	六點	六點	六點
四十一分	十七分	十六分	九分	四分	六分	四十八分	十二分

芒種	夏至	小暑	大暑	立秋	處暑	白露	秋分
日出	日入	日出	日入	日出	日入	日出	日入
上午	下午	上午	下午	上午	下午	上午	下午
六點	七點	六點	七點	六點	七點	六點	六點
十六分	九分	三十分	十一分	三十分	十五分	十八分	三十九分

寒露	霜降	立冬	小雪	大雪	冬至	小寒	大寒
日出	日入	日出	日入	日出	日入	日出	日入
上午	下午	上午	下午	上午	下午	上午	下午
六點	六點	六點	五點	六點	五點	六點	六點
四十五分	三十一分	十三分	十九分	三十四分	四十一分	四十五分	十四分

It begins again!' The historian goes on to make the following observation: 'Those who calculated the calendar made of this date [25 November 105 BC] the first starting-point.'[1] Ssu-ma Ch'ien also states that at first the Han dynasty (founded 207 BCE) continued to use the Ch'in calendar, which started the year with the tenth month.

Thus it is possible to see that the Twenty-Four Joints and Breaths are very much the backbone of the whole of calendrical science.

HONG KONG CALENDAR OF THE TWENTY-FOUR TERMS OR DIVISIONS OF THE YEAR, THEIR START AND THEIR END

[Reading from top right to bottom left in right-hand column on p. 65.]

1. *Li Ch'un – Beginning of Spring*
   Start at 7.01 a.m. End at 6.14 p.m.
2. *Yu Shui – Constant Rain*
   Start at 6.53 a.m. End at 6.22 p.m.
3. *Ching Che – Awakening of Insects*
   Start at 6.41 a.m. End at 6.29 p.m.
4. *Ch'un Fen – Spring Equinox*
   Start at 6.26 a.m. End at 6.35 p.m.
5. *Ch'ing Ming – Bright and Clear*
   Start at 6.12 a.m. End at 6.40 p.m.
6. *Ku Yu – Rain Showers*
   Start at 6.00 a.m. End at 6.46 p.m.
7. *Li Hsia – Beginning of Summer*
   Start at 5.46 a.m. End at 6.52 p.m.
8. *Hsiao Man – Small Harvest*
   Start at 5.42 a.m. End at 6.49 p.m.
9. *Mang Chung – Sowing of Seed*
   Start at 5.39 a.m. End at 7.06 p.m.
10. *Hsia Chih – Summer Solstice*
    Start at 5.40 a.m. End at 7.10 p.m.
11. *Hsiao Shu – Minor Heat*
    Start at 5.45 a.m. End at 7.11 p.m.
12. *Ta Shu – Great Heat*
    Start at 5.52 a.m. End at 7.08 p.m.
13. *Li Ch'in – Beginning of Autumn*
    Start at 5.58 a.m. End at 7.00 p.m.
14. *Ch'u Shu – End of the Heat*
    Start at 6.03 a.m. End at 6.49 p.m.
15. *Pai Lu – White Dew*
    Start at 6.08 a.m. End at 6.34 p.m.
16. *Ch'iu Fen – Autumn Equinox*
    Start at 6.20 a.m. End at 6.19 p.m.
17. *Han Lu – Cold Dew*
    Start at 6.17 a.m. End at 6.04 p.m.
18. *Shuang Chiang – Frost*
    Start at 6.24 a.m. End at 5.51 p.m.
19. *Li Tung – Beginning of Winter*
    Start at 6.32 a.m. End at 5.43 p.m.
20. *Hsiao Hsueh – Minor Snow*
    Start at 6.14 a.m. End at 5.39 p.m.
21. *Ta Hsueh – Great Snow*
    Start at 6.50 a.m. End at 5.40 p.m.
22. *Tung Chih – Winter Solstice*
    Start at 6.58 a.m. End at 5.44 p.m.
23. *Hsiao Han – Minor Cold*
    Start at 7.04 a.m. End at 5.55 p.m.
24. *Ta Han – Great Cold*
    Start at 7.05 a.m. End at 6.00 p.m.

Section 6

CHARTS FOR WRITING
TWO AUSPICIOUS
CHARACTERS IN 100 WAYS

The power of the written character is known wherever writing has been practised. In traditional Chinese culture this reached considerable heights. Any piece of paper with writing on it was considered important and wilfully to destroy any writing was deemed the act of a barbarian. As we shall see in Section 10, the use of writing as a charm or talisman also features in Chinese thought. There are two other factors which come to bear on this section: first, the development of writing as an art form in itself, which leads to both a vast diversity of styles and an ability to utilize words in a decorative pattern; secondly, the authority or power that certain characters have because of their meaning. Certain characters are highly charged with meaning in a way which is difficult for non-Chinese to grasp. Their role is perhaps best seen in the following example: Chinese ceramic spoons or bowls will often have a character – or, in the case of a bowl, four characters – painted on them, usually associated with longevity, health, wealth and happiness; they are not there just for decoration. The idea of writing such words in English on spoons or bowls would never dawn upon the English – unless it is a commemorative article, in which case by dint of association it becomes more charged with meaning.

The calligraphy charts of the two characters shown on pp. 68–9 are often used as backdrops to domestic shrines or as decoration for temples. The two characters are 'good luck' and 'longevity'.

百福全圖

太極圖
鐘鼎文
王子安
王棄篆
遲父鐘
主屑章
宋友門
萬古文
李長吉
徐楷文
勁曹奇
蒼頡文
王子敬
上帝文
即華篆
瑞章文
江緣溪
景雲書
洵屋文
東虞文
復古文
帝上文
帝印文
蒙古文
欽古文
存童文
方受文
高篆文
登天文
小篆文
羊歡文
度樂文
老君文
高麗文
星斗文
三佛文
古數章
五禺文
偃波文
社中文
許慎文
鐘聶
五敬文
南鼎文
張仲匜
陳蒼書
萬庚書
胡文員
周鼎文
星中書
擇父鐘
湯誠齋
蜈鬲書
鳥跡文
古福篆
垂露文
正帝文
圭章文
米差作
鳳尾文
魯篆文
刻符文
故書文
石鼓文
張芝文
菉學文
紫霄文
白然文
流香篆
連鉄文
澤光文
虹乞文
重篆文
上元文
古篆文
飛霞文
王澡文
岑參文
獅形文
柏子文
象形文
漆書文
奇字文
金錯文
會示文
大當文
著草文
可祿文
燕祖蛇
高捨文
古烏文
龍鳳文
上大常
皇杼文
平簡文
屈平書
科斗文
六書文
四川文
泰篆文

百壽全圖

Section 7

THE BISCUIT POEM OF LIU PO WEN

(Consultant Adviser to the First Emperor
of the Ming Dynasty)

The strange title of this section is explained in the first few lines
of the account as given below. Liu Po Wen, the Chinese
Nostradamus, was an adviser to the first Ming Emperor, Chu
Yuan-chang. Liu Po Wen was also known as Liu Chi, and it is
this name which is used in the actual text of the prophecy. Liu
Chi is reputed to have met a sticky end, despite the pledges of
the Emperor given in the poem. Fearful of Liu's knowledge
and power, the Emperor had him executed.

The prophecy is reputed to date from $c.$ 1370 CE and to
foretell in a cryptic manner the fortunes of the ruling houses of
Ming and Ch'ing. Apart from its inclusion in the Almanac
(which appears to be of relatively recent date) the prophecy is
also available with various commentaries and interpretations
in small booklet form in a couple of Chinese editions. It seems
to have the sort of fascination that, say, the Book of Daniel or
Revelation has for Christians. As with the Book of Daniel, it is
possible to see that while purporting to be written in a former
time, it is in fact of quite recent date. In the case of Daniel, this
was supposedly written $c.$ 550 BCE in Babylon. It tells with
remarkable accuracy the fate of various empires until about
160 BCE. From then on it becomes very vague. It is likely that
Daniel was in fact written $c.$ 160 BCE as propaganda against the
invading Greeks. It uses history to show that all empires will
fall before God. Similarly, the prophecy of Liu Pei Wen claims
to date from 1370 CE and is remarkably accurate until the fall
of the Ch'ing dynasty in 1911. From then on it gets very vague
and ill-defined. It seems likely that the prophecy arose from
the chaos of the early Republic, the rise of Communism and
the Japanese invasion as an attempt to answer fears and to
show that all would eventually be well. It is interesting that in
one of the books of commentary the last line of the commentary on the last section of the prophecy concerns the calendar.
It says that one of the signs of change will be when the lunar
calendar is done away with and the Western one is introduced.
The calendar was changed thus under the first years of the
Republic. Furthermore, the Court, including the traditional
office charged with constructing the lunar calendar, was

cleared out of the Forbidden City in 1924. Perhaps this gives us a point at which the prophecy arose.

The prophecy is very difficult to understand as it relies upon puns and games using various characters to make up a totally new character which then reveals a name. In the translation we have given the true meaning where this was discoverable. In square brackets we have then given historical explanations and, where appropriate, we have also explained how the text reads in the original and what methods are used to arrive at its true reading. Thus anyone trying to read the Chinese text will need to bear this in mind. For non-Chinese readers, we thought it important to give the prophecy followed by an explanation rather than an exact translation of the Chinese text.

The great founding Emperor of the Ming dynasty was eating a biscuit in his palace one day. Just as he took the first bite, a servant came to say that Consultant Liu Chi wished to speak to the Emperor. The Emperor covered the bowl and sent for Liu Chi.

The Emperor asked Chi: 'Sir, you are good at predictions, calculating and so forth. Do you know what is covered with this bowl?'

Chi calculated on his fingers and said, 'It looks like the sun, or like the moon, and one piece has been bitten by a golden dragon [the Emperor].' The Emperor removed the bowl and revealed the biscuit.

[The dialogue continues thus:]

EMPEROR: *'Tell me, what will be the future of my country?'*

CHI: *'Boundless is your rule. Myriad are your sons and grandsons. Why do you ask me about the future?'*

EMPEROR: *'From ancient times it is said that the destiny of a land is fixed either for good or bad. Is it true that one man under Heaven [the Emperor of China] can bring good or bad luck to the country?'*

CHI: *'Our Ming dynasty is very prosperous and controls the earth. But there will be wars in the south. The north side will be all right because the north side has your eldest son the Prince. He has a good-fortune star Wen Sing. [This refers to the capture of Peking early in the Ming dynasty.] The west side is strongly defended.'*

EMPEROR: *'So this is good.'*

CHI: *'In my opinion, although your castle is strong and sturdy a swallow can easily fly over it.' (Chi is referring to the Emperor's fourth son, Yen Wang.) Chi then wrote three songs of prophecy.*

'When Yen Wang comes to be the Emperor, there will be

71

peace. *[This refers to Yung Lo who was the first Emperor's fourth son and rebelled against the first Emperor's grandson. Yung Lo waged a fierce civil war until his victory in 1403 when he captured Nanking. He is also referred to in the text by his Title of Reign, Yung Le.]* When the old, bald person comes to advise (Minister Yao Kuang) all will be well. Because there is no war, nearly half the heroes (members of the Kan Chung Society) will disperse. On the north side many Mongols will attack, killing many people. Therefore the Emperor should attack by himself and gain peace. *[Yung Lo himself led a number of successful attacks on the Mongols and associated tribes.]* The senior officers will admire the Emperor's skill – but if once he slips, they will rebel. *[In 1449 the Mongols attacked again, seizing the Emperor. A new Emperor was found and he repulsed the invaders.]* So defend the Empire and the Mongols will not attack. (The north side will be strongly and bravely defended by you.) Tomorrow strengthen your borders.' *[A major rebuilding of the Great Wall took place in the mid-Ming period.]*

EMPEROR: 'How is China now?'

CHI: 'This is a very bad time.'

EMPEROR: 'How and why is it so bad?'

CHI: 'Lots of people are hungry. Yet the Emperors *[Tai Tsung, Ying Tsung, Wu Tsung and Shih Tsung are meant in particular – c. 1449–1566]* live in luxury, are well fed and live long. At that time there will be a Prime Minister called Wei. He will cause trouble, death and conflict amongst the good officials. He will run pirate ships.' *[This refers to Wei Chung-hsien (1568–1627). A eunuch, he rose to terrible power. In the text he is named obliquely. The text reads '8000 women ghosts trouble the Palace'. The characters for '8000 women ghosts' are 八千女鬼. Combined together they make the character 魏. This is Wei.]*

EMPEROR: 'Will father and son fight over the country?'

CHI: 'No. The last of your name will hang himself from a tree. *[This is referred to cryptically in the text thus: 'The T square hangs on the tree.' The character for 'tree' is 木. Put a T square hanging from it and you have 朱. This is the character Chu, which is the family name of the Ming Emperors.]* The country will be attacked by a person called Shun. Then your country will be nearly finished.'

EMPEROR: 'What do you mean by nearly finished?'

CHI: 'When myriad sons and myriad grandsons go, that will be the end (meaning the son of Emperor Wan Li and the grandson, Ch'ung Cheng, the last Emperor). The Manchu will take over. Li Tzu-ch'eng will also attack. *[This is referred to cryptically thus: 'Eighteen sons will attack.' The characters for 'eighteen sons' are 十八子. Combine these and they form the character 李, Li. Li led a major revolt in the provinces* of Shensi, Hupei and Honan at the end of the Ming dynasty, from 1630 to 1644. In 1644 he captured Peking, effectively ending the Ming dynasty. This laid the way open for the Manchu to invade and set up the Ch'ing dynasty. The rest of Li Tzu-ch'eng's name is also found by puns, e.g., 'The eye with a line above.' The characters for 'eye' and 'line' are and 目 / respectively. Combined they make 自, Tzu.] The eldest son of the Emperor will attack the country. People would rather study than fight. The year of Mao Tzu and Chi Ch'ou will be very bad. Every house will be deserted. Many will go hungry. A warlord will control the city (Wu San-kuei).' [This refers to the Ming general Wu San-kuei. The last Emperor called him to assist Peking. Before he arrived, Li had taken Peking. Wu surrendered to the Manchu and together they drove Li from Peking.]

EMPEROR: 'Hunger is not important. That is normal.'

CHI: 'The western side will attack. There are no honest advisers. Your countrymen will see the country go downhill day by day. There will be no luck in the country and the cunning people will be scheming all the time. The general will flee and cross the Yellow River seeking refuge.'

EMPEROR: 'Will there be trouble on Coal Hill, because extra soldiers can be sent if necessary?' [This refers to the Forbidden City.]

CHI: 'No, there will now be peace. [The Ch'ing dynasty will be founded.] There is a lucky star which blesses the country for half of six hundred years.' [The Ch'ing dynasty lasted nearly three hundred years, from 1644 to 1911.]

EMPEROR: 'So they rule for half of six hundred years. This is good. I don't want any more. Why don't you write down your ideas and put them into a sealed envelope for us to open in times of trouble? If you are too embarrassed to say something, write it down and I'll put it in my treasury for my son or grandson to open if necessary.'

CHI: 'I had just the same idea!'

Chi made up a song for the Emperor which said: 'During this period there will be war with Japan and trouble with eunuchs. The Mongols will rule for 280 years. Wu San-kuei and his followers have been surrounded. [Wu rebelled against the Ch'ing dynasty in 1673 and was followed by two other provincial rulers in a war known as the Revolt of the Three Feudatories. They were not defeated until 1681.] There will be twenty-three people to protect the eight directions.' [The figure 23 means the Three Feudatories.]

EMPEROR: 'Will the twenty-three be honest and will the people fare well?'

CHI: 'I will tell you honestly. If the twenty-three are

dishonest, then your Ming dynasty is finally over.' [The revolt sought to re-establish the Ming dynasty but eventually crumbled through mistrust.]

The Emperor was very surprised. 'Who is in charge of China?' he asked.

CHI: [*This entire section consists of the characters for 2 and 8 followed by one other character. Whilst the cryptic code of some of it is clear, at other points it is not.*] 'The Ch'ing will last 280 years. There will be 2–8 major wars.' [*They include, according to the commentary, the White Lotus (1796–1804, Buddhist Triad Society); the T'ai-ping (1850–65); Moslems (1855–70); Kashgar (seized in 1758–59); England (the Opium Wars of 1840 and 1859); England and France (1860); Russia (at various times); Japan (1894–95).*]

EMPEROR: 'The Mongols – will they really last over two hundred years?'

CHI: 'The Ch'ing dynasty will be in charge. [*The text reads: 'The rain water grass head.' The characters are* 雨水草頭 . *They make Mau,* 滿 , *the family name of the Ch'ing.*] They will come to China in the eighteenth year of Shun Chih. [*This was the first Ch'ing Emperor, who had ruled the Mongols from 1627. In 1644 he was thus entering his eighteenth year.*] In the 18th year of Shun Chih fire and water will fight each other. The next Emperor (K'ang Hsi) will rule (for sixty-one years). [*K'ang Hsi, 1662–1723.*] So use the men of your own province as they are more loyal.'

EMPEROR: 'You use the men as water to kill the fire. Will the son-in-law attack?' [*K'ang Hsi's eldest son often tried plotting against him.*]

CHI: 'No. Because water and fire will compromise, there will be peace in the country. But some people will be dishonest and cunning and cause trouble. Also many people will go hungry. Under Yung Cheng [1723–36] and Ch'ien Lung [1736–96] things will get better.'

EMPEROR: 'Will Mongolia cease to be?'

CHI: 'Not yet, although people will have a hard time. But the luck of the country is going well. All the people will be of one heart and working towards the same goal. (This is during Chia Ch'ing [1796–1821].) After this time many will die. Monks and nuns will become revolutionaries. The British will invade with cannons. [*Text says: 'The fire dragon will cross the river and make it too hot to bear.' This refers to the British bombardment of forts in 1840.*] (This period is called Tao Kuang [1821–51].) There will be many disasters. Hung will attack. [*Hung Hsiu-ch'uan led the T'ai-ping rebellion. His name is found by yet another cryptic use of characters.*] It will be especially bad in the years of the Ram, Monkey, Pig and

Dog. Sorrow will abound. The moon's light will be dimmed during the next period (called Hsien Feng). [This refers to the crushing of the vast T'ai-ping rebellion of 1850–65. The rebels called themselves Ming, which means 'bright'. The character is constructed from the characters for moon and day. Hence the pun and cryptic reference. Hsein Feng ruled from 1851 to 1862.] In the next period (T'ung Chih [1862–75]) people will go hungry and there will be many disturbances. But the country will be built up again. [Following the defeat of the T'ai-ping, the country was more settled although revolts occurred in many places.] But beware. For a woman carrying a baby will be in charge.' (Kuang Hsu [1875–1908].) [During this time the country was ruled by the Empress Dowager Tz'u-hsi whose son Kuang Hsu was only four years old when he came to the throne. Tz'u-hsi dominated the last decades of the Ch'ing.]

EMPEROR: 'And will Mongolia still exist or not?'

CHI: 'Things will get better. The people will be happy with the Emperor.

'In the end it is the White Flag which will kill the Mongols. [The text says '99 catties'. The character for 100 is 百 . Take away 1 and the character becomes 白 , 'white'. The White Flag was the Ming flag, but refers here to the overthrow of the Ch'ing by the Revolution of 1911.] The capital will move. [Because of feuding warlords, Nanking was for a time the Republic's capital.] It is a troubled time. Moslems, Han, Tibetans, etc., are at war. There is a big hole between the mountains and it holds 108,000. If anyone gets there, they will be all right. If not, then hard luck. [A possible reference to Hong Kong.] A big general [this is supposed to be Hsuan T'ung, also known as Pu Yi, or one of his restorationist generals] on a horse will come and kill the bad men and protect the honest. The people will enjoy peace.'

EMPEROR: 'Will Mongolia still be there?'

CHI: 'Mongolia will have been defeated long ago. Everything will be well and music will play. There will be an Emperor for five hundred years and a holy man will come to sort out all the problems. All will be peaceful. Everyone will have enough money. The Mongolians in the north will still have a difficult time because they were defeated by the eight groups' army. Everyone will be free to enjoy themselves. The luck of the country will go well. All things will be plentiful. At this time there will be a lot of learning. It will be like a monkey splashing, a chicken on a perch or a dog barking [instances of exuberance]. The country will have excellent poets and generals. If a war comes, it will make the people flee a thousand miles. So the subjects should be loved as though brothers. Train for posterity and for whatever comes.'

Section 8

THE YELLOW EMPEROR'S POEM OF THE FOUR SEASONS

This set of figures represents one of the most simple and general forecasts in the Almanac. It is not to be taken too seriously. To work it, you need to know what 'hour' you were born in – that is to say, which of the Twelve Earthly Branches is yours. Then you find the picture for the season in which you were born. Reading from top to bottom the pictures represent spring, summer, autumn and winter. Let us say your 'hour' character is Tzu (子), and you were born in the winter. This means looking at the fourth picture. Here, Tzu (子) is shown in the small circle on the Emperor's belly. You then look up in the columns on the left the general forecast for those born on the Emperor's belly.

The figure represented in the pictures is that of Huang-ti – the Yellow Emperor (*c.* 2650 BCE), first of the Five August Emperors. He is credited in legend with enormous powers of control. Ssu-ma Ch'ien, the historian, speaks of his causing 'beings in movement and in repose, divine beings, great and small, everything on which the sun and moon shine, to become calm and docile.' What better person to use!

The poem reads down each column, starting on the right:

Born on the Emperor's head,
No troubles in life at all.
Even the poor will get rich,
Enough clothes and food.

He always gets senior post,
An excellent mind for planning.
Women will be very steady and good,
Marrying into high class (educated husband).

Born on the Emperor's hand,
Money enough for a business.
Gentlemen help him, even when travelling,
Home gives him every comfort.

When he first starts something it is so-so,
But later very successful.
Money will come from all directions.
When old, all is success.

春 季

夏 季

秋 季

冬 季

生在黃帝頭
慶世多高位
君子好籌謀
一世永無憂
小人多富貴
女人平穩好
衣食自然週
嫁得俊儒流

生在黃帝手
初年平平穩
營謀本錢夠
積聚十分有
財帛四方來
出外貴人逢
家中百事有
老大則到手

生在黃帝肩
衣祿隨時好
一生富萬千
晚景有庄田
中年財帛有
兄弟多得力
前苦後頭甜
兒孫衣頭繼

生在黃帝腹
中年衣食貴
晚年多享福
衣食自然足
文武兩邊隨
快活盡榮華
老大得黃金
笙歌連舞曲

生祿隨衣食
中年衣食貴
晚年多享福
衣食自然足
子孫必新食好
中年衣食好
老大明多得黃金
文明多進步

黃帝門風多改換
父母當奇珍
此是貴人身
初年勞碌多
晚景享榮多
中年辛苦極
也不缺衣食

生日日路上行
未免腳掃拂
作事無利益
一世也平安
踏破荒山嶺
中年辛苦極
也不缺衣食

女生在黃帝足
人嫁兩夫
男人妻兩續
修行免勞碌
一世也平安
踏破荒山嶺
不宜居祖屋
雛祖方成福

Born on the Emperor's shoulder,
Throughout life is wealthy.
In middle age, what riches!
Lots of sons and grandsons.

Well dressed at all times,
Old age brings properties and farms.
All his brothers come to help.
In old age he has every comfort.

Born on the Emperor's belly,
He is well dressed and fed.
Personal assistants, bodyguards at all times,
For ever holding parties and dancing.

In middle age, more variable fortune,
In old age he enjoys a comfortable time.
Longevity makes him happy and glorious
And brings him yet more good fortune.

Born on the Emperor's girth,
He has such loving parents.
In middle age, well dressed and fed,
In old age he has gold.

He moves, is promoted many times,
For he is a nobleman.
His son and grandson very modern,
Thriving in the progressive world.

Born on the Emperor's knee,
He receives no reward for his labours.
When young, such difficult jobs.
Few clothes he has but at least he has some.

Day after day, no time to rest,
By middle age, worn and tired.
But old age brings wealth;
Middle age brings terrible bad luck.

Born on the Emperor's foot,
Things come easily to him,
Avoiding difficulties, preserving himself from dangers.
It is not suitable for him to live in his ancestor's house.

If a woman, then two husbands.
If a man, married twice.
If he lives far from his ancestor's house,
He will be more comfortable in his old age.

Section 9

TIME OF SUNRISE AND SUNSET OF THE TWENTY-FOUR JOINTS AND BREATHS OF THE YEAR

For details of the Twenty-Four Joints and Breaths, see the Introduction, p. 30, and Section 5. The list included in this section of the Almanac provides a further aid to farmers by giving sunrise and sunset times according to readings based on Kwangtung (Canton).

CHARMS

(Sections 10, 17 and 44)

The use of charms has been a long-established part of Chinese religion. The Almanac itself is a charm. By hanging it from a doorpost or bed, evil is warded off. Hence the red (lucky colour) loop of string at the top of each copy. It is also used in other ways. For instance, a pregnant woman who is suffering badly may have a copy placed on her stomach. In certain cases, a copy will be put under the pillow of a sick person. The colours, characters and illustrations used for the Almanac's cover are all bound up with its properties as a charm against evil and misfortune.

Within the book itself there are three sections containing charms. Their functions vary enormously although their method of use remains virtually the same.

The charm itself cannot be used by just anyone. It is customary to seek the help of a fortune-teller, a diviner, a Taoist or Buddhist priest or an astrologer. In many cases the person involved will fulfil several of the above functions. The room or building will have been prepared by the burning of incense. The practitioner will then select the most appropriate and powerful charm. These are either charms associated with Chang Tao-ling (see below) or linked to one of the gods. The charm is written on yellow paper using red ink. This must be done with due reverence in order to invoke the power of the particular deity.

The charms begin in several formal ways. Those in the Chang Tao-ling section begin with Chen (鎮), meaning 'to repress' or 'to reduce to submission'. It is imposing order on the chaotic. In the later sections some of the talismans begin with Ch'ih (勅), 'to order' or 'to command'. In Section 44 all the charms to protect against illness according to the month begin in this way. The term Ch'ih is one of the earliest ones used in charms. Combined with Kwei – ghost or demon – it appears in the literature of the Han period (207 BCE–9 CE).

Certain charms begin with Cheng (正). The word Cheng means 'first' and is used in Taoist literature to describe the Tao – the first principle of universal order. This gives a hint at the functional concept underlying the use of charms. In their most potent form they combat the forces of disruption and chaos which threaten order.

It is also worth noting that charms are deemed more

powerful if they also have a representation of lightning (or if possible two representations). This is usually done by elongating the final stroke or strokes of the principal charm character into a twisting line denoting lightning. There are two concepts linked with this usage. First, the primeval chaos as described in the traditional creation story is disrupted by a bolt of lightning erupting into the midst of the dark mists. The effect of this bolt is to shatter the darkness. From this Heaven and Earth emerge; from them the creative forces of yin and yang arise. So, at the beginning of time, chaos is transformed into order by lightning. (A similar function of creative power over chaos appears in the complex story of the killing of Emperor Hun-tun, whose name means 'chaos', by the emperors Shu and Hu. Shu-hu means 'lightning', and at the death of Hun-tun the world emerged.)[1]

Secondly, the Thunder God is a major figure of order and correction. With his lightning he strikes down wrongdoers, especially those who threaten the divine order. In Buddhist mythology, lightning is pictured as shattering false teachings and beliefs. Again, the emphasis is on re-establishing order.

The charms often end using language reminiscent of former Imperial Edicts. Formulas such as 'Let the Law be obeyed; let this order be respected and executed straightaway' are used.

Once the charm has been written out, it is usually burned. The ashes are mixed with water and either sprinkled or drunk. Certain charms are pasted up to prevent the entry of evil spirits or other intruders such as birds or mice. The charms contained in the Almanac are there to be copied. They are not seen as being efficacious in their printed form. It is only when they are correctly and reverently written out in appropriately coloured ink that they become effective.

Whilst charms and talismans are used by Buddhist monks and nuns, it is the Taoist influence that lies most forcefully and systematically behind charms and their power. Taoism traces the use of charms and talismans back to the earliest figures of civilization. In the strange collection of apocryphal Taoist writings called *Ku Wei Shu* (*Old Mystery Books*, c. 100 CE), the role of charms and talismans is mentioned in connection with the last two of the legendary Five Emperors – Yao and Shun – and the mysterious Emperor who founded the Hsia dynasty, Yu the Great. Of Yu the Great, the story goes that there was a great and terrible river flood which devastated most of China. Yu was assigned the duty of fighting the flood and for ten years, sparing neither himself nor his men, he struggled to contain the river. In the end, he was helped by the gift of a talisman chart. Painted with red characters on green material, it showed how the river should flow. Whoever controlled this talisman – called the Ho-t'u – controlled the stars, rivers and the Five Elements. This talisman, having achieved its purpose under the rule of Yu, was then buried on Mao Shan.[2]

One of the central documents of religious (rather than philosophical) Taoism is the Ling-pao Five Talismans. These great charms (one of which was the talisman given to Yu) control all creation and in some texts are credited with the act of creation itself. Like so many of the most powerful charms in Taoism, they can only be used with great caution. But the idea expressed in this description of their original formation captures the sense of order and authority which lies at the heart of the use of charms:

> The heavenly writings, jade characters,
> Flew off and disappeared into the primordial breath
> Of the mysterious void,
> Where they congealed and became Ling-wen,
> 'Writings which bear spirit and life'.
> Joined to the eight trigrams, they became harmonious tones.
> Joined to the five talismans, they become chang charms.[3]

There are numerous books within Taoism concerned with the construction and use of charms, such as the *Ch'i-men Tun-chia*, which contains talismans and charms for the Nine Stars and the Twenty-Eight Constellations. But the key figure in all Taoist works and practice of charms is Chang Tao-ling.

Chang Tao-ling was born in 35 CE and is traditionally believed to have ascended to Heaven to become an Immortal in 157 CE. Legend says that by the age of seven he understood the *Tao Te Ching* (the great Taoist classic reputed to be written by the sage Lao Tzu, in the sixteenth century BCE), alchemy, feng-shui and astronomy. He established a school of practical or 'religious' Taoism in Kiangsi province. His organization of Taoism into something resembling a formal religion entitles him to be called the founder of religious Taoism. He is often known as Chang Tien-shih – Heavenly Master Chang – a title still used by his descendants.

When Chang ascended to Heaven he left behind his seal, his sword, a mystic book and a collection of charms. It is these which form the basis of Taoist charm and talisman study. There is a selection of these charms in the Almanac (see below). It is known that one of Chang Tao-ling's most favoured methods of healing (healing was the core of his school at Kiangsi) was to make the patient write out all the sins and failures of his life, and then wade out into a river, clutching the written confession, and thus cleanse himself of his sins. In this action the roots of written charms as well as the use of water can be traced. Charms derived from Chang Tao-ling are deemed the most efficacious.

Finally, it is worth noting the basis upon which modern Buddhist monks teach students the use of charms. The attacks by Western missionaries, scientists and sociologists plus the reforms forced upon Buddhism by the Communist system within China have led to great caution regarding charms. Stung by charges of superstition and fraud, the modern Buddhist-trained diviner or astrologer who uses charms does so as an integral part of Buddhism. As explained earlier, charms are meant to restore order. It is very much this ordering and controlling function that is stressed today, occasionally even to the extent of regarding charms as being psychologically helpful if nothing else.

Section 10

CHANG T'IEN-SHIH, CATCHER OF GHOSTS, AND HIS CHARMS

The charm immediately below the portrait of Chang T'ien-shih (see p. 84) is put on the wall to protect the home. The bottom right-hand charm is inscribed: 'Place on a well to ensure clean/lucky water.' The third charm, on the bottom left, is inscribed: 'Hundred Different Things Charm', meaning it covers everything.

INCANTATION

The person faces east and recites the following incantation, clenches his teeth three times, holding the water in his mouth, then spits it out.

'*The universe and yin–yang are wide, the sun comes out from the east. I use this charm to get rid of all the evils. My mouth spits out strong fire, my eyes can shine out rays like the sun. I can ask the Heavenly Soldiers to catch the devils and get all sickness out of the house. Heavenly Soldiers can suppress evils and create luck. Let the Law be obeyed; let this order be executed straightaway.*'

張天師符

書符法○叩齒三通含淨水一口向
東噴之○咒曰赫赫陰陽日出東
方勅書此符盡掃不祥口吐三昧
之火眼放如日之光捉怪使天蓬
力士破疾用鎮煞金剛降伏妖怪
化吉爲祥急急如律令勅

鎮衣冠雜履怪符

硃書此符佩帶大吉

百解消災符

鎮宅淨水神符

上半·右起

一、鎮床帳枕被等怪符　　硃書此符佩帶大吉

二、鎮灶釜甑等怪神符　　硃書此符貼廚房吉

三、鎮牛馬犬畜等怪符　　硃書此符貼怪處吉

四、鎮禽鳥入人家等符　　硃書此符貼大門吉

五、鎮鳥獸污衣冠等符　　硃書此符佩帶大吉

下半·右起

六、鎮器皿物具等怪符　　硃書此符壓怪處吉

七、鎮舟車等速靈怪符　　硃書此符壓怪處吉

八、鎮野獸入人家等符　　硃書此符貼門上吉

九、鎮鷄鵝鳥等怪之符　　此符壓栖井窩上吉

十、鎮諸般總怪之靈符　　此符與見怪人佩吉

[Whenever you make use of any of the ten charms shown on p. 85, you should also put charms 1 and 3 up in your house at the same time.]

1. *To be carried whenever you move your bed – to protect bedding*
2. *To be hung on the kitchen wall when you are installing a new stove – to protect kitchen implements*
3. *To be put on the wall of animal enclosures to avoid sickness*
4. *To be hung on the main entrance door to prevent the entry of birds and other flying creatures*
5. *To be carried on the person to prevent birds and animals coming near and soiling your clothes*
6. *To be put up around the house if objects keep getting lost*
7. *To be put inside a car or boat to avoid accidental loss*
8. *To be hung on the main door to prevent the entry of wild animals*
9. *To be put up at places where clothes are drying and at wells to prevent their being soiled by birds*
10. *To be carried on the person to give added power in avoiding all the above misfortunes – protecting the person from disturbed people*

Section 17

CHARMS TO PROTECT THE FOETUS AND SPIRITS GUARDING THE STAGES OF PREGNANCY AND CHILDHOOD

To protect the mother and child the Almanac carries basic but powerful charms for both pregnancy and the early months following birth. With these charms are two contrasting parts. First, simple information is provided by illustrations showing the foetus's development month by month, plus a full-page illustration of how the foetus is fed by the umbilical cord (not shown here). For many women this advice, simple as it is, is the only information of its kind they will receive about what is happening during pregnancy.

受胎之圖式

保胎靈符

一月
二月
三月
四月
五月
六月
七月
八月
九月

出世圖

此符內聖人刻令等照樣各字宜騰為明如
孕婦有犯胎神者時符化火調水服之即愈

太歲諸神符救諸內全

六甲
靈符

大犯
五方

The second part consists of two lists. The first gives the deities who guard the child on each day for the first twelve months of its birth. The second list gives the Twenty-Six Malignant Gates, which are shown in more graphic details in Section 13.

Section 44
CHARMS

The majority of these charms are written on yellow paper or very thin tissue. They only last a short while, whereas those of Chang Tao-ling last all year. Below are descriptions of the main application and method of using these charms. They are numbered from right to left, top and bottom.

1. This charm is used to protect one's house, so that evil influences cannot enter or attack it. Write it on red paper and stick it onto the wall.
2. A charm to purify water in a well, etc. Write it on tissue or yellow paper, burn the paper and put the ashes into the water.
3. If anyone is suffering from a fever which makes him feel alternately hot and cold, copy this charm onto paper. If the illness is severe, burn the paper, put the ashes into water and drink it; in other cases, carry the charm in the pocket or hang it round the neck with red string.
4. If you feel that there is a strange influence or a bad spirit in the house, affix this charm to the affected part of the house: it will drive the bad spirit away.
5. To protect her unborn child, a pregnant woman should burn this charm and drink the ashes in a bowl of cold water.
6. This charm is effective for eye ailments and abdominal pains. Write the charm on a piece of paper, burn it and put the ashes in a bowl of cold water. If the eyes are affected, use the water to bathe them; for abdominal pains, drink the water.

北斗紫光夫人座鎮

用紅紙書衝祀奉其畜神則不犯之

淨水靈符

玉華司勅令∴鳥破穢宋劉瀞

此淨水符係玉華司勅令∴九鳳破穢宋劉二將軍清淨水照歘書用火化下應驗

治發冷靈符

廠速退

此符或食或佩即好

鎮煞靈符

靈漸耳∴戩日遊大將軍押煞靈

此符能趕煞制壓神攘胎效驗甚速若有觸犯胎神將符照寫粘於動作之處即安

安胎靈符

奉勅靈符救母内子全

此符内聖人勅令等照樣各字宜騰寫明如孕婦有犯胎神者將符化火調水服之即愈

眼熱肚痛靈符

勅令中却犯神

此符用清水化　眼熱洗　肚痛食

犯符生人（月別）

正月生人犯符	二月生人犯符	三月生人犯符	四月生人犯符	五月生人犯符	六月生人犯符	七月生人犯符

正月生人
正月生人犯子丑寅申方位有木石磚瓦動吐土當天禮儀請符起吉係三四十月修造熱嘔動

二月生人
二月生人犯子寅卯辰未酉戌方有木石板撞着飛天鑀刀五鬼主病眼痛右手痛四五骨痛脚痛請符起吉係八十一月修造

三月生人
三月生人犯子丑辰午未酉方有木門肚痛左手脚痛欄坆拆卸四肢寒冷請符起吉係正六月雞栖牛十二月修造

四月生人
四月生人犯子丑辰午未酉亥方有木倉牛欄門石灶壁四肢不安請符起吉係二月子脚痛肚痛主心痛口痛左腰往社門用木修造眼痛腰

五月生人
五月生人犯寅卯申戌亥方神主生病眼寶燭水飯請符起吉係三四心口腰脚痛大門不香火祖九月修造夜

六月生人
六月生人犯寅卯心口先不安用果酒請符起吉係三四九腰脚有睡不寧月修造安

七月生人
七月生人犯辰午未申方有板竹壁飲食火神土神主病安時行急症請符起吉係三六九月心肚痛頭痛修造不神

The next set of charms is used by those who, after starting a building or repair job, find themselves becoming ill. They should look up the month of their birth, and if they find that they have offended by working at an unpropitious time, they should affix the relevant charm to the work and finish it in the month recommended. The charms for the first three months, starting from the right, read as follows:

A person born in the first month will offend if he does anything to do with wood or stone, bricks, a ceiling, a door or a stove during the Tzu, Ch'ou, Yin or Shen days. He may suffer from eye or abdominal troubles, a painful left leg, fever and shivering or vomiting. The work should be completed in the third, fourth or eleventh month.

A person born in the second month will offend if he does anything to do with wood, stone, a board or knives, during Tzu, Yin, Mao, Ch'en, Wei, Yu or Hsu days. He may suffer from eye troubles, an ailing right hand, a painful back or legs or a bump on the head. The work should be completed in the fourth, fifth, seventh, eighth or eleventh month.

A person born in the third month will offend if he does anything to do with a wooden door, a chicken coop, a byre, breaking down a room partition or a bed during Tzu, Yin, Wu, Shen or Yu days. He may suffer from problems with the left eye, left hand, abdomen, right leg or coldness in the limbs. The work should be completed in the first, sixth, seventh or eleventh month.

張仲卿	李文卿	十二月生人犯符	十一月生人犯符	十月生人犯符	九月生人犯符	八月生人犯符

（各欄符籙圖）

十二月：犯神斬煞
十一月：犯神觀斬煞
十月：犯神鬼煞
九月：犯神速起
八月：犯神速起

丙寅日得病　東北方冲着五道傷神過死鬼無頭鬼傷神骨肉疼痛身熱不安　用白錢五百神馬水飯果酒齋雜金銀衣襲寶燭向北方送大吉

甲子日得病　往傷神男女傷神家神祖先不安主病寒熱往來四肢沉重骨痛病身　五百紙馬水飯果酒向北方送神黑錢果

十二月生人　犯寅卯辰午未申方板木香火　灶石飛來凶星飛來心痛請符起吉係　左眼熱左

十一月生人　犯寅卯辰巳申酉方代眼不安方撞着眼　無肚痛死左鬼脚請痛符沉起重吉作係悶冷熱正三四八月修造

十月生人　犯丑辰午申戌方肚痛左脚痛飲　食栖不井安神生請佛符道起香吉火係鍊三釘五七主腰

九月生人　犯寅巳未申亥方有木倉牛馬羊撞着凶星五石主右鬼　急眼痛症谷左倉腰神痛請左脚痛符起吉係背痛三七月修造

八月生人　犯丑卯午未酉亥方位有石頭壁　痛邊心痛左脚床痛難籠房厨灶請符起吉係病頭痛右眼頭痛五月修造口壁

司馬卿	龐諸卿

丁卯日得病　四肢沉重睡卧不安傷神馬水飯果酒寶燭向東方設送吉

乙丑日得病　東北方冲着刀兵傷神外傷神頭痛嘔吐氣急神馬水飯果酒沉重睡卧不安東北方設送大吉

The third set of charms relate to those who suddenly fall ill or become uncomfortable. They should look up the day on which the trouble began under its Earthly and Heavenly signs. The full cycle of sixty days is given in the Almanac, with a specific charm for each possible combination. Below are translations of the first four (they run from top to bottom, right to left, on the far left). (Shang Shens are evil spirits.)

If you fall ill on a Chia Tzu day, this means you are opposed by evils from the north, Wu Tao Shang Shen and Kuo Wang Shang Shen [male and female spirits]. This will make your home's ancestors restless. It will cause fever, heavy limbs and painful bones. Use this charm and some shiny new coins, with 500 pieces of paper money, rice, fruit and wine. Pray towards the north and burn all these things; throw away the coins. This will give great fortune.

If you fall ill on a Yi Ch'ou day, you are opposed by the north, a knife and soldiers, male and female Shang Shen. This will make the Stove God and the Earth King unhappy. It will cause headache, vomiting and breathing trouble. Use this charm and white (new and shiny) coins, 200 pieces of paper money, rice, fruit and wine. Pray towards the north. This will give great fortune.

If you fall ill on a Ping Yin day, you are opposed by the north, male and female Shang Shen, new ghosts and headless ghosts. This will cause bone complaints, muscle pains. Use this charm and white coins, 500 pieces of paper money, a bowl of clear water, rice, fruit, wine, a vegetarian dish, gold and silver paper and paper clothes. Light candles and pray facing north. This will give great fortune.

If you fall ill on a Ting Mao day you are opposed by the east, tree Shang Shen and Lok Shui Shang Shen. Your home buddhas will be distressed, your bamboos and trees on the east side will have a bad spirit around them. This will cause bone complaints, heavy limbs and disturbed sleep. Use this charm and white coins, 200 pieces of paper money, a bowl of water, rice and fruit. Light candles and pray towards the east. This will give great fortune.

Section 11

THE TWENTY-EIGHT
CONSTELLATIONS AND
FORTUNES

We have already dealt in some detail with the Twenty-Eight
Constellations in the Introduction (see pp. 36–7). Below we
give a translation of part of this section. Each constellation has
first the creature name, then the name of the soldier hero
associated with it. Then come details of whether it is a good or
bad influence. Below this is a more detailed explanation – we
have provided two complete examples. (The soldiers' names
are in phoneticized Cantonese pronunciation.)

1.	*Crocodile*	*Tang Kin*	*Good fortune*

*Everything you do goes well. If you study, you will gain
success and honour. You will marry well and have
faithful sons. Beware of having anything to do with the
dead. This will cause disaster and two more people will
die.*

2.	*Dragon*	*Ng Hon*	*Bad fortune*

*If you marry or bury someone, within ten days you will
have a terrible disaster. This disaster will harm your
children. Your daughter-in-law will be a widow.*

3.	*Badger*	*Kar Fok*	*Bad fortune*
4.	*Fox*	*Kwaing Hop*	*Good fortune*
5.	*Dog*	*Kan Sun*	*Bad fortune*
6.	*Wolf*	*Sunm Rang*	*Good fortune*
7.	*Hare*	*Fong Yee*	*Good fortune*
8.	*Porcupine*	*Chu Yau*	*Good fortune*
9.	*Rat*	*Chai Chuen*	*Bad fortune*
10.	*Leopard*	*King Tan*	*Bad fortune*
11.	*Griffon*	*Yik Yin*	*Bad fortune*
12.	*Bat*	*Kin Hung*	*Bad fortune*
13.	*Pheasant*	*Kwing Sun*	*Good fortune*
14.	*Gibbon*	*Chong Foo*	*Good fortune*
15.	*Cock*	*Ma Mou*	*Bad fortune*
16.	*Crow*	*Lan Lung*	*Good fortune*
17.	*Horse*	*Woo Sing*	*Good fortune*
18.	*Earthworm*	*Wong Leung*	*Bad fortune*
19.	*Deer*	*Chan Chuen*	*Good fortune*
20.	*Monkey*	*Foo Chuen*	*Bad fortune*

21.	Snake	Do Mo	Good fortune
22.	Stag	Yin Kau	Good fortune
23.	Sheep	Wong Ban	Bad fortune
24.	Tapir	Yam Kwang	Bad fortune
25.	Swallow	Lee Chung	Bad fortune
26.	Ox	Man San	Good fortune
27.	Tiger	Kai Tong	Bad fortune
28.	Pig	Lan Chun	Good fortune

THE FOUR ARRANGEMENTS OF CONSTELLATIONS

The Four Arrangements contain between them the Twenty-Eight Constellations. Each arrangement comprises seven of the constellations. They figure in aspects of both traditional medicine and in the martial arts, the links with the soldier heroes being of significance. The Four Arrangements are seen as being in the shape of four animals and are also associated with the four seasons and the four directions (see pp. 96–7).

1. Green Dragon Shape

This is linked with the east and with spring. It represents the first seven constellations.

2. Tortoise Snake Shape

This is linked with the north and with winter. It represents the fourth block of seven constellations.

3. White Tiger Shape

This is linked with the west and with autumn. It represents the second block of seven constellations.

4. Vermilion Bird Shape

This is linked with the south and with summer. It represents the third block of seven constellations.

東方蒼龍七宿

1

北方玄武七宿

2

西方白虎 七宿

3

南方朱雀 七宿

4

Section 12

FORTUNE-TELLING
BY PHYSICAL SENSATIONS

The experience of a flushed cheek, a burning ear or the feeling of 'someone walking over your grave' is known to us all. In China these sensations were accorded a greater significance than in the West. While we in the West have traditions such as if your ear burns someone is talking about you, China developed a highly complex system of fortune-telling based upon these sensations.

The most important aspect of this system is remembering when you first felt the sensation. For example, you may have a tic in your left eye which starts at 8 a.m., thus falling within the 'hour' of Ch'en (see pp. 34–5). You would then consult the appropriate block of this chart, looking up the character for Ch'en under 'Tic in the eye'. The reading following this tells you what a tic in the left eye at this time means.

Below are translations of the first three blocks, which are shown on p. 100. The titles of the other nine sensations covered are as follows: burning cheeks; someone 'walking over your grave'; being startled; sneezing once; suddenly remembering you have left an article of clothing somewhere; a pot or kettle boiling over or burning; smouldering wood falling from the fire; being startled by a dog; being startled by a flock of birds.

A Tic in the Eye

Tzu
: In the left eye, this means a nobleman will come to see you. If the right eye, you will be invited to a big party (feast).

Ch'ou
: In the left eye, this means something will happen to worry you. If the right eye, then someone is thinking of you.

Yin
: In the left eye, this means a friend will come from afar. If the right eye, a happy event awaits you.

Mao
: In the left eye, this means a special guest will come. If the right eye, then everything will go well.

Ch'en
: In the left eye, this means a close friend will come from afar. If the right eye, then expect a slight injury.

Szu	*In the left eye, this means you will go to a feast. If the right eye, you will have a quarrel or a disaster.*
Wu	*In the left eye, this means you will eat and drink heartily. If the right eye, beware or there will be a disaster.*
Wei	*In the left eye, this means you are safe and plans go well. If the right eye, then you will have a minor happy event.*
Shen	*In the left eye, this means you will lose money. If the right eye, then you will be thinking of your loved one very much.*
Yu	*In the left eye, this means a guest is coming. This is also true for the right eye, but from far away.*
Hsu	*In the left eye, this means a guest is coming. If the right eye, then you will go to a big gathering.*
Hai	*In the left eye, this means a friend is coming. If the right eye, beware trouble in court.*

Ringing in the Ears

Tzu	*In the left ear, this means that your girlfriend or loved one is thinking of you. If in right ear, then you will lose money.*
Ch'ou	*In the left ear, this means you will have a quarrel. If the right ear, then you will have a more serious dispute.*
Yin	*In the left ear, this means you will lose some money. If the right ear, then you will be rushed off your feet.*
Mao	*In the left ear, this means you will have a feast. If the right ear, then a friend will come to visit.*
Ch'en	*In the left ear, this means you will go on a journey. If the right ear, then a friend is on his way.*
Szu	*In the left ear, this means a terrible and tragic event will befall you. If the right ear, then all is well (luck is coming).*

眼跳法

時	左	右
子時	左有貴人	右有飲食
丑時	左有憂心	右有人思
寅時	左遠人來	右喜事至
卯時	左貴客來	右平安吉
辰時	左遠客來	右主損害
巳時	左有凶惡	右有飲食
午時	左主飲食	右有凶事
未時	左有小喜	右主吉昌
申時	左有女思	右有損財
酉時	左有客來	右遠客至
戌時	左有客至	右有聚會
亥時	左主官非	右主飲食

耳鳴法

時	左	右
子時	左女思	右主失財
丑時	左主口舌	右主失財
寅時	左主心急	右主心急
卯時	左主客行	右主客至
辰時	左主客至	右主大吉
巳時	左主大吉	右主凶事
午時	左主飲食	右有親來
未時	左遠人來	右主行人
申時	左主喜事	右主喜事
酉時	左主大吉	右主飲食
戌時	左主大吉	右主客至
亥時	左主大吉	右主飲食

耳熱法

時	占
子時	主來商量事
丑時	主臨身大吉
寅時	主相會大吉
卯時	主來相見吉
辰時	主有財喜，大通達吉
巳時	主失財物，之事不利
午時	主喜事來吉
未時	主有相求之事
申時	主酒食宴樂
酉時	主有婚姻事
戌時	主口舌之事
亥時	主有詞訟之事

Wu	*In the left ear, this means you will receive a letter from far away. If the right ear, then a relation will come to visit.*
Wei	*In the left ear, this means you will have a drink or a feast. If the right ear, then a friend from far away is coming.*
Shen	*In the left ear, this means you will go on a journey. If the right ear, then you can expect a happy event.*
Yu	*In the left ear, this means you will lose money. If the right ear, then you are in for good luck.*
Hsu	*In the left ear, this means you will have a feast. In the right ear, then a friend is on his way.*
Hai	*In the left ear, this means good luck. If the right ear, then feasting will come your way.*

Burning Sensation in Your Ear

Tzu	*A monk or nun will come to meet you to discuss things.*
Ch'ou	*You are in for a happy event of your own and very good fortune.*
Yin	*You will have a festive gathering with good fortune to follow.*
Mao	*Someone is coming from afar to meet you about some lucky thing.*
Ch'en	*You are about to have a financial windfall.*
Szu	*You are about to lose money and whatever you do will be unsuccessful.*
Wu	*You will have a feast and a happy occasion.*
Wei	*A friend of yours will seek your help.*
Shen	*You will go to a happy banquet.*
Yu	*Someone is coming to discuss marriage with you.*
Hsu	*You face an argument (quarrel).*
Hai	*You face prosecution in court.*

Section 13

THE INFLUENCE OF THE FIVE ELEMENTS IN CHILDHOOD, FOLLOWED BY THE TWENTY-SIX MALIGNANT GATES

We have already spoken of the fundamental role of the Five Elements in Chinese thought (see Introduction, pp. 32–5). Here we can see this in action, albeit in a very simple and basic way.

Each day has an element assigned to it. It is therefore usual for people to know not only their day characters but also the element. Those who cannot remember can work it out from their Heavenly Stem as each stem is related to a specific element (see p. 34).

To work this chart, all that is needed is to find the appropriate block and picture which relates to your element. From top to bottom they run: Metal, Wood, Water, Fire, Earth. Having found that, find the number of the month in which you were born. The position on the plant which has this is then related to the short, cryptic poem associated with that block. Thus, someone born under the element Wood will look at the second block. On this plant, if his birth month is the sixth month, he is at the base of the plant. The poem alongside tells him that this means he will have many girlfriends! This chart is not accorded great reverence and is more in the nature of mild amusement than that of serious intent.

Under Metal

On the base, very strong. On top, out of control. The wind blows, you waver. You will be unnerved.

Under Wood

On the base, happy child. This child strong and sturdy. On the base, long life. Good job and clothes always.

Under Water

On the base, many girlfriends. On top, so much anxiety. Disturbs parents with frequent crying. Needs 'honoured parent' or will have short life.

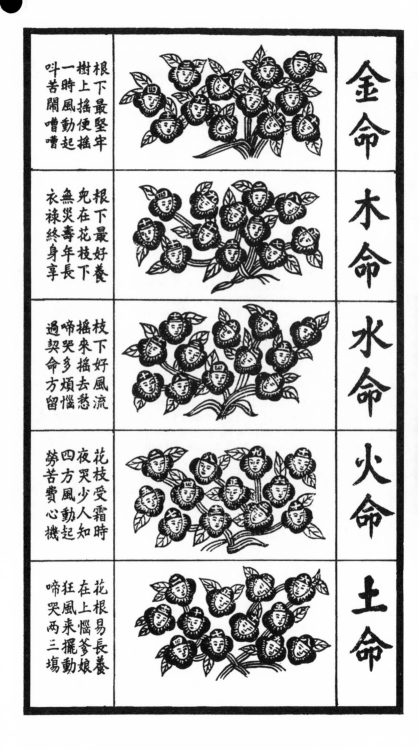

叫苦鬧嘈嘈 一時風動起 樹上搖便搖 根下最堅牢		金命
衣祿終身享 無災壽年長 兒在花枝下 根下最好養		木命
過契命方留 啼哭多煩惱 搖來搖去愁 枝下好風流		水命
勞苦費心機 四方風動起 夜哭少人知 花枝受霜時		火命
啼哭兩三塲 狂風來擺動 在上惱爹娘 花根易長養		土命

Under Fire

On the flower, snow falls. No one cares if baby cries. When grown up, working hard. Yet no real reward at all.

Under Earth

Base of flower, easy child. On top, parents don't like. Cause of so many arguments. Thrice the winds destroy the crops.

THE TWENTY-SIX MALIGNANT GATES

Following the Five Elements chart comes a collection of twenty-six small but dramatic pictures. In twelve of them a sinister devil figure seeking to harm a young child can be seen. And this figure sums up the whole collection. For this is concerned with the twenty-six difficulties or dangers which face children. The rearing of young children has long been beset with troubles and early deaths. This is reflected in this diverse collection of natural and supernatural disasters. The term 'gate' is used on all these pictures, rather as Westerners might talk of 'hurdles'. Charms, amulets and caution have been the traditional ways of preventing harm. One interesting device is often used. Children are not given a name until they are one month old. On this day, a big feast is held and the child is named. However, the name is often very odd, especially if the child is a boy. He might be called Cow Face, Monkey Nose or another such term. The reason for this is to confuse evil spirits, who are deemed to be constantly on the lookout for children they can steal – i.e. kill. To put off the evil spirits, children are given these odd names in order that the devils will not think this child is good enough to steal.

Gates numbers 9–18 are as follows (reading down the page, starting top right):

9. Hundred-Dates Gate

Children to whom this applies should avoid playing around gates.

10. White-Tiger Gate

These children should not be allowed to use or come near knives, scissors or similar sharp implements.

11. Fire Gate

Keep children born on these dates away from fire, boiling liquids and other hot things.

| 關柱四 | 凡亥年正二月辰巳時生人犯此忌坐欄杆竹椅太早 | 百日關 | 凡正月寅巳時生人犯此百日内忌出入門前 |

| 雷公關 | 凡寅午申酉辰未亥時生人犯此忌驚聞羅鼓雷公及大擘叫 | 白虎關 | 凡金木水火土生人犯此主多血光灾厄 |

| 短命關 | 凡子辰年巳時生人犯此主多驚怖夜啼之患 | 湯火關 | 凡子午卯酉年午時生人犯此忌疮痲之患 |

| 斷橋關 | 凡正二月寅卯時生人犯此忌過橋汲水照影 | 天狗關 | 凡八字五行全者生人犯此月内怕聞犬吠聲 |

| 千日關 | 凡午年寅申巳亥時生人犯此忌三歲上高落低之患 | 浴盆關 | 凡正二三月申時生人犯此忌沐浴太早 |

12. Sky-Dog Gate

Until the child born on these dates is a month old, do not let it get near or hear a dog.

13. Bath Gate

Do not bathe children born on these dates when they are around a month old.

14. Four-Poles Gate

Children born on the relevant dates should not be placed on any construction involving poles.

15. Thunder-God Gate

Children born on these dates should be kept from hearing thunder, drums or other loud noises.

16. Short-Life Gate

A child born on these dates will cry from fear every night while a baby.

17. Broken-Bridge Gate

Children born on the relevant dates should avoid crossing bridges, and particularly should not lean over to look at their reflection in the river.

18. Thousand-Dates Gate

When this child is around three years old, do not let him climb on anything, not even someone's shoulder.

Section 14

AUSPICIOUS AND INAUSPICIOUS DATES FOR VARIOUS ACTIVITIES

This section is a catchbag of activities which have auspicious or inauspicious facets. For instance, the following advice is given about when to shampoo your hair, and what will befall you if you wash your hair on certain days.

What will befall you if you wash your hair on any given day of the month:

Day 1	Short life	Day 17	Black face
Day 2	Good fortune	Day 18	Robbed
Day 3	Great wealth	Day 19	Nothing good
Day 4	Hair-colour disease	Day 20	Poor
Day 5	Hair falls out	Day 21	Sick
Day 6	Harm your face	Day 22	Good luck and
Day 7	Get into trouble		fortune
	with the police	Day 23	Great fortune
Day 8	Long life	Day 24	Quarrel
Day 9	Good marriage	Day 25	Damage your eyes
Day 10	Promotion	Day 26	Great fortune
Day 11	Bright, clear eyes	Day 27	Good time
Day 12	More bad luck	Day 28	Fighting and
Day 13	Have a son		arguing
Day 14	Earn money	Day 29	Good news
Day 15	Good fortune	Day 30	Haunted
Day 16	Great bad luck		

Other topics covered in this section include days for visiting the tailor, bed making, visiting the sick and trading.

Section 15

DEITY IN CHARGE OF YOU FOR THE YEAR ACCORDING TO YOUR AGE

The influence of the planets (amongst which Chinese thought places the sun and the moon – the Great Yang and the Great Yin) has long been a feature of astrology in both the East and the West. However, as this rather brief and quite simplistic section shows, the planets do not occupy a major role in Chinese astrology.

The system used in this section relates age to a specific planet which is then seen as being the star which will exert influence over you for the year. These stars should not, however, be confused with the auspicious and inauspicious stars of Section 20.

The section contains nine illustrations of the planet deities plus a fortune-telling poem which gives some indication as to your fortune for this year. Prefacing the section is a poem followed by a description of how to deal with your year planet.

This star is your life; it is good to light the lantern.
It can bless you, keeping you safe and bestowing fortune and long life.
Male or female, if this year's star is good, you should offer sacrifice.
The nine planets respond to honest prayers.

The description advises that if you have a good star, then through prayer and abstention from eating meat all will go well. If you have an evil star, then earnest prayer will help avert disasters.

The second page of this section contains a list of the ages which are influenced by each planet (see p. 110, the two columns on the left). (Remember that the Chinese count themselves as being one year old at the time they are born.) The list of ages for each planet is divided into two, one for men (on the right) and the other for women (on the left). For the Earth Star (fifth pair of blocks) the associated ages for men are 11, 12, 29, 38, 47, 56, 65, 74, 83 and 92; for women the ages are 14, 23, 32, 41, 50, 59, 68, 77, 86 and 95. The prediction alongside the Earth Planet God's picture (see opposite, centre left) runs as follows:

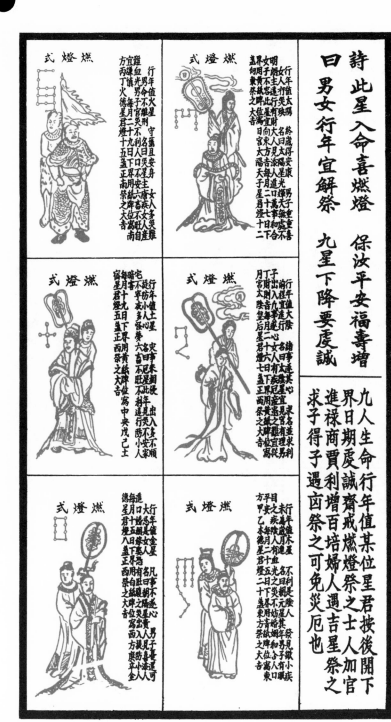

詩　此星入命喜燃燈　保汝平安福壽增
　　日男女行年宜解祭　九星下降要虔誠

九人生命行年值某位星君按後開下
界日期虔誠齋戒燃燈祭之士人加官
進祿商賈利增百培婦人遇吉星祭之
求子得子遇凶祭之可免災厄也

式燈燃

明朗女人行年值此星打昊喜陽宜向東方吉陽天子星君二十七日和燈吉合不二盡向南宜丙丁火德星君二十九日燈正南祭之大吉

式燈燃

行男值火星守舊目安身女人多災產難雞血光男不離刑每月二十不利人口不安方宜丙丁火德星君二十五日燈正南祭之大吉

式燈燃

子前入九曜退行月丁星則太陽皇后星二十六日有太歲星燈七日有疾病宜見官事宜用黃紙牌位寫中央黃色祭之大吉

式燈燃

宅不防身上心事退行小人多怪害六畜不旺不利年每月十九日燈五月下界用西方紙牌位寫中央戊己土

式燈燃

目疾男行年女星新星值木星人身不遂痛人日光二月二十燈五日下界用方甲乙木德星君東方祭之大吉

式燈燃

大行年值女星凡事不遂心男子喜逢可德星君每月十五日燈八月下界用西方紙牌位寫西方庚辛金祭之大吉

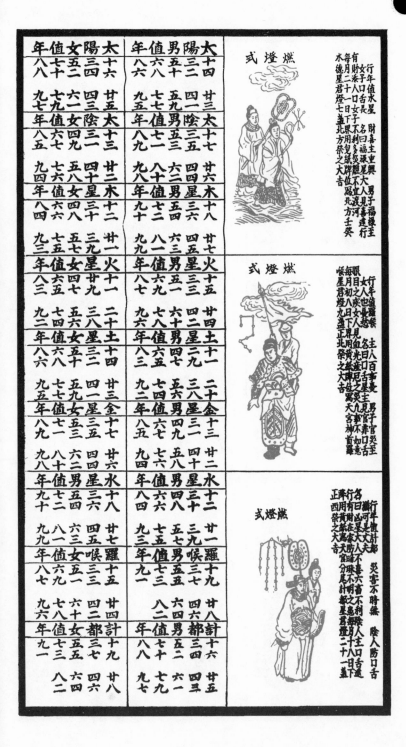

燃燈式（九曜值年燈圖）

值年星君歌訣

水德星君（第一圖）
行年值水星，財喜主重興，男子福祿全，女子口舌長，大人見喜遠行，多疾病，不宜渡河……囚死方壬癸。水德星君每月二十日燈一盞，界北方壬癸，禳之大吉。

羅睺星君（第二圖）
行年值羅睺星最惡，主人百事憂，眼目有疾，女恐口舌，男子官災至，非口舌血光黄腫……寫灸天九宮神首羅睺。羅睺星君每月初八日燈九盞，界正北方，禳之大吉。

計都星君（第三圖）
各行年值計都……有日官災至，不喜六畜不利，陰人口舌……計都星君每月……日燈……盞，界西……方，禳之大吉。灾害不時無，陵人防口舌。

值年九曜星年歲表

星	值男年	值女年
太陽	十四 廿三 三二 四一 五十 五九 六八 七七 八六 九五	十六 廿五 三四 四三 五二 六一 七十 七九 八八 九七
太陰	十七 廿六 三五 四四 五三 六二 七一 八十 八九 九八	十三 廿二 三一 四十 四九 五八 六七 七六 八五 九四
木星	十八 廿七 三六 四五 五四 六三 七二 八一 九十 九九	十二 廿一 三十 三九 四八 五七 六六 七五 八四 九三
火星	十五 廿四 三三 四二 五一 六十 六九 七八 八七 九六	十一 二十 廿九 三八 四七 五六 六五 七四 八三 九二
土星	十一 二十 廿九 三八 四七 五六 六五 七四 八三 九二	十四 廿三 三二 四一 五十 五九 六八 七七 八六 九五
金星	十三 廿二 三一 四十 四九 五八 六七 七六 八五 九四	十七 廿六 三五 四四 五三 六二 七一 八十 八九 九八
水星	十二 廿一 三十 三九 四八 五七 六六 七五 八四 九三	十八 廿七 三六 四五 五四 六三 七二 八一 九十 九九
羅睺（喉）	十九 廿八 三七 四六 五五 六四 七三 八二 九一	十五 廿四 三三 四二 五一 六十 六九 七八 八七 九六
計都（都）	十六 廿五 三四 四三 五二 六一 七十 七九 八八 九七	十九 廿八 三七 四六 五五 六四 七三 八二 九一

The person under this planet will have many disasters which will harm him. Nothing will go smoothly and you should beware of petty little men. This is also a bad year for your home. There will be no calm but rather many nightmares. Your cattle will be poor and travelling bad. Beware lest little men harm you. On the 19th of each month use yellow paper and write down the charm Chung Yung, Mao Chi, Tu and light five lamps. Face to the west and worship. This will help avert disasters.

The whole section is known as 'Lighting Lamps'. Through the offering of chants and lighting a specified number of lamps, good fortune is accrued or disaster averted.

Section 16

FENG-SHUI TABLE OF AUSPICIOUS AND INAUSPICIOUS DATES

See Section 1, pp. 46–50.

Section 17

CHARMS TO PROTECT THE FOETUS AND SPIRITS GUARDING THE STAGES OF PREGNANCY

See Charms, pp. 86–8.

Section 18

OLD MR CHOU'S BOOK OF AUSPICIOUS AND INAUSPICIOUS DREAMS

The correct title of this section is in fact 'Chou Kung's Book of Auspicious and Inauspicious Dreams'. The epithet 'Old' is rather appropriate here – for Old Mr Chou is none other than Chou Kung, the Duke of Chou, who is reputed to have assisted in the compilation of the *I Ching* (*The Book of Changes*) and is supposed to have lived *c*. 1020 BCE. Chou Kung's association with the *I Ching*, one of the most ancient and mysterious of the divination books of China, means that he was seen as a major figure in divination by later generations. While we can be fairly certain that this great early mathematician was not responsible for the dream interpretations, it is of significance that he is nevertheless associated with them. He lends them authority and dignity as well as status within the overall scheme of divination.

The dream interpretations associated with Old Mr Chou are very well known and his name and its link has passed into the language in a number of ways. For instance, a teacher finding a child dozing during lesson time will often inquire if the pupil has 'been to visit Mr Chou' – i.e. been dreaming.

The interpretations of the dreams would puzzle any Freudian, as they consist entirely of auspicious and inauspicious messages. The format of the dreams is also of interest, reflecting, as one would expect, the Chinese way of life and beliefs. So, for example, there are explanations for dreams about the 'soldiers of Heaven', about 'a monk giving you cash' (normally, of course, it is the monks who are given money), or about 'a kang being broken' – the kang is the old-fashioned stove-cum-bed made of bricks. There are dreams about 'honouring your parents' and of kowtowing to your wife. The Chinese enjoyment of puns (easy in a language in which the same basic sound can mean up to nine different things) also comes out, for example, in a pun on the sounds for 'coffin' and 'financial windfall'.

Considerable authority is given to these interpretations, although it is important to stress that dreams, while valued, have not been accorded the same significance as in many other cultures. On occasions, a dream has been an instrument of revelation – but rarely just on its own. Emperor Wu, who overthrew the Shang to found the Chou dynasty (c. 1028 BCE) had a dream which coincided with his other divinations: 'It would seem that Heaven is going by means of me to rule the people. My dreams coincide with my divinations; the auspicious omen is double. My attack on Shang must succeed.'[1] In the *Shih Ching* (*The Book of Poetry*) only three poems, all found together in the 'Decade of K'e Foo' section, mention or make use of dreams and interpretation. There is a passing reference in the *Analects* of Confucius and one further instance in the *Shu Ching* when Emperor Wu-ting (c. 320 BCE) dreamed of an assistant whom, when he awoke, he described and found. These are the only references in the Classics. Compare this with the Bible and the difference is staggering. In Genesis alone there are over thirty references to dreams and their role in each instance is of great import. Helpful indicators dreams may be, but they are not by any means regarded by the Chinese as the most important way of foretelling the future.

In Old Mr Chou's Book of Dreams there are seven categories of dreams. The opening third of each category is given below.

1. The Heavens and the Weather

If you dream of the sun or moon just rising, then your family will be fine, prosperous, well educated and have important jobs. If you dream of the sun or moon setting, then your servants will cheat you.

If you dream of thunder, then the Thunder God, Lei Kung, is calling you. This means good fortune. If you dream of a dark, cloudy, drizzly day, then someone is going to die or be killed shortly. If you dream of a phoenix, that means you will receive an important letter from far away, with news.

If you see the sky door to Heaven and through it espy the soldiers of Heaven, then know that a nobleman is coming to help you. If you dream of a shooting star, this means your family will be struck with sickness. If this doesn't happen then you will be in trouble in the courts instead. If you see a multicoloured cloud, then good fortune will come to the family. If you dream of the stars without any clouds, then yet again, good fortune. A star going slowly into a cloud means you will have a child. If you see clouds coming from all four directions, then this means your business will do well.

2. Features such as Houses, Gardens, Forests, etc.

If you dream of the forecourt to the house, with bamboo trees growing healthily, then there will be continuous good news. If

you dream of lying on a large stone, then there will be good
fortune. *Dreaming of playing with small stones means you will
have a child. A dream of trees dying but new growth springing
up beneath means your children and grandchildren will grow
up well and they will be numerous. If you see the grass and
trees growing well, then the family is happy. If you dream of
crossing a bridge hand in hand, then your wife will be
pregnant. Dreaming of walking to town or market with your
wife means you will soon buy a property. If you see a bridge
which is damaged, then you will soon face a prosecution in
court. If you dream of an empty town, this is very dangerous.
You could be murdered. If you see a monk giving you cash,
then your job is going to go well.*

*You dream of an orchard bowed down with ripe fruit. This
means that your sons and grandsons are safe and well. Dreams
of a garden growing well mean good fortune. You are standing
under a tree. A nobleman will come to help you soon. If you
see that a kang is broken, then this means someone is about to
die. If you dream of collecting water from a well and the water
is clear, then you will have good fortune. If, however, the
water is cloudy, then beware, for danger is around. If you see
a new tomb and the coffin [there is a pun on 'coffin' and
'windfall'], then any worry you have will now be over. If you
see a new coffin taken out of a tomb, then you will have good
fortune. If the soil around the tomb is bright, then good fortune
will occur; but if the soil is dull, beware, for this means
danger. If you see someone putting a body into a coffin, then a
windfall will come to you. A hillfire means you will be
promoted, but leaves falling from a tree means your family is in
danger and someone will be killed.*

3. Gods, Fairies, Spirits, etc.

*If you dream of visiting a temple, then this will mean
extraordinary good fortune. To dream of seeing statues of the
Buddha on an altar means very good fortune.*

*To see a dead person rise out of a coffin is good, for this
means you will earn much money. To dream of a monk, nun or
instructor reciting the Buddhist sutras is to be sure of good
fortune. To dream of yourself with a female spirit – a devi –
means you will have a fine son from your real wife.*

4. The Human Body

*To dream of honouring your parents means great good fortune
and prosperity. To see a naked person means very good fortune.
To dream of no teeth, but new ones beginning to grow,*

means you will have many sons and grandsons. To dream of a woman with her husband in the water means good fortune. To see any female genitals means you will have a quarrel in the family or with your neighbour. To dream your wife is pregnant means she will have or is having an affair. To see yourself and your wife honouring each other means you will be divorced.

Hair turning white or falling out means you will grieve about your son and grandson. To see a hand or foot with a bleeding boil is good fortune. But to dream of your teeth falling out means your parents are in danger. Dreaming of saying goodbye to your brother means a quarrel. To see yourself going along with a woman means you will lose money. Dreaming of sex with any woman means you will have unclean thoughts. Dreaming of eating only vegetables means great danger is in store.

5. Being Out of Harmony with Someone – Music

To dream of someone blowing a flute or banging a drum means a party will happen. To dream of a sick person crying or laughing means that their sickness is about to go. To dream that you or anyone kills a chicken, goose or duck means very good fortune.

To dream of someone killing a pig is very good fortune, but killing a lamb is a sign of evil and danger. To dream of being killed is very good fortune. To dream of killing yourself with a knife or axe is also very great fortune. To dream of family quarrelling at home means the family will split and some will go away.

6. Living Creatures, Birds, Animals, etc.

To dream of a snake becoming a dragon means a nobleman will come to help. If a snake bites you, this means lots of money. To see a lot of snakes means you will plot a devious plan. To see a heron flying into the heavens means you will have a quarrel. To dream of a parrot calling you means a major quarrel. To see a swallow flying to you means a friend will come to see you from far away.

To see a door with dragons is very great fortune and prosperity. To dream of a phoenix means a noble will come to help. If a bird flies at your stomach, then you will have a son. If any bird flies into your family house, then there will soon be danger for you. To see a peacock is good fortune. To dream of a hen hatching an egg means happy news and rejoicing. To see a hen standing on a tree means lots of money.

7. Clothing, Jewellery and Miscellaneous Items

To dream of a ship or boat going swiftly means that shortly you will become both rich and a noble. To see your clothes all dirty with mud means your wife's pregnancy will be problematic. To see a fish break a boat means bad fortune. To dream of vehicles not moving any more means that any application you have made will be turned down. To dream of a boat going under a bridge means good fortune, as does seeing a lamp or candle lit. A clear mirror means good fortune – but dreams of a cloudy one augur no good at all. Expensive hairpins being knocked against each other means your wife will leave you.

To dream of a bamboo-leaf roof covering means you will have certain worries. To see your belt fall off means all will be well. To dream of lying on a boat means danger. To see your vehicle broken or reversed means you will have debts or compensation to pay. To dream of a patient being put into an ambulance is very dangerous. If any vehicle moves off, all is well. To dream of picking up money means good fortune. To see a needle and thread means everything is successful. To dream of a golden hairpin shining brightly means you will have a noble son.

Section 19

THE WEATHER AND FARMING FORECASTS

This is a purely agricultural section, reminding us of the basic original function of this calendar. The lists give details of the wind and rainfall expected during each month, plus details of when to sow certain crops. In recent copies of the Hong Kong editions of the Almanac, such agricultural parts have been dropped, marking the shift in occupation of most readers.

Section 20

THE AUSPICIOUS AND INAUSPICIOUS STARS FOR THE YEAR

Running as a constant thread through much of the fortune-telling are the good and bad stars. They are featured prominently in the 'house' sign for each person for this year (see Section 3). They occupy two of the eight subdivisions of each day in the main calendar. They occur as factors in many other divination processes. The stars are seen as minor officials within the complex heavenly system or bureaucracy of the Ministry of Time over which T'ai Sui (the planet Jupiter) rules. Included in this system are, of course, the Twenty-Eight Constellations. The influence of the good and bad stars can be compared to that of faithful servants of the Crown who carry out their duties according to the specific task they are assigned.

The stars each have a name, such as Heavenly Horse or Bright Star, but more importantly they have a special function – a blessing or a curse which they carry with them.

The section is broken into three subdivisions. First come the good stars – eighty-eight in number. Then come four stars which can go either way – fellow-travellers, as it were. Finally come the evil stars. There are 162 of these, reflecting the fact, says tradition, that evil outweighs good in the affairs of the world. Below we give a translation of some of the good stars and their blessings. (The titles have been left in Cantonese.)

1. *Tin Tak Hap – Heavenly Virtue Harmony*
   This star blesses everything you may do.

2. *Yuet Tak – Moon Virtue*
   Blesses everything except hunting and fishing.

3. *Tin Tak – Heaven Virtue*
   Same as 1.

5. *Ng Hap – Five Harmonies*
   Good for marriage and trading.

6. *Sam Hap – Three Harmonies*
   Same as 1.

8. *Tin Yan – Heaven Grace*
   Same as 1.

10. *Yuet Yun – Moon Grace*
    Same as 1.

11. *Iu On – Seeking Quiet*
    Generally good; especially good for setting up a statue of a god.

13. *Yick Ma – Courier's Horse*
    Good for long journeys, moving house and consulting a doctor; generally good.

14. *Ng Fu – Five Riches*
    Good for opening a new business, for trading and in general.

18. *Fuk Sang – Lucky Birth*
    A suitable time for praying to the gods and for marriage.

19. *Sing Sam – Holy Heart*
    A good time for praying to the gods and for visiting the cemetery to show respect for one's ancestors.

22. *Wong Yat – Vigorous Day*
    Suitable for planting.

26. *Tin Ma – Heaven's Messenger*
    A suitable time for long journeys and for moving house.

27. *Tin Koan – Heaven's Officer*
    A good time to apply for a prestigious new job.

28. *Yung Tak – Yang Virtue*
    A time to give donations to the poor and to help the needy.

29. *Yum Tak – Yin Virtue*
    Same as 28.

31. *Tin Choi – Heaven's Wealth*
    A good time to open a new business, to pray for wealth and to make other prayers.

36. *Look Yee – Six Rites*
    A time to give speeches and to carry out the duties of your office.

Section 21

CUP DIVINATION CHART OF T'U TI (EARTH GOD)

The term 'cup divination' is not a particularly helpful one, but it is difficult to describe this method succinctly. The equipment used is in fact two shaped pieces of wood. About 3–5 inches long, they have a straight flat side and a curved side making a solid bowl shape. In the illustration (see p. 120) they can be seen in the hands of the Earth God. When thrown, the sides are interpreted as yin or yang, depending on which way they fall, and from this the answers are found. This activity usually takes place within the precincts of a temple as it is a very powerful form of divination or oracle. It is not to be undertaken lightly. Before going to the temple and the diviner, it is customary for the inquirer to abstain from meat for three days prior to the visit. Some will fast for the three days. Joss sticks are also regularly burned throughout these three days and are always offered at the consultation. After washing their hands, the inquirer and the diviner will then formally put the question to the cups and throw them on the floor three times. The answers given are related to two important sets of messages. First, the first character below the resulting set of three 'answers' gives a direct reference back to the Twenty-Eight Constellations (Section 11). By looking up which constellation is referred to, it is possible to get an immediate sense of whether the answer will be auspicious or inauspicious. Secondly, below the 'answer' are two sets of poems, one cryptic and one explanatory. The first four examples are given below. This method of divination is highly thought of and is consulted at times of major personal decisions.

The cups are thrown three times – one up, one down is called Sheng; both down Yin; both up Yang.

土地枑圖

福德祠

廿八宿

聖陰　聖陽　陰陰　陽陰　陰陽

角聲三弄　無雪心寒
勸君休慮　合卷人安

亢宿金龍　行子丑宮
藏身在未　急避他鄉

氐頭偷看　暗想佳人
任君舌巧　恐未成親

房生瑞草　孕婦且喜
合卷皆慶　麒麟是子

解曰

貴人扶事有理後有遇時前程
得路喜得平安到老雙全

缺月圓圓枯木再生慢行且步
諸事難成

往事勞心求財問事家敗人亡
食無求飽居無安

牛郎織女難會佳期好事難得
不可向前

斷曰

婚好
病安
孕男
行人至

病安
至財有
婚不成

訟吉
財無
婚難
人未至

訟吉
病安
孕男
人未至

1. Sheng, Sheng, Yin

You are too worried in yourself –
No snow falls, yet you are feeling cold.
Don't fret so much, everyone will be well.

Explanation: You will have a nobleman to espouse your cause.
Your future is very bright, and you and your spouse will
continue to fare safely.

In brief: Marriage will go well; the sick person will recover; if you
are pregnant you will have a boy; a nobleman will help you.

2. Sheng, Sheng, Yang

This time is not fit for anything, because of the unlucky dragon star.
You must avoid doing anything.

Explanation: The moon is not full, the trees are dying. If you
wait for the trees to regrow you will have a very long wait.
You will labour hard with little result.

In brief: The sick person will survive; a nobleman will come to
help; you will have some money; marriage will be unsuccessful.

3. Yin, Yin, Yang

You will look sideways at your beloved, not full in the face.
The one you love is always in your mind.
You may ask someone to put in a good word with your love
But marriage will still be a failure.

Explanation: Even if you work very hard you will receive no
reward for your labours. If you pray for wealth you will not
get it; if you ask the god how your family will fare, the answer
is badly. You will always be hungry and in need of a place to
live; there will be no luxuries in your life.

In brief: If you are involved in a legal dispute, the result will
be fair; money and marriage will both go badly; you will
receive no help from noblemen.

4. Yin, Yang, Yin

If you ask about your wife's pregnancy
She will fare well.
She will bear you a son.

Explanation: In every other matter, your chances are poor at
this time. Do not attempt to take things further for now.

In brief: Court cases will go fairly well; those who are ill will
recover; if there is a pregnancy, a boy will be born; noble help
is not forthcoming.

Section 22
COIN PREDICTION

Prediction by the use of coins has a long tradition in China, the best-known example of this method of prediction being the *I Ching* or *The Book of Changes*. The *I Ching* began as a series of orally transmitted verses based on the trigrams attributed to Fu Hsi, who, according to Chinese tradition, was the father of our present civilization, teaching men the skills of agriculture, fire making and community living. Each trigram or group of three broken and unbroken lines relates to some aspect of nature, society and the individual.

The *I Ching* as it is known today was assembled in the eleventh century BCE by King Wen, the founder of the Chou dynasty. It was arranged by that time into sixty-four hexagrams or groups of six lines, with short verses which King Wen amplified with more detailed commentary. After the king's death his son completed the expansion with detailed commentary on the individual lines of each hexagram.

Around the sixth century BCE Confucius came into contact with the *I Ching* and was so impressed by it that he and his disciples wrote an extensive work of criticism on it known as *The Ten Wings*.

The use of the *I Ching* as an oracle can vary in form. One method involves an elaborate casting of the stalks of the yarrow plant, a procedure which may take half an hour or more to derive the appropriate hexagram. The method using coins is a much simpler form of this procedure.

Whichever method is used, adequate mental and spiritual preparation is essential when using the *I Ching*; in fact, such preparation and an attitude of serious inquiry are vital factors in most methods of prediction in Chinese and Western traditions. First, incense is burned and the question which is to be answered is addressed directly to the *I Ching*. The person making the inquiry should pray, making mention of his or her identity and circumstances. The coins or stalks must be passed through the smoke of the incense before being thrown. All this induces a receptive and meditative frame of mind in the questioner.

When coins are used for the *I Ching*, they are usually ancient Chinese coins, which are round with a square hole in the middle; the circle represents Heaven while the square represents Earth. They are engraved with four characters on one side: this is the yang side. The other side either has two characters or none: this is the yin side. Coins used for *I Ching* prediction should be kept separate and only used for this purpose, as it is believed they will absorb influences from those who handle them which may affect their validity.

Three coins are used, and these are thrown six times in all to derive the six lines of the hexagram. The lines are determined from the bottom upwards. If the coins fall so that one yang face and two yin faces are upwards, this is an unmoving yang or unbroken line. One yin face and two yang faces make up an unmoving yin or broken line. Three yang faces mean a moving yang line, three yin faces a moving yin line. The hexagram is drawn up with the moving lines marked, and the interpretation of the hexagram read. This represents the present situation. Each moving line is then changed to its opposite – i.e. yin becomes yang and yang becomes yin. This reflects the idea that anything taken to the extreme becomes its opposite. A new hexagram is formed which represents the potential situation. When the interpretation of this hexagram has been read, the inquirer can find out how the situation depicted in the first hexagram can become that of the second hexagram by studying the meanings of the moving lines. These are referred to by looking at the interpretation beneath the original hexagram according to the position of the line.

The coin prediction system given here is a much simpler one, using only one throw of five coins which have characters on one side and a picture on the other. It is best used for answering questions about job applications, exam results, legal matters, illness, money-making, finding missing persons, marriage and trading, although it can also provide more general predictions. The overall answer is given a grade ranging from top top, the best possible outcome, to bottom bottom, absolute disaster, with flat being halfway between these. The poem gives a metaphorical picture of this overall answer.

Below are the translations of the first six of the thirty-two combinations (running from right to left on pp. 124–5).

且守君子分　勿用小人言　九事皆當謹　作福保安然

第七進求卦上上
說言未遂　謀事不成　出行錯悮　考試不利　訟事不利　病人不安　婚姻難成　求財不利

國治人安泰　家財漸漸興

第八進保卦上上
求官得位　謀事有成　訟得理宜　病人安痊　進財求望吉　孕生貴子　有福亦平安　婚姻成　家宅吉　交易成　家宅大吉

好德承天佑　門招喜氣新

第九獲安卦中吉
求官得祿　謀事有成　訟事和　病人安　有人相助力　求財十分　婚姻有成　交易成　獲福盡歡欣

目下如冬樹　枯落未開花

第十遂心卦中吉
訟事和吉　病人無妨　求財易　行人至　看看春色動　求財十分　婚姻成　交易合　六甲生男　漸漸發萌芽

時逢融和氣　衰殘物再興

第十一災散卦大吉
求官得位　謀事大吉　訟可和　病即愈　更逢微細雨　求財十分　婚姻成就　交易合　家宅安　春色又還生

災散福門開　無邊喜氣來
出行六分　謀事成就　訟事和　病不妨　目下相逢處　求財七分　六甲生男　婚姻成　交易合　須當得橫財

金錢卦

彩鳳呈祥瑞
第一星震卦上上
麒麟降帝都　禍除通福至　喜氣自然舒
求官得位　考試得意　訟事有理　病即寧
求財十分　尋人得見
婚姻得成　買賣十分

從革宜更變
第二從革卦上平
時來合動遷　龍門魚躍過　凡骨作神仙
求官小就　謀事有成　訟事有和　病人無妨
求財八分　走失有望
婚姻百成　交易有功

動作因風便
第三曲直卦下平
求謀可託人　若逢戊己土　事事得遂心
謀事先成　訟事宜和　病人無妨
求財不多　尋人不見
婚姻可定　交易大利

船放江湖內
第四潤下卦小平
灘邊獲寶珍　更宜將大用　災散福來居
謀事可成　訟事宜和　病人安
求財八分　尋人得過
婚姻有成　交易有成

此卦向南方
第五炎上卦下下
災危不可當　官司多不利　目下有災殃
生意得利　訟事和吉　婚姻不成
求財落空　尋人不見
交易不遂　行人不至

第六稼穡卦平平
求謀有害　出行平下　求財落空　婚姻不成
訟事無理　尋人不見

[Key: C = characters, P = picture]

1. CCCCC: Top Top

The phoenix flies freely
The unicorn comes to rest on your land
All misery will leave you
And fortune will replace it
A happy atmosphere surrounds you.

You will get a good job in future
Your exam results will be good
You will win in court
Sickness will depart
Money-making goes well
You will find whoever you are looking for
Marriage will be successful
Making deals will go well.

2. CPPPP: Top Flat

If your job is bad, you'd better change it
But first wait till the time is right
All will go well
You will be free from trouble.

You will have a fair chance of getting a job
If you apply for something, you will succeed
Trouble in court will result in a compromise
A sick person will recover
You will make quite a lot of money
*If you are looking for someone, you have a fair chance of finding
    them*
Marriage will go well
You will make a deal successfully.

3. PCPPP: Bottom Flat

The tree moves because the wind blows it
If you ask for help, it will be given
Anything you do in the year of Wu Szu
(Which belongs to the element Earth)
Will be successful.

If you want a job, you will get it
Your application will be successful at the first attempt
If you are patient in court, you will reach a compromise
A sick person will recover
Not much chance of making money
A missing person will not be found
Engagements will prosper
Very good for making deals.

4. PPCPP: Small Flat

The boat is in the middle of the pool
On the beach are priceless treasures
Use that wealth wisely and well
Then you will have fortune and not misery.

You will earn money from your commerce
Applications will succeed
You will make a large profit
Those who are ill will be safe
You will not have legal problems
You will find the missing person you seek
Marriage will go well
You will succeed in making deals.

5. PPPCP: Bottom Bottom

This prediction faces south
You are in for great disasters
You will lose everything at law
There is no chance of winning
Something terrible is coming to you soon.

If you apply for something new, you will lose what you already
    have
Travelling will go fairly well
You cannot make any money
Your marriage will break down
You will be taken to court and lose
A missing person will never be seen again
Deals will be broken
You will not get help from a nobleman
No one will visit you.

6. PPPPC: Flat Flat

Don't listen to those who spread gossip
Think everything out for yourself
If you do so, everything will be well
You will have no trouble.

Serious plans will not be successful
Journeys will not go well
Exams will be failed
You have a poor chance in legal disputes
The sick will not recover quickly
Success in marriage is difficult to achieve
Money-making is unsuccessful.

Section 23

MASTER YUAN T'IEN KANG'S CHART OF THE SPIRITUAL VALUE AND WEIGHT OF YOUR BONES

This series of charts represents a very particular style of Chinese fortune-telling which is unknown in the West. According to this tradition, perfected by Master Yuan T'ien Kang, each person has a spiritual weight – a Heavenly weight – to their bones. By adding together the weights, a divination can be achieved. The predictions are of a very general nature and are considered as interesting rather than as crucial or decisive.

The procedure is as follows. As usual, it is necessary to know certain of your Eight Characters – in this case the two characters for the year (see Introduction, p. 31).

The first page of Master Yuan T'ien Kang's chart consists of four tables. The top half of the page lists the pairings for the years on the basis of the sixty-year cycle. Under each pairing of Heavenly Stem and Earthly Branch is a weight. The weights are, of course, given in Chinese categories. These are explained below. The bottom half of the first page contains three lists. On the right, the months; in the middle, the days of the month; on the left, the 'hours'. Each has below it a specific weight.

The method of divination is quite simple. Taking your Eight Characters you find the pairing of Heavenly Stem and Earthly Branch for your year. This gives you the first weight. Next, you look up the month number, and that gives you the next weight. Then you find your day – the third weight. Finally, the 'hour' gives you the fourth weight. You add these together and that gives you the spiritual or Heavenly weight of your bones.

Having now discovered the weight, you turn to the following pages (see pp. 130–31). Here, using the shorthand version of the characters for numbers, are all the possible varieties of weight combinations. Once you have found the correct one for you, the poem below gives you the prediction.

Let us follow an example through:

新輯算命不求人

袁天罡先師神數稱骨分量照年月日時推算

(年數)

鼠 甲子	丙子	戊子	庚子	壬子
牛 乙丑	丁丑	己丑	辛丑	癸丑
虎 丙寅	戊寅	庚寅	壬寅	甲寅
兔 丁卯	己卯	辛卯	癸卯	乙卯
龍 戊辰	庚辰	壬辰	甲辰	丙辰
蛇 己巳	辛巳	癸巳	乙巳	丁巳
馬 庚午	壬午	甲午	丙午	戊午
羊 辛未	癸未	乙未	丁未	己未
猴 壬申	甲申	丙申	戊申	庚申
雞 癸酉	乙酉	丁酉	己酉	辛酉
犬 甲戌	丙戌	戊戌	庚戌	壬戌
豬 乙亥	丁亥	己亥	辛亥	癸亥

(月數)

正月六兩	二月七兩	三月八兩	四月九兩
五月五兩	六月六兩	七月九兩	八月五兩
九月	十月八兩	十一月九兩	十二月五兩

(日數)

初一五兩	初二兩	初三兩	初四兩	初五兩	初六兩
初七兩	初八兩	初九兩	初十兩		
十一兩	十二兩	十三兩	十四兩	十五兩	
十六兩	十七兩	十八兩	十九兩	二十兩	
二一兩	二二兩	二三兩	二四兩	二五兩	
廿六兩	廿七兩	廿八兩	廿九兩	三十兩	

(時數)

子兩　丑兩　寅兩　卯兩　辰兩　巳兩
午兩　未兩　申兩　酉兩　戌兩　亥兩

以上年月日時配準依數合查算出一身之榮枯評定百年之貴賤善排八字合計兩數成骨輕重

此命終身運不通 苦心竭力成家計 到得那時在夢中 勞勞作事盡皆空	平生衣祿是綿長 前面風霜多受過 後來必定享安康 件件心中自主張	此命推來是不同 中年還有逍遙福 不比前時運未通 為人能幹異凡庸	若使中年命運濟 得寬懷處且寬懷 那時名運一齊來 何用雙眉皺不開	為人心性最聰明 衣祿一生天數定 不須勞碌是豐亨 作事軒昂近貴人	萬事由天莫苦求 當年財帛難如意 須知福祿賴人修 晚景欣然便不憂	名利推求竟若何 命中難養男和女 前番辛苦後奔波 骨肉扶持也不多	衣祿無窮天數定 東西南北盡皆通 中年晚景一般同 出姓移居更覺隆	此命推求旺末年 平生原有滔滔福 可卜財源若水泉 妻榮子貴自怡然

What is the general forecast for a man born at 4 p.m. (Shen 'hour' – 申) on the 26th day of the 1st month 1928?

1928's Heavenly and Earthly characters were Wu (戊) Chen (辰).
The spiritual weight for Wu Chen is 1 liang 2 chin.
Month 1's weight is 6 chin.
The 26th day's weight is 1 liang 8 chin.
4 p.m. (Shen's weight) is 8 chin.
The total weight = 4 liang 4 chin.

Turning to the table of weights and poems (see above) we find the following prediction under 4:4 (兩):

Everything is controlled by Heaven.
You have good control over yourself.
There is not much money when you are young.
But in your old age, good fortune will attend.

Below are further examples taken from Master Yuan T'ien Kang's calculations.

三兩

勞碌碌苦中求　東奔西走何日休
若係終身勤與儉　老来稍可免憂愁

難得祖基家可立　中年衣食漸能周
忙忙碌碌苦中求　何日雲開見日頭

初年運寒事難謀　漸有財源如水流
到得中年衣食旺　那時名利一齊收

早年作事事難成　百計勤勞枉用心
半世自如流水去　後来運至得黃金

此命福氣果如何　僧道門中衣祿多
離祖出家方為妙　終朝拜佛念彌陀

生平福量不週全　祖業根基覺少傳
營事生涯宜守蕉　時来衣食勝從前

不須勞碌過平生　獨自成家福不輕
早有福星常照命　任君行去百般成

此命般般事不成　弟兄少力自孤行
雖然祖業須微有　来得明時去不明

一身骨肉最清高　藍袍脱去換紅袍
待到年將三十六　早入鱉門姓氏標

Example 1

A man born on the 16th day of the 9th month 1943 at Wei hour.

Look up the chart for 1943 = Kuei Wei. Look in top section of the chart: Kuei Wei = 7 chin.
Month = 9th = 1 liang 8 chin.
Day = 16th = 8 chin.
Hour = Wei = 8 chin.
Add these together = 4 liang 1 chin.

Turn to next pages to look up 4 liang 1 chin (四兩) (see opposite). This gives the following prediction:

You will have a strange life, a difficult life.
You are a very helpful person.
In your middle age you will have considerable fortune.
Your old age will be even better than the rest of your life.

Example 2

A woman born on 28th day of the 12th month 1955 at Tzu hour.

Look up the chart for 1955 = Yi Wei. Turn to chart of weights:
Yi Wei = 6 chin.
12th month = 5 chin.
28th day = 8 chin.
Tzu hour = 1 liang 6 chin.
Total = 3 liang 5 chin.

Turn to the chart on following pages (see p. 131). The prediction under 3 liang 5 chin (三兩) is:

When you are young, you will not have much fortune.
You will not be able to enjoy the fruits of your ancestors' property.
Be cautious in the use of your income.
Your old age will be better than the earlier part of your life.

Section 24

LUCKY DIRECTION FOR THE DAY

This chart is referred to in Section 1, p. 50. It contains fengshui details for each day of the sixty-day cycle, plus which good or evil stars are in which particular direction for that day.

Section 25

T'IEN KANG – DAY
CALCULATION ON THE HAND
FOR FORTUNE-TELLING

The use of this prediction system requires a time and date. If
the eventuality inquired about involves a time and date, these
are used. If not, the time and date when the inquirer visits the
fortune-teller are used.

The hand is marked with characters which correspond to
the 'hours' of the day (see p. 134) – these are, of course, the
Earthly Branches.

First, the correct start position is found by using the table
under the diagram:

1st and 9th month – begin Ch'ou
2nd and 8th months – begin Tzu
3rd and 7th months – begin Hai
4th and 6th months – begin Hai
5th month – begin Yu
10th and 12th months – begin Shen
11th month – begin Mao

Using the hand, the fortune-teller counts in a clockwise
direction starting on the character for the month in question –
in the case of the 5th month, for example, he would start on Yu
(酉). Including that first character, he counts off the
appropriate number of days – for, say, the 4th day of the 5th
month he would count four characters starting on Yu; this
leaves him on Tzu (子). The fortune-teller then looks at the
'hour' concerned. He starts from the new position which he
has reached, in this example Tzu. He then refers to the list of
Earthly Branches, finds again the character for the month, and
then counts from that character to the character for the 'hour'
in question. If the hour is, say, 8 a.m., it falls within the 5th
'hour' of the Chinese clock, which is Ch'en. The start character for counting is Yu, the character for the 5th month, which
is also the character for the 10th 'hour'. From Yu (the 10th) to
Ch'en (the 5th) are seven 'hour' characters. Therefore the
fortune-teller will count out round the hand seven positions
starting on Tzu, which brings him to Wu (午).

The resultant position indicates the answer to refer to on the
next page of the chart (not shown here). These answers are
divided into categories according to the question asked, as

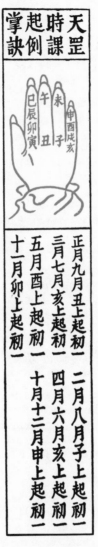

正月九月丑上起初一　二月八月子上起初一
三月七月亥上起初一　四月六月亥上起初一
五月酉上起初一　十月十二月申上起初一
十一月卯上起初一

follows: wealth; travel; trade negotiations; buying and selling; whether you have anything in your hand (a game); whether you will find lost things; location of lost things; legal disputes; going to seek wealth; luck or disaster on entering or leaving a building; when will the sky become clear?; whether a child will be male or female, and whether it will have good luck or disaster; whether it will rain or not; what is in your hand?; whether an illness is serious; whether a tic in your eyelid is lucky or not; how to avoid being the subject of gossip; straying animals.

Section 26

CHILD TALK (A STORY ABOUT CONFUCIUS)

K'ung Fu-tzu, Master K'ung or, to give him his family name in full, K'ung Ch'iu, does not feature greatly in the Almanac. He is only given prominence in one other place, as the greatest of his family name in 'The Hundred Family Names' (Section 32). As is mentioned in the Introduction, Confucian filial and structural concepts permeate the book in the form of assumptions about home life, duty, business, etc. They even enter into the very fabric of dreams. Yet Confucius, to use the Latinized form of his name, gets little prominence. Even here he is seen more as a foil to the young boy's wit and sharpness of mind than as the greatest moral philosopher of the classical tradition. The Almanac was often the butt of Confucian attacks and was not infrequently opposed because of its superstitious aspects. Moreover, those responsible for the construction of the more popularist elements of the Almanac came largely from the Taoist and Buddhist groups. As we saw at the end of the Introduction, 'A scholar should not concern himself with almanacs, but should act as the situation demands.' It is therefore not surprising that Confucius plays such a minor role in the Almanac.

The section entitled 'Child Talk' is a most unusual one for the Almanac. The story behind it is told in the translation below. It goes on to explore in question and answer format many core philosophical and intellectual issues, not, it has to be said, in any particular depth. Nevertheless this section is unique in the Almanac for introducing concerns of the mind and intellect.

Confucius, whose surname is K'ung and whose given name is Ch'iu, and whose personal name is Chung Ni, had his school in the west of Lu [a kingdom in China]. One day, when he was taking his pupils out for a ride in a cart, he encountered several children playing in the road. Among those children only one wasn't playing. Confucius stopped his cart and asked, 'Why aren't you playing?'

The child answered, 'Whenever we play, it is not good, because my clothes might get damaged and so this will ruin my parents' good name. So when I play, my effort won't get any reward. Why should I play? Instead, I am just using small pieces of slate to try to build a castle on the road.'

小兒論

孔子名丘字仲尼。設教於魯國之西。一日率諸弟子御車出遊路逢數兒嬉戲中有一兒不戲孔子乃駐車問曰獨汝不戲何也。小兒答曰凡戲無益衣破難縫上辱父母。下及門中。必有鬥爭勞而無功豈為好事。故乃不戲遂低頭以瓦片作城孔子及勒車問焉。汝年尚幼何多詐乎小兒答曰人生三歲分別父母兔生三曰走論道。下車而問焉。汝居何鄉何里何姓何名當車避於城避不當城避於車孔子乃勒車之曰何不避車乎小兒答曰自古及今豈為地阱畝魚生三曰遊於江湖天生自然豈謂詐乎孔子曰吾居敝鄉賤地姓項名橐。何字。小兒答曰吾欲共汝同遊汝意下未有字也孔子曰吾欲共汝同遊汝意下如何小兒答曰家有嚴父須當事之。家有慈母須當養之。家有賢兄須當順之。家有弱弟須當教之。家有明師須當學之。何暇

Then Confucius scolded him, saying, 'Then why don't you get out of the way of my cart?'

The child answered, 'Ever since history began, I have only heard that a cart will avoid a castle, not a castle a cart.'

Then Confucius got out of the cart and said to the child, 'You are so young and already so astute.'

The child answered, 'When human beings have lived for three years, they already start becoming independent of their parents. When rabbits are three days old, they walk along the field. When fish are three days old, they swim to the sea. This is all natural – why do you say I am astute?'

Then Confucius said, 'Where do you live and what is your name?'

The child answered, 'I live in a poor village and my surname is Hsiang Wei. I don't have my personal name yet.'

Confucius said, 'I wish to ride along with you. How about it?'

The child answered, 'My home has a respectable father: he needs me to serve him. My home has a kind mother: she needs me to look after her. My home has an elder brother: I should obey him. My home has a younger brother: I should teach him. My home has a learned teacher, I should learn from him. How should I have time to ride with you?'

Confucius said, 'My cart has thirty-two chessmen. Shall we gamble with them?'

The child answered, 'If the Emperor gambles, people in the country won't bother about him. If an official likes to gamble, it will affect the administration. If a learned person loves to gamble, all his knowledge will be useless. A person of average wealth, if he loves to gamble, will lose all his family's wealth. If a servant loves to gamble he will receive punishment. If a farmer loves to gamble, the harvest will not be on time. That's why I don't want to gamble with you.'

Then Confucius said, 'I want to talk to you about ruling [a play on words is being made here; the word used can mean both 'ruling' and 'levelling'] the whole country. How about it?'

The child answered, 'You can't level the country because it has high mountains, lakes and rivers, and has masters and servants. If you level high mountains, all the birds and animals will have no home. If you fill up the lakes and rivers, all the fish will also have no home. Without ruling officials, there will be a lot of gossip and mistakes in the country. If you get rid of the servants, everything will be in a mess.'

Confucius replied, 'Do you know in this country which fire has no smoke, which water has no fish, which mountain has no rocks, which tree has no branches, which man has no wife, which girl has no husband, which cow has no horns, which horse has no reins, which male has no female, and which female has no male? Who is the gentleman, who is the rascal? What is the meaning of less than enough? What is the meaning of more than enough? Which city has no market? Which person has no name?'

The child answered, 'A glowworm has no smoke, well water has no fish, a mountain of earth has no rocks, a dying tree has no branches, a saint has no wife, a virgin has no husband, an earth cow has no horns ['earth cow' means the lumps of clay used to bolster up embankments], a wooden horse has no reins, a bachelor has no female, a spinster has no male. Winter days are less than enough, summer days are more than enough. A palace has no market, a rascal has no name.'

Then Confucius asked, 'Do you know how the world came to be? The meaning of yin–yang? What is left, what is right? What is external, what is internal? What is father, what is mother? What is husband, what is wife? Where does the wind come from? Where does the rain come from? Where do the clouds come from? Where does the fog come from? What is the distance between the sky and the earth, how many thousands of miles?'

Then the child answered, '$9 \times 9 = 81$, this is how the world came to be. $8 \times 9 = 72$, this is how the yin and yang start and end. The sky is father, the earth is mother. The sun is husband, the moon is wife. East is left and west is right. Outside is external, inside is internal. The wind is from the forest, rain from the pastureland, the cloud from the mountain and the fog from the earth. The distance between the sky and earth is many thousands of miles. East, west, south, north have their own settling place.'

Section 27

ETIQUETTE IN WRITING
LETTERS, INVITATIONS, ETC.

The formal style of most traditional Chinese writing is reflected here. Just as handbooks for addressing people correctly have long been found in the West, so in China. In Chinese traditional society the art of letterwriting became highly elaborate with formulas of address being developed appropriate to the rank of the person receiving the letter. It is important to remember that, for many people, their grasp of written Chinese may be quite basic. In many places where the Chinese live overseas, there are professional letterwriters, as there are in Hong Kong, Taiwan and indeed in many parts of China. For those who are literate but unsure of the correct style, this section provides models for most social occasions and is a very real help in many circumstances.

In the following example, a bride's family thank their son-in-law for his gifts and say that they will give him a set of gifts in return. The gifts are examples and may vary. The message should be written on a red card.

I give you this thanks card and one hat, a pair of shoes and a piece of cloth, some money, sweets and a cake.

Name
Signature

Section 28

PRONUNCIATION GUIDE TO ENGLISH

As explained in the Introduction, the Almanac is often the only readily available source of reference in many homes. It has thus come to include much which is of a useful nature, such as the stages of the foetus in pregnancy (Section 17; see p. 86) or the reasons for eclipses (see Section 39). Another addition has been this dictionary of English. It has two functions. Each English word has beside it on the left the equivalent word or phrase in Chinese. This is useful. Below each English word is placed a character or characters which are supposed to provide a pronunciation guide. This is not so useful! For instance, to replicate the sound of the English word 'want' it suggests 王, which is pronounced 'wong'! The dictionary is certainly of help in translation of a very basic kind, but as a pronunciation guide it falls into the category of those splendid nineteenth-century European travellers' dictionaries which contained phrases such as 'My postillion has been struck by lightning.'

黄金	Gold 告路	二金	Quinea 堅拿	从大金	Gold dollar 告路打罅
港幣	Hongkong dollar 香港打罅	英磅	Pound sterling 旁士他令	先令	(s) Shilling 司令
便士	(d) Pence 便士	美元	United States dollar 腰噠士打罅	磅	Pound (lb) 旁
盎斯	Ounce (oz) 盎斯	公吨	Metric ton (M/T) 也推力吞	公担	Quintal (Q) 坤吐
公斤	Kilogramme (kg) 奇路古林	公兩	Hectogramme (Hg) 客吐古林	加侖	Gallon (Gall) 加侖
公里	Kilometre (Km) 奇路笏他	公尺	Metre (M) 笏他	公分	Centimetre (Cm) 新地笏他
公厘	Millemetre (mm) 美利笏他	味	Metre (M) 笏他	碼	Yards (yd) 丫蔓
呎	Foot (ft) 福	吋	Inch (in) 烟台	一担	One picul 温俾哥
一個	One piece 温庇斯	一箱	One case 温企士	一張	One sheet 温士噠
一条	One bar 温爸	一堆	One pile 温批路	一份	One share 温些路
一滴	One drop 温都笠	一尺	One foot 温福	一丈	Ten feet 吞飛
一打	Dozen 打臣	一个骨	Quarter 括他	中意	Like 拉克
唔中意	No like 奴拉克	買乜貨	What do you want to buy? 屈都要王施悲		
老定	Honest 奧坭斯呢	貴	Dear 爹	幾錢	How much cash? 嘩抹治加示
俾夠	Pay up 披鴨	唔夠	Not enough 納阿夜拿夫	減	Deduct 爹突
俾錢	Give cash 鈒加示	添	Add 压突	無現錢	No cash 奴加示
要	Want 王	最好	Best 悲斯脱	計數	Count 康脱
貨物	Cargo 卡哥	好生意	Flour tshng 夫羅哩脧	要靚的	Want best 烏突啤士

THE SECRET BOOK OF CHU-KO'S SPIRIT CALCULATION

(Fortune-Telling from the Number of Strokes in Your Name)

According to its own account, 'The Secret Book of Chu-ko' is the most powerful and authoritative method of divination in the Almanac. It is also one of the most complicated both in terms of the method used and in interpreting the end result. The preface to this part of the Almanac talks of the book being copied from 'the old times' (see below). The book is credited to Chu-ko, the legendary founder of an early sect of religious Taoism known as Pei-chi or Pole Star. He is also credited, in his full name of Chu-ko Liang, with being the founder of the military magic called Wu-tang Shan. This is better known through one of its forms – T'ai-chi Ch'uan. Chu-ko is supposed to have lived during the Three Kingdoms period (221–65 CE). In fact, the earliest reference to him does not appear until just before the T'ang dynasty (618 CE) and the major manual of Wu-tang Shan and thus of T'ai-chi Ch'uan dates from the Ming (1368–1644 CE). Obviously Chu-ko was a useful name to attach to an old document in order to give it even greater authority, rather as revolutionary Judaism in its battle against the Seleucids (169–64 BCE) looked back to the legendary figure of Daniel.

The methodology of this form of divination is explained in part in the translation below. However, it may be helpful to readers to have it even more clearly stated. The core of the procedure is the writing of three characters. These can be any three characters, but they need to be linked to a question. Below we have given two examples. Someone wishes to open a restaurant and wants to know if it is wise to open this year and if business will prosper. To get an answer, the inquirer writes the name of the proposed restaurant – in this case 'The Golden Phoenix'. In the second example someone wishes to know whether next year will be a good or bad year. In this instance the inquirer writes his own name, P'eng Ma-tin. If someone is about to travel on business and wishes to know whether the journey and trade will go well, he might write either the name of his destination or the commodity he wishes to sell. The only rule is that it must be three characters – no less, no more.

Each character is then divided up into the number of strokes it takes to write it. Every character has a specific way in which it is written and a set number of strokes of the pen. For instance, the character for 'middle' is constructed thus:

中 丶 冂 口 中

In the example of The Golden Phoenix restaurant, the first character – gold – has 8 strokes. As it is the first character it is given the hundreds position = 800. The second character has 13 strokes. As this has to fill the tens slot, it is reduced to a single number by taking away 10. This leaves 3 = 30. (Any number which exceeds 9 is reduced to a single number by taking away 10.) The third character has 11 strokes – less 10 = 1. This fills the single digit position. Hence the secret number of these three characters is 831.

The magic number of charts in this section is 384 as there are deemed to be 384 predictions contained therein. It is thus necessary to reduce the secret number of the three characters to a figure of 384 or less before the divination can start. Thus 831 − 384 = 447 (still too high). 447 − 384 = 63. This gives the starting figure.

With this starting figure of 63 the process can begin. Following the two pages of preface and explanation (see pp. 144 and 146), come twenty-four pages of charts (see p. 148). These charts start off by being nearly full of characters, each ascribed to a specific number. The charts, three to a page, go up by blocks of 100 each. Hence the first three charts go from 1 to 100; 101 to 200; 201 to 300. In all, the charts go up to 12,700. Taking in our case the starting figure of 63, you find the character ascribed to 63. Write this down. Next you add 384 to 63 to find the second number. This will be 447. Write this down. Again add 384 to 447 giving you 831. Write down the character ascribed to this. Then add another 384 to 831 giving 1215. Write down this character. And so on, adding 384 each time. As you progress through the charts the number of characters in each block shrinks, and increasingly the charts are composed of noughts. Eventually the last part has only six characters and ninety-four noughts. You continue to add 384 to your last figure until you land on a nought. This means your message from the divination has ended.

You now need to interpret the message which the process has given you. The diviner will break the message into lines of four or more characters. Each line then becomes a sentence. Having found a meaning to each line and to the overall poem, the diviner may still have to give you an interpretation of the poem for the final message to be received.

秘本諸葛神數

是書係舊時抄本紙皆破碎。乃遠代之遺
傳世不多覩相傳為漢諸葛武侯所作共
有三百八十四籤按三百八十四爻其中
句法長短不一寓意深遠變化無窮判斷
吉凶如應斯響較之金錢馬前等數實有
霄壤之別余什襲珍藏視同拱璧今友人
有家庭圖書集成之輯內有藝術彙編一
篇搜輯豐富多為真本秘本該主人再三
以此書付梓相商因想禍福吉凶人所共
有。先賢傳授此書本以指人迷惑故未敢
自秘謹錄一通詳加校對搜殘補缺以供
同好惟願占者誠心禱告無不靈驗如神。
慎勿以兒戲為之致損此書之價值也。

民國七年七月　吳縣江陰香謹識

【占法】

(甲)報字　凡占卦者。必先報字。報字
不拘何字。必以三字為度不可報四
字。亦不可報二字。

(乙)計算　將所報之字。先寫於紙上。
數其筆畫。以便查字其法有三。

(一)第一字作百數例如報求財運三字。求
字筆畫作百數。財字作十數。運字作
個數。餘仿此舉例如左。

求	百位
財	十位
運	個位

(三)凡字筆畫在九筆以內者照算。在
十筆以外者。減十筆算(二十筆同)
若恰在十筆或二十筆。俱照一筆計
算。例如求財運字。求字七筆計算。
財運字十二筆。財字減去十。九筆。
照算。餘仿此舉式如下。

We must stress, as the preface to this section itself does, that this is not a game or a toy. It is regarded by believers to be of enormous power and authority. We do not recommend that it is used by anyone in a playful or lighthearted manner.

PREFACE

This book has been copied down through the ages from the old times. In the old times, only a few fragments of it were preserved and very few people knew of it or how to use it. According to legend, during the Han period it was written down by a man called Chu-ko Wu Hou and consists of a total of 384 predictions. Some of these prediction poems are short, some long but they all contain powerful explorations of both good and bad fortune. It is also very accurate and if you compare it with the fortune-telling of Chin Ch'ien or Ma Ch'ien you will find this method is more accurate. A friend of mine has a large library of books on many similar subjects but he says that this book is the most valuable and accurate of them all. The book of Chu-ko is able to tell everyone whether they will have good or bad fortune. It can also lead people to avoid evil things and guide them to fortune and safety. Those wishing to use it should be honest in order to ensure the utmost accuracy. Do not play with this book or else you will destroy its value.

Written on 7th month of the 7th year of the Republic at Wu Hsien by Chang Yin Hsiang (1918).

INSTRUCTIONS

The following are the key points given in the instructions:

The inquirer should give three words – not two and not four. Ask the inquirer to write these on a piece of paper and then work out the number of strokes. There are three parts to the procedure.

1. The first character is in the hundreds column. The second character is in the tens column. The third is in the single column.
2. If the character number goes up to 9, count as up to 9. If it goes to 10 or more, take away 10. If exactly 10 or 20, then it is equivalent to 1.
3. This book has only 384 predictions. So if the numbers of the three characters are more than this, take away 384 from the total number until you come below 384. Then use the figure you have arrived at to start divination. Continue to add 384 to each total figure until you reach 0. Then you have the poem.

（三）此書照大易三百八十爻作為三百八十四爻度過於三百八十四計算減後仍多須減去三百八十四計算減後仍多再減之必減至不過三百八十四為止。假如三百八十五數除去三百八十四數即作一數。例如求財運三字為七百九十二數減去三百八十四為四百零八數仍過法數須再減三百八十四為二十四即照二十四查。

餘倣此舉例如下。

報字據	求財	運
	九	二
減去	七	四
存	〇	八
再減	八	四
存		二

（因）查字　數已計定即可查字。其法有

二

（一）第一字照三字合計之數為何數即在何數中查起查得之後記之於紙再加三百八十四查查至有圈無字則籤已完畢。

（二）若第一字之數為○則須加三百八十往下再查。如求財運三字第一次為二十四再加三百八十四即是有○無字凡遇此等須再加三百八十四往下再查即得矣。

【實例】

（甲）報字　須寫正楷記在紙上。假如報出「求財運」三字占有

（乙）計算　財為第二字作十筆作為一百數九十二筆作為九十二數依法凡運為第三字作七筆為百數作七百數三字合成七百九十二數依法凡過三百八十四數須除去多數此數過三百八十四數須除兩個三百八十四得數為二十

（丙）查字　四。二十四為第四字字中第五萬第百回依法一行一為第八逢一第千六二八再加四即查以三百八十四百字為數其中第五萬第百回翻着無字者為完

（丁）籤詩　求財運三字竣即得籤詩如左。

（戊）演式　意誠心誡　求財運三字意誠心誡要平安防出入。

意	誠	心	誡
二八四	二八四		
八二四			
〇八四			
三八四			
八七九三			
一五三八			
一九三八			

誡	要	平	安	防	出	入
九八	二四					
四〇二	八四					
三八六	二八四					
〇三四	八三四					
三八六	加					
四三二	加					
六三三	加					
五〇一	六〇					

Example 1

Someone wishes to open a new restaurant this year. Will he be successful? The diviner asks for three characters associated with this venture. The proposed restaurant's name is The Golden Phoenix. This gives the following three characters: 金鳳凰 . Their values are 8, 13, 11, which gives a total of 831. This must then be reduced by subtracting 384 = 447. Reduce again by subtracting 384 = 63. This is the start.

Turning to the charts, and adding 384 each time the following message is spelt out (★ = end of sentence):

(a)   63 = /
(b)   447 = 湖
(c)   831 = 海
(d) 1215 = 意
(e) 1599 = 悠
(f) 1983 = 悠 ★
(g) 2367 = 烟
(h) 2751 = 波

(i)   3135 = 下
(j)   3519 = 釣
(k)   3903 = 鈎 ★
(l)   4287 = 若
(m) 4671 = 逢
(n) 5055 = 龍
(o) 5439 = 與
(p) 5823 = 兔 ★

(q) 6207 = 名
(r) 6591 = 利
(s) 6975 = 一
(t) 7359 = 齊
(u) 7743 = 圖
(v) 8127 = 0 ★

The characters spell out the following poem:

The pool and the sea are calm.
There is a slight mist in the early morning.
If you meet the Dragon or Rabbit years,
Then your name will be famous and you will be wealthy.

The interpretation is as follows. The first two lines signify all is calm and peaceful. Nothing much is happening. The last two lines tell quite clearly when it would be advisable to open such a restaurant. If this year is not Dragon or Rabbit then do not open this year.

Example 2

A person wishes to know whether the coming year will be auspicious or inauspicious for him. The diviner asks for the three characters of his name. They are 影 馬 田 . Their values are 12, 10, 5. This gives 215. Now the question must be asked specifically, otherwise the general use of a name will not be seen as specific enough to gain a clear answer. 'Will next year be good or bad for me?' As 215 falls below 385, this can be the start number.

(a) 215 = 安
(b) 599 = 坦
(c) 983 = 路
(d) 1367 = 平
(e) 1751 = 麦 ★
(f) 2135 = 寞
(g) 2519 = 中

(h) 2903 = 一
(i) 3287 = 雁
(j) 3671 = 胞 ★
(k) 4055 = 桃
(l) 4439 = 花
(m) 4823 = 逢
(n) 5207 = 驟

(o) 5591 = 雨 ★
(p) 5975 = 水
(q) 6359 = 畔
(r) 6743 = 女
(s) 7127 = 頻
(t) 7511 = 啼
(u) 7895 = 0 ★

The poem reads:

> *The road is straight and steady in front of you.*
> *The wild goose is flying through the clouds in the sky.*
> *There is a sudden shower over the peach tree.*
> *At the riverbank there is a girl calling loudly.*

The interpretation is that you cannot achieve what you want all by yourself. You should seek help from others; with that help, you will be successful.

Section 30

LISTS SHOWING FOUR DIFFERENT STYLES OF WRITING CERTAIN CHARACTERS

This section is a further element of the practical educational dimension of the Almanac. Preserved in its middle is a classic-style primer. This is the sort of book that all students starting on the long and hard path to the Imperial examinations would have used. Similar to the nineteenth-century primers beloved of English educators, it contains simple proverbs or statements just like those which adorned the copperplate primers of English schools. 'A fool and his money are soon parted' is the general level and style. Since the Imperial examination ceased in 1912 and the whole Confucian style of education decayed until overthrown by the new regime in 1949, this primer is of some historical interest. It also has a very pragmatic function. It contains a considerable number of characters (twenty-eight pages worth) in the four main styles. As can be seen in Section 6, there are scores of different styles, but these are the four most common.

The first is the ordinary, everyday standard style as used in most books, newspapers, etc. It is known as the general style.

The second is classical and was brought to perfection in the seventh to twelfth centuries CE. It is sometimes referred to as T'ang style. This is used on special posters or for formal inscriptions.

The third is the famous 'grass' style, scourge of all those trying to learn to read Chinese. This is a form of shorthand combined with personal-correspondence style and is used extensively for ordinary writing.

The fourth and final style is Shang or oracle-bone style. The origins of Chinese writings are traced back to the oracle bones of the Shang dynasty (1523–1028 BCE). In order to obtain oracles, the shoulderblades of oxen or the shells of tortoises were marked with either grooves or holes. The shell or bone was then asked a specific question and then a red-hot tool was placed in the groove or into the hole. The resultant cracks were then interpreted by the diviner. The diviner looked for 'pictures' which answered the question put and he would complete or draw out 'latent' pictures he saw in the cracks. These provided the answers. From these answer pictures the written language developed.

天地玄黄　天地玄黄　天地玄黄　天地玄黄
宇宙洪荒　宇宙洪荒　宇宙洪荒　宇宙洪荒
日月盈昃　日月盈昃　日月盈昃　日月盈昃
辰宿列張　辰宿列張　辰宿列張　辰宿列張
寒来暑往　寒来暑往　寒来暑往　寒来暑往
秋收冬藏　秋收冬藏　秋收冬藏　秋收冬藏
閏餘成歲　閏餘成歲　閏餘成歲　閏餘成歲
律呂調陽　律呂調陽　律呂調陽　律呂調陽

Section 31
TELEGRAM NUMERATION OF CHINESE CHARACTERS

The difficulties posed by Chinese characters when using modern communication techr ues are many and vast. Anyone who has seen a Chines. typewriter will understand.

This problem first became a major one when the telegraph was invented. There is no way that characters as such can be sent by telegraph or by telex. Instead, a system of numeration of characters was devised. All the main characters are given a number and a Chinese telegram consists of a string of numbers which are then turned into their character equivalents. The Almanac lists nearly 8000 numbered characters. The system is also used by Western publications which cannot print characters but wish to indicate the specific characters behind, for example, someone's name, as in reports of government officials carried in the *BBC Summary of World Broadcasts – Far East*. There have been various attempts to abolish or fundamentally alter the writing of Chinese characters in the last sixty years, but none has ever been fully accepted. Thus the numeration system provides a vital bridge between the grace of the character and the needs of communication.

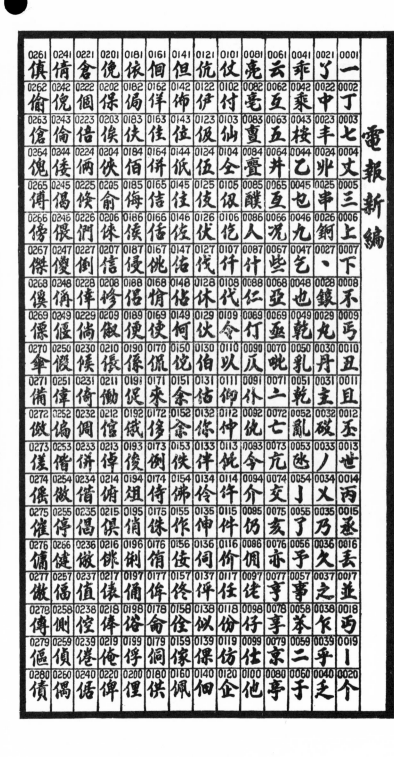

電報新編

Section 32

THE HUNDRED FAMILY NAMES

This section is so titled because it is common to talk in terms of the 'hundred family names' or the 'three hundred family names' as a generic phrase for the whole people.

The significance, antiquity and power of the surname in Chinese society is not readily grasped by those from other cultures. Through a Chinese surname, a person is linked to a vast network of people, many of whom will be completely unknown, but who will help if contacted in the family name.

The use of surnames stretches back into the earliest records. We know the family names of K'ung Fu-tzu and of that semi-mythological figure Lao Tzu. Indeed, so strong is and was the sense of family name ties that when members of the same family name – Li – became the founders of a new dynasty, the T'ang (618–906 CE), they heaped honours on Lao Tzu. Indeed, part of the official acceptance of Taoism was made possible because of the Li family emperors' desire to honour their distant ancestor.

Given the extent to which filial piety and family honour are features of such early material as went to compose the *Shu Ching*, some parts of which date from between the tenth and sixth centuries BCE,[1] it is fairly safe to assume that family names were fixed facets of the family system as far back as the Shang dynasty (1523–1028 BCE). In the English world fixed surnames only go back to the late Middle Ages.

The family name is always associated with a particular place. It is still common today to find Chinese villages where either all or the majority of the population have the same family name.[2] These villages, often walled, physically represent the family members' need for one another. The outside world was hard and hostile. It was only through the family that one could expect help and care. This is mirrored in all the great Chinese domestic novels such as the eighteenth-century *The Dream of the Red Chamber* or the modern *China Men* by Maxine Hong Kingston.[3] Most Chinese today can tell you where they come in the line of descent from the founder of their village or area and take you back even farther – in many cases thirty to forty generations back – to the original family area.

In many places where the Chinese have settled overseas, the family link has proved both the means for migration and a major form of welfare and support in a strange land.[4] Through funeral arrangements, filial payments and general help, the

154

ties with the wider family are maintained and stressed – not least at the major festivals.

This section actually contains some 576 names complete with brief details about the area from which the family originally came. Ranged along the top of each page are three pictures. These show three people whose family names appear on that page and who are considered the most famous person of that line. Below is a translation of twenty-four names and places plus details of the three famous men shown on the first page of this section (see p. 156). The pronunciation is Cantonese. Reading down from the right:

Chiu	*from Tien Shui county*
Chin	*from Pan Shing county*
Suen	*from Lok On county*
Lee	*from Long Sai county*
Fung	*from Che Ping county*
Chan	*from Wan Chuen county*
Chu	*from Ho Lan county*
Wai	*from Ho Dong county*
Ch'u	*from Pui Kwok county*
Chun	*from Tien Soy county*
Yau	*from Ng Hing county*
Hoi	*from Ko Yeung county*
Hung	*from Dong Lo county*
Cho	*from Chin Kwok county*
Yim	*from Tien Soy county*
Wah	*from Mo Ling county*
Chik	*from Dong Hoi county*
Tse	*from Chan Lau county*
Chow	*from Fan Yung county*
Yue	*from Kong Ha county*
Wan	*from Long Nga county*
So	*from Mo Kung county*
Poon	*from Wing Yung county*
Kot	*from Kut Yan county*

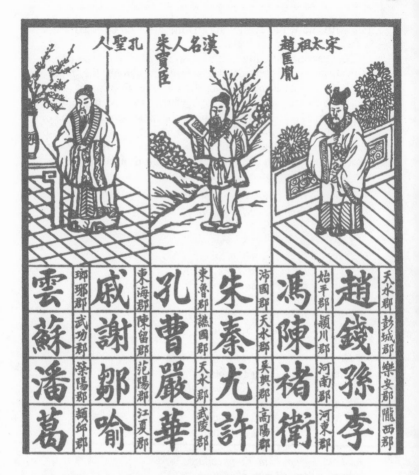

The three ancestors are, from right to left (in Wade-Giles):

1. *Chao Family – Chao K'uang-yin*
   The first Emperor of the Sung dynasty [960–1126 CE].

2. *Chu Family – Chu Mai-ch'en*
   Foremost scholar of the Han dynasty [207 BCE–9 CE].
   [Legend tells of his being very poor – in fact a homeless beggar. He saved up and bought books for study and eventually rose to great fame and fortune.]

3. *K'ung ★Family – K'ung Sheng-yen [Holy Man K'ung]*
   [Best known as Confucius.]

   ★ Hung in Cantonese.

Section 33

MISCELLANEOUS ACTIVITIES AND THEIR MOST AUSPICIOUS TIMES

This section contains a vast range of activities, many associated with farming, with details as to the best days on which to undertake them. The list covers weaning children, building, buying animals, crops, travel, etc. – a true miscellany of everyday actions for which guidance might be required. We give two examples; in the second the pronunciation is Cantonese.

How to See if a Cat is a Good Cat or Not

The best cat has a short body, charming eyes and a long tail. Its face should have a haughty expression like a tiger's. Its voice should be strong, so that when the rats hear it they will die instantly. When its claws come out, they should be capable of digging up tiles. If a cat has a long body, it will not stay long at home; it will go to another family. A cat with a long face will kill chickens. A wide tail means a lazy cat.

Good Stars and Bad Stars for Marriage

Good stars are: Wong Tao, Sang Hei, Yick Hau, Chuk Sai, Yin Yang Hop, Yan Man Hop, But Chung, Sing Yat.

  Bad stars are: Tin Kau, Yeut Yim, Tin Wor, Yeung Cheung, Yum Cheung, Yan Kag, Pei Ma Sark, Ngau Kau, Yeung Chor, Yum Chor, Check Hau, Chung Song, Chung Fuk Yat.

Section 34

HOW TO JUDGE PEOPLE BY THEIR HABITUAL ACTIONS

This section anticipates in some ways the section on physiognomy (Section 40). In physiognomy it is not just the face which tells you of a person's character, but his or her whole body. By astute reading of how people behave, their mannerisms and 'little ways', you can often judge their personality quite accurately.

The sections opens with wordly advice as follows:

What the learned people of old said or wrote down is valuable and worth remembering. It teaches people to learn about whatever they may encounter. We can use the ancient experiences to help ourselves in our present lives. If you know a great deal about yourself and others, you will always be successful. Whatever you do, first be sure it will have no ill effect on others; do not just think about yourself but put yourself in the other person's place. To enjoy yourself with others, it is best to be with your closest friends. If you want to give advice to others, you should approach those who trust you. Although you may know many people, not many are really honest with you. If we always value our friends as much as when we first met them, our friendship will always remain. If you live close to the river, you will know the character of the fish well. If you live in the forest, you will know the different songs of the birds. Those who don't keep their promises are not friends to make. If you fall on hard times, it would be like a piece of gold changing to iron and vice versa. If you learn one word, it is worth a thousand units of gold, and so whatever you learn, use it well.

The section then proceeds to take certain characteristics, certain mannerisms, and to provide an interpretation of these. In total, thirteen examples are illustrated by use of woodblock pictures, whilst their meaning and significance are spelled out. For instance, the second illustration shows a man riding a horse (see p. 160). The text tells how getting to know someone is like riding a horse. All may go well at first, but it is only after you have travelled a long way, endured various incidents and come to know the horse's strengths and weaknesses that you can claim really to know the horse. So it is with a friend. The seventh picture in the set shows two crabs. Beware, says the

読書須用意

繪圖增廣賢文

昔時賢文，誨語諄諄。集韻增廣，多見多聞。觀今宜鑑古。無古不成今。知己知彼，將心比心。酒逢知己飲，詩向會人吟。相識滿天下，知心能幾人。相逢好似初相識，到老終無怨恨。近水知魚性，近山識鳥音。易漲易退山溪水，易反易覆小人心。運去金成鐵，時來鐵似金。讀書須用意，一字值千金。逢人且說三分話，未可全拋一片心。有意栽花花不發，無心插柳柳成陰。畫虎畫皮難畫骨，知人口面不知心。錢財如糞土，仁義值千金。流水下灘非有意，白雲出岫本無心。當時若不登高望，誰信東流海樣深。路遙知馬力，久見人心。兩人一般心，有錢堪買金。一人一般心，無錢難買針。相見易得好。久住難為人。馬行無力皆因瘦，人不風

力馬知遠路

但將冷眼看螃蟹

暗處一燈

text, of people who move like crabs. They are not straight-forward but seek to get round you by indirect moves. The eleventh picture in the set is accompanied by the following advice:

If a rich man has a large house and he lights every room in it, what use is that? He would be better to use his wealth to put one light on a dark street corner to help everyone, rather than keeping his lights for his own use.

This section is considered to be full of very sound and worthwhile advice even by those who find other sections of the Almanac unimportant.

Section 35

HOW TO RUN A SMALL BUSINESS

This section forms part of the block of moral and ethical teachings which cluster together in the middle of the Almanac. As with the other sections in this group, it speaks of an ideal person, living according to Confucian rules and strictures. Within Confucian thought, right behaviour was crucial to civilized life. Confucians, as we see in the introduction to this block, saw themselves as models of conduct and sought through office to mould behaviour. It is, therefore, not surprising that this part concerned with small businesses contains little of what we would see as practical guidance, but lots of proverbs and homilies. The following is a translation of part of the first page of this eight-page document.

All young people like to go off trading. By doing this they can make more money to feed more mouths. You must be honest so that your every word is trusted. You should not be quick-tempered but able to remain calm under pressure. If someone scolds you, even when you have done nothing wrong, you should bear it with patience. Do not get drawn into arguments, and especially not into fights. Smile for everyone. Wherever you are, at home or at the shop, be cheerful with everyone. If someone argues with you, be patient and smile. If someone calls for you, reply, do not ignore him. If you call for someone, it should be done politely. If during the day you have too much work to do, let your assistants do some of it for you, but always check it over yourself. If you finish all your work, go and help those who have not finished yet. Do not think in terms of 'his work' or 'my work'. Work hard at all times.

Section 36

CHU TZU'S GUIDE TO
MANAGING YOUR HOME

In the Introduction we discovered how the Almanac gives a unique opportunity to glimpse values and patterns of traditional Chinese life. This section is perhaps the most interesting in this regard. While the likelihood of anyone's ever having lived up to this guide is small, it does capture and illustrate fundamental concepts, ways of living and beliefs in a quite fascinating way. If much of the Almanac is folk Buddhism and folk Taoism, then this surely is folk Confucianism. The illustrations not only cover the tasks outlined in the text but also provide a model for a day's behaviour from rising early (note the sun just coming up) to reverencing the ancestors before retiring. The text draws out wider social implications of proper behaviour. The Confucian ideal is here made accessible by exactly the same method as Mao Tse-tung used to explain the Communist Manifesto to peasants: vivid woodblock pictures, with a text which is very short and to the point.

You should rise at daybreak and water down the dust in your front and back yards, then sweep it away. You should keep inside and outside your house tidy.

In the evening you should prepare to sleep, and, of course, before going to sleep should lock all doors and windows; you should check everything yourself.

When you eat your food, you should remember that it is not easy to grow it; remember that every material of your clothing is difficult to produce. Prepare things before you need them; do not wait to dig a well until you are thirsty.

You should not be extravagant in buying food for yourself. It is all right to have a guest to dinner, but do not have your guest stay overnight.

Do not have a wasteful amount of food and drink. Do not buy an over-ornate house or an expensive farm.

Ignore gossiping women. Do not hanker after a young girl's beauty: it does your home no good if you are greedy.

Do not employ handsome servants. Do not allow your wife to use make-up. Although your ancestors are not physically present, treat them with respect and honesty.

All children should go to school. You should save constantly to enable your grandchildren to have a good education.

Do not be greedy about money or drink it away. When you do a little trading, do not cheat your customers.

*If you see your neighbour in need, try your best to help. Do not
be miserly with servants or relatives or you will soon lose your
home.*

*When you have something to give to your brothers, uncles or
cousins, do not show favouritism. When you are teaching your
juniors, do so sincerely.*

*Do not listen to women's talk; if you do, you are not a man. If
you love money more than your parents, you are not truly their
child.*

*When you choose a son-in-law, you should not ask him to give
you too much money. Your daughter-in-law should be well
mannered; this counts for much more than beauty.*

*Do not envy the rich or lord it over the poor. Try to avoid legal
wrangles.*

*When you are working outdoors, do not talk too much or you
will get into trouble. Do not cheat those weaker than you.*

*Do not be a glutton or you will get sick. Do not kill more
animals than you need for food. Do not be lazy.*

*Do not keep the company of bad youths or you will suffer for
it. Seek the company of your elders instead; if there is trouble,
they will help you.*

If someone gives you advice, listen patiently. If you are involved in an argument, bear in mind that you may be wrong.

When you have helped someone, do not keep it in mind, but if someone helps you, you should remember it.

Let others have a little leeway. When you are happy do not show off. Do not be jealous of other people.

Do not be overoptimistic about your chances. If you want to help somebody, do not make a big fuss about it. If you do so, you are not a real help. If you try to disguise your cruelty by a façade of kindess, you are even more cruel. If you mistreat other women, your wife and daughter will suffer.

If you attack people behind their backs, it will rebound upon your son and your grandson. If your home is happy then everything will go smoothly.

If the country collapses, you will have no home.

If you are self-sufficient, you do not need to depend on anyone else. The aim of study is to increase knowledge, not the mere attainment of high position. If the King and the citizens work together, there will be peace and prosperity. Whether you are successful or not, you should try to be content.

Section 37

TRADITIONAL MEDICAL PRESCRIPTIONS

The treatment of various ailments by traditional medicine is now increasingly widely accepted in the West. In China, traditional and Western medicine have long worked side by side. It is surprising that so little of it has entered into the Almanac. This short four-page section is all there is.

It is impossible to try to discuss Chinese concepts of medicine, health and the body in so short a space. Nor is it wise to translate directly the prescriptions given here as they contain no real details of method of preparation or ingestion.

The prescriptions or recipes are for a wide range of common ailments such as asthma, high blood pressure and arthritis and are regularly used in homes today.

Section 38

ASTROLOGICAL CHARTS

The six star charts given in this section are an interesting mixture of astrology and astronomy. Five of the charts show the positions of the stars in the night sky. The other chart deals with the Twenty-Eight Constellations and the Four Arrangements.

The first chart (p. 168) shows the stars in their groupings and gives the interpretation and Chinese names of each group, names such as the Phoenix and the Little Horse. The second chart (p. 169) shows the Four Arrangements of the Twenty-Eight Constellations in relation to the shapes of the Four Creatures (see Section 11). The remaining four charts (not shown here) show the night sky for the four seasons, starting with spring and ending with winter.

The charts do not, with the exception of the second one, attempt to deal with the sources of the good and bad stars, or the planets. They are really information charts of a scientific nature with traditional Chinese names. The six charts neatly capture the relationship between the 'scientific' knowledge of astronomy and the 'beliefs' about astrology – all part of the same continuum.

星 座 圖

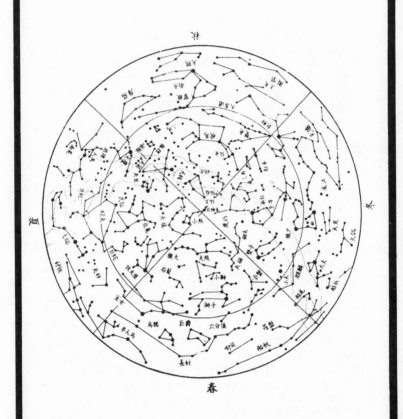

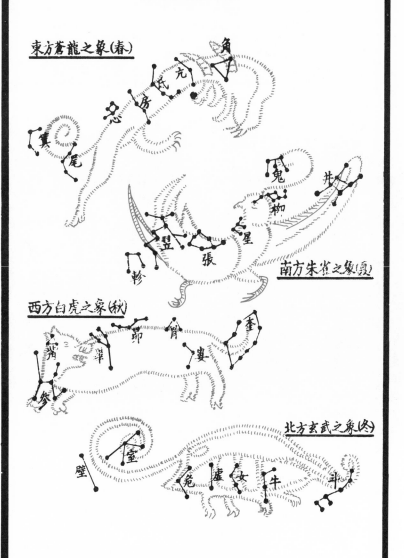

Section 39
<u>ECLIPSES, ETC.</u>

This section is, like the previous one, essentially scientific and informative in its orientation. Eclipses and other celestial phenomena, often a source of fear because they are considered to be omens and harbingers of ill luck, are here considered as natural and explicable events, a curious intrusion in a volume closely concerned with omens and good or ill luck.

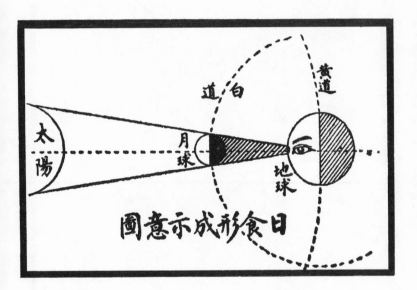

Section 40

PHYSIOGNOMY, PALMISTRY AND FORTUNE-TELLING

The highly complex and detailed world of Chinese physiognomy and palmistry deserves a full book of its own, not least because of the attacks upon it by some of China's greatest philosophers. It is a very well-developed art and still exercises great attraction both inside and outside modern China.

The Almanac itself devotes some ten pages to the two topics, consisting mainly of charts and very simple details. The level of the material is basic and popularist rather than serious and detailed. Professional physiognomists and palmists do not regard these charts very highly. It is expected that those wishing to have a proper reading will go to a professional rather than rely on these charts.

The history of physiognomy and palmistry – but more particularly of physiognomy – is an intriguing one. There is no mention of it in the Classics and the first reference to it comes in the vitriolic and highly acclaimed attack launched upon it by the Confucian philosopher Hsun Tzu in the third century BCE. Hsun Tzu was a major critic of superstitious practices, which he saw as arising from the traumatic events surrounding the end of the Chou dynasty, the period of the Warring States and the early stages of the rise of the brutal but efficient Ch'in. The stable pattern had been broken and was in need of being recast. From this disorder, new ideas – such as physiognomy – arose to answer certain basic questions and to provide a key to aspects of life no longer safely covered by the older rites.

In order to get a picture of some of the dimensions of physiognomy, it is intriguing to read Hsun Tzu's attack:

Formerly there were no physiognomists, and the word is not found in any books. Ku-pu Tze-k'ing and T'ang-ku began to examine the appearance, the stature and the complexion of persons, in order to deduce therefrom their good or evil destiny, and whether they would live a long or short life. Ignorant folks believed such nonsense, but in ancient times the practice was quite unknown, and books make no mention of it. It would be much better to speak of the heart rather than examine the countenance, better still to discourse on men's intentions rather than the heart, for the heart is better than the countenance, and a man's intention is better than the heart itself. If the intention is upright, the heart is likewise good.

Even if a man's appearance be against him, but the intention of his heart is good, he is a superior man. On the contrary, given a man enjoying all exterior advantages, if his intentions are perverse, he is a worthless individual. There is nothing more desirable than to be a superior man, and nothing more despicable than to be a worthless person.

Therefore, a man's exterior, be he of high or low stature, gaunt or stout, gifted with fine features or ugly as a toad, exerts utterly no influence upon his good or evil fortune. The Ancients never noticed such twaddle, and writers did not even mention it in their books.[1]

Hsun Tzu's view never carried the day; nor, it seems from current reports in the mainland Chinese press, does its latter-day successor, rationalistic Communism. Reports of physiognomy being practised are quite common in newspapers and in radio broadcasts.

The major texts of present-day physiognomy see themselves as stemming from the great Sung dynasty (c. 960–1279 CE) book *T'ai-ch'ing Shen Chien* (*The Mysterious Mirror of the T'ai-ch'ing Realm*, attributed to Wang P'o and reputed to have been written in the sixth century; however, it assumed its final form in the Sung dynasty) – copies of which in abbreviated form are regularly printed today – and the works of Yuan Chung-ch'e, the fourteenth-century physiognomist. The handbooks of the modern physiognomists are highly detailed, giving complete breakdowns of every conceivable variant of physical features such as eyebrows, moles, etc. However, physiognomy is not just concerned with the face. The whole body is studied (see in this connection Section 34); the face plays the major but not the only role. The weight, stance and shape of the body give the initial indications, while the face provides more detailed information. There is an old proverb that 'Your face reflects what is in your heart.'

The selection given below, and indeed the total selection given in the Almanac, is but the tip of the iceberg.

YOUR ANNUAL PERSONAL FORECAST CHART

If you want to know your annual good luck forecast, select whether male or female and, if male, then read the figures on the left-hand side of the face; if female, on the right-hand side.

Aged 10–11

On the middle ear. If the ear curls out or protrudes in any way, you will have very bad fortune.

Aged 12–14

If the earlobe is curled, then you will have a long life.

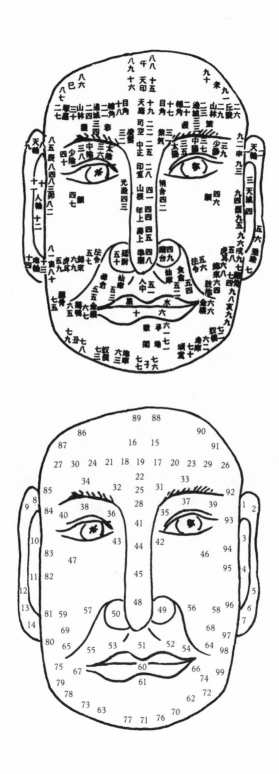

痣的相法

面痣圖解

出現在臉的部痣

1、2、3──跟雙親、上司及長輩皆無法和睦相處。

4──欠缺思考力、且生活無法安定。

5眉毛上方──因受親友連累而吃虧、財運不佳。

6眉毛內──主聰明，才藝超群、富貴且具有財運。

7眼皮上──主家庭不和、是屬於破財之相。

8鼻樑上──主經濟苦難、且須防色難。

9鼻頭上──主色難、且須防突發事故。

10人中──子孫運薄弱。

11鼻樑側面──病難之相。

12口角邊──會招來跟飲食有關的災厄

13眼下──為子女操心辛勞、或無緣。

14下唇下──會因飲食中毒而身亡。

15下巴──居住經常變動、生活不安定。

16唇上──須注意色難及飲食難。

17額骨上──恐怕會喪失社會上的名譽。

18額角──長期在國外旅行時須特別注意。

19眼尾──色難之相。

20兩眼之間──主短命、且可能犯罪。

21法令──主腳部疾患、且須防水厄。

22鬢角──旅行中會遭遇災難之相。

23耳內──賢而多貴，男女皆吉。

MOLE POSITION PHYSIOGNOMY CHART

[This chart is not particularly approved of by professionals.]

If the mole is in:

Position 1–3
He will not obey his parents, manager, elders and others in authority. He will never be in harmony with elders or those in authority.

Position 4
He will never use his brain and will be very difficult to live with.

Position 5
He will never be particularly successful because he is burdened by the bad behaviour or errors of his parents. This is also true as regards financial matters.

Position 6
This means he is clever and a skilled artist, which brings wealth and nobility. He is also lucky with money.

Position 7
This means he will never be happy because of arguments within the family and bad luck with money.

Position 8
He will have both financial and sexual troubles of a major kind.

Position 9
He will have sexual problems and should be careful because some major problem will arise suddenly.

Position 10
He will not have many sons or sons-in-law.

Position 11
He will always be unwell.

Position 12
Disaster and misfortune will overwhelm him through drinking and feasting.

Position 13

He will always be harassed by worries about his children. Furthermore, he will not be welcomed by the family.

Position 14

He will die from eating poisoned food.

Position 15

He will constantly be moving and his living standards will fluctuate greatly.

Position 16

He will have great problems caused by sex, drink and feasting.

Position 17

He will lose his good name.

Position 18

He should always take care when travelling overseas.

Position 19

He is a flighty gentleman!

Position 20

His will be a short life and much of that will be spent in prison.

Position 21

He will have trouble with his legs and must beware of drowning.

Position 22

He will encounter various disasters while travelling.

Position 23

He is both noble and learned. This is very good.

Section 41

SONG OF INTERPRETING PERSONALITIES

This section complements both Section 34 and 40. It is a series of mnemonics in rhyme, concerning certain physical features and physical mannerisms which give clues to someone's personality. Many of the rhymes are very cryptic and short but contain, for the most part, useful information. Below are a few examples.

Teeth evenly spaced and sized,
This person will have good food and will dress well.

Well-shaped, longish ears,
This indicates long life.

The heel doesn't touch the ground when walking,
This indicates a short life.

The corners of the mouth turn down,
This person will be friendless.

Eyes longer than eyebrows,
No brothers to help this person.

Eyebrows low, nearly touching the eyes, dozy appearance,
This man will always be afraid of his wife.

THE CALENDAR AND RELATED CHARTS

Sections 42 to 46

The last two fifths of the Almanac consists almost entirely of charts and details concerning the calendar and its use in relation to the seasons, the Western calendar and, most important of all, fortune-telling and divination. The only material not related to the calendar is the section on charms (Section 44; see pp. 88–93) and the final section, the Spring Festival Cow and the geomancer's compass for the coming year (see pp. 214–15).

The core is the calendar itself – the oldest and most significant part of the Almanac. It is because of the authority of the calendar, as we saw in the Introduction, that other material has come to be gathered around it, forming the current Almanac.

The calendar itself is distinctive, with its mixed black and red printing covering forty-eight pages. The red lettering denotes auspicious aspects such as fortunate 'hours', lucky days, benevolent stars and so on. The function and use of the calendar are explained below.

Coming before the calendar are a number of associated charts and sections. Some are very closely related to the calendar itself. For instance, Respected Master T'ung's chart (Section 42) is central to the interpretation of the descriptive term for the day. We explain the precise function of this chart below (see p. 187 onwards), but a brief general description here may help.

Section 42

RESPECTED MASTER T'UNG'S METHOD OF CALCULATING DAYS

The chart contains at the top a set of twelve descriptive terms. These twelve recur throughout each month of the year. They give a basic outline of the type of day it is going to be. The twelve descriptive terms are:

建寅日　往亡不利起造結婚姻納采主家長病招官司六十日一百二十日內損小口一年內見重喪百事不宜

除卯日　逢離死別　不宜起造婚姻犯之六十日內損家長招官司三五年內見凶冷退主兄弟不義各業分散惡人相

滿辰日　天羅富為天羅又云甲辰雖有氣却與戊辰同然集中宮百事皆忌犯之主起首殺人退財大凶餘辰日亦不吉

平巳日　小紅沙有朱雀勾絞到州星犯之主招官司損家長宅女娘婦三五年內重重不利破財大凶田蠶不收產死自縊被惡人尅削

定午日　黃沙有黃羅紫檀天皇地皇金銀庫樓田塘月財庫貯星蓋照宜起造安葬移徙開張出行婚姻六十日一百二十日內進橫財田產或因附寄成家大作大發小作小發主田蠶大收穫金銀庫滿

執未日　天賊有朱雀勾絞六十日一百二十日內損六畜傷驛馬成惡疾乙未煞集中宮惡忌起造入宅婚姻開張修整等事

破申日　有朱雀勾絞招官司口舌退牲財三五年內見寡婦醜事庚申正四廢更凶

危酉日　辛酉正四廢不宜用事惟丁酉有天德福星蓋照宜安葬還福應出行開張參官見貴吉只不宜起造及婚姻嫁娶等事乃比和之日也餘酉日均不可用

成戌日　天喜却是地網諸事不宜犯之主家長病人口不義冷退又云丙戌戊戌庚戌壬戌煞集中宮犯之主首殺人兄弟不義死別生離尤忌起造婚姻入宅婚

收亥日　有勾絞不宜用事犯之損家長害子孫六十日一百二十日內主南方白衣刑害男女多夭大凶惟地支與月建陰陽合德者次吉

開子日　甲子自死之金五行陰忌之日壬子木打寶瓶終是北方沐浴之地不宜起造婚姻入宅開張等事戊子丙子庚子三日惟水土生人用之大吉內有黃羅紫檀天皇地皇金銀寶藏財庫貯聯珠衆星蓋照六十日一百二十日內得大財貴人接引受職祿謀事大吉旺六畜益財產亦宜安葬

閉丑日　不利婚姻起造防虎蛇傷馬驛馬踢成惡疾貧病大凶

1. Build
2. Get rid of
3. Full
4. Flat
5. Steady
6. Carry on
7. Destroy
8. Danger
9. Success
10. Collect
11. Open
12. Close

Beneath these comes one of the Twelve Earthly Branches which occur two or three times each month. The chart is divided into the twelve months, of which the first is shown here (p. 179).

Below this comes the detailed prognostication for each day of that month which has these two characters (i.e. the descriptive term and the Earthly Branch). Examples are given below (pp. 190–94). While the details are intelligible to the general reader at one level, they require the interpretation and explanation of a professional fortune-teller to draw out their true meaning, especially in relation to the other details contained within the actual calendar. T'ung's chart marks the start of the main calendrical section of the Almanac.

Following the tables for each month comes a feng-shui chart containing details of auspicious directions related to the Heavenly and Earthly characters and their days. This section is also ascribed to Master T'ung.

Section 43

THE YIN AND YANG CALENDAR COMPARISON TABLE FOR THE PRESENT CENTURY (PAI CHUNG CHING)

This is the next most significant table in this series of charts. Yin and yang are symbolized by the sun and the moon, which harks back to one of the most ancient ways of expressing these concepts (see Introduction, pp. 32–5). This is a table of comparison between the Chinese lunar and the Western solar calendars. The following is a translation of the preface to the tables which cover twenty-eight pages in the Almanac, taking us almost up to the calendar itself.

PREFACE

The Pai Chung Ching is the fortune-teller's vital memory book. It contains, for those wishing to know how to calculate their birthday according to the lunar and solar calendars, a comparison of these calendars. For anyone in business who needs to work out both sets of dates, the Pai Chung Ching is essential. According to the stories of its history, it used to be based on the Peking longitude and latitude of east 116° 25'. It used the Peking longitude of 116° 25' as its basis. The Nanking observatory gives its east longitude as 120°. Everyone now follows the Nanking rules. After all, why use differing calculating points? So we now use the 120° as a standard point. Thus, since 1905, Yi Szu year at the New Year start, this has been used as the base. It can be used until the year 2000. The total of years covered is ninety-six, so for ordinary use it is fine.

The Pai Chung Ching is especially useful for fortune-tellers who need to work out quickly the eight characters of a person's year, month, day and 'hour' of birth but who do not have with them one of the books which lists every single day of every year over the last 100 years and for the next twenty to thirty years. Using the details in this set of tables, a competent fortune-teller will be able, with the minimum of difficulty, to work out your eight characters. It should be pointed out, however, that if you were born before 1904 you are out of luck. The chart starts then and goes up to, as the preface says, the year 2000. (Charts for 1985–92 are shown on pp. 182–3.)

乙丑年 一九八五

正月小 庚寅	二月大 己未	三月大 己丑	四月小 己未	五月大 戊子	六月大 戊午	七月小 丁亥	八月小 丁巳	九月大 丙戌	十月大 乙卯	十一月小 乙酉	十二月大 甲寅
子戌 十四子驚蟄 二二月	巳未 十四子春分 二二月	卯巳 初二子清明 三一月	酉亥 初一子穀雨 三一月	寅辰 初六寅立夏 五 月	申戌 初四午小滿 五 月	丑卯 廿一寅芒種 六 月	未酉 廿二午夏至 六 月	寅辰 初七子小暑 七 月	申戌 初八午大暑 七 月	卯巳 廿四子立秋 八 月	酉亥 初六寅處暑 八 月

丙寅年 一九八六

正月小 甲申	二月大 癸未	三月大 癸丑	四月小 癸未	五月大 壬子	六月大 壬午	七月小 壬子	八月大 辛亥	九月小 辛巳	十月大 庚戌	十一月小 庚辰	十二月小 己酉
辰午 十一酉雨水 二 月	亥丑 十六卯驚蟄 二 月	巳未 十七酉春分 三 月	亥丑 十二卯清明 三 月	辰午 十七酉穀雨 四 月	戌申 十二卯立夏 五 月	辰申 初九寅小滿 五 月	酉亥 初八午芒種 六 月	卯巳 廿三酉夏至 六 月	申戌 初一子小暑 七 月	寅卯 初六酉大暑 七 月	酉未 廿一亥立秋 八 月

丁卯年 一九八七

正月大 戊寅	二月小 戊申	三月大 丁丑	四月小 丁未	五月大 丙午	六月大 丙子	閏六月小 丙午	七月大 乙巳	八月大 乙亥	九月大 甲戌	十月大 甲辰	十一月小 癸酉	十二月小 癸酉
戌子 廿二申立春 二一月	辰午 廿二申雨水 二 月	酉亥 初二卯驚蟄 二 月	卯巳 初二酉春分 三 月	申戌 初七卯清明 三 月	寅辰 初九未穀雨 四 月	未酉 廿二辰立夏 五 月	丑卯 廿一酉小滿 五 月	未酉 廿二卯芒種 六 月	午申 十二子夏至 六 月	子寅 十七酉小暑 七 月	巳未 廿一亥大暑 七 月	亥丑 十四子立秋 八 月

戊辰年 一九八八

正月大 壬寅	二月小 壬申	三月大 辛丑	四月小 辛未	五月大 庚子	六月大 庚午	七月小 己亥	八月大 己巳	九月小 己亥	十月大 戊辰	十一月大 戊戌	十二月小 戊辰
戌子 初三申立春 二一月	辰午 初三申雨水 二 月	酉亥 初三酉驚蟄 二 月	卯巳 初五卯春分 三 月	申戌 初八酉清明 三 月	寅辰 初一子穀雨 四 月	未酉 初九午立夏 五 月	丑卯 十一子小滿 五 月	未酉 十五寅芒種 六 月	子寅 十二午夏至 六 月	申子 十三寅小暑 七 月	寅辰 十八寅大暑 七 月

己巳年 一九八九

月	大小	干支
正月	大	丁酉
二月	小	丁卯
三月	小	丙申
四月	大	乙丑
五月	小	乙未
六月	大	甲子
七月	小	甲午
八月	大	癸亥
九月	大	癸巳
十月	大	壬戌
十一月	大	壬辰
十二月	大	壬戌

庚午年 一九九〇

月	大小	干支
正月	小	壬辰
二月	大	辛酉
三月	小	辛卯
四月	小	庚申
五月	大	己丑
閏五月	小	己未
六月	小	戊子
七月	大	丁巳
八月	小	丁亥
九月	大	丙辰
十月	大	丙戌
十一月	大	丙辰
十二月	大	丙辰

辛未年 一九九一

月	大小	干支
正月	小	丙戌
二月	大	乙卯
三月	小	乙酉
四月	小	甲寅
五月	大	癸未
六月	小	癸丑
七月	小	壬午
八月	大	辛亥
九月	小	辛巳
十月	大	庚戌
十一月	大	庚辰
十二月	大	庚辰

壬申年 一九九二

月	大小	干支
正月	小	庚戌
二月	大	己卯
三月	大	己酉
四月	大	己卯
五月	大	戊申
六月	大	丁丑
七月	小	丁未
八月	大	丙申
九月	小	丙子
十月	小	乙巳
十一月	大	乙亥
十二月	大	甲戌

甲子日（冲庚午）

時	神煞
甲子	金匱、日建
乙丑	寶光、天乙、日合
丙寅	白虎、日馬
丁卯	玉堂、日刑
戊辰	天牢
己巳	元武
庚午	司命、日破、不遇
辛未	勾陳、天乙、日害
壬申	青龍、路空
癸酉	明堂、路空
甲戌	天刑、旬空
乙亥	朱雀、旬空

丙寅日（冲壬申）

時	神煞
戊子	青龍
己丑	明堂
庚寅	天刑、日建
辛卯	朱雀
壬辰	金匱、不遇、路空
癸巳	寶光、日害、日刑、路空
甲午	白虎
乙未	玉堂
丙申	天牢、日破、日刑、日馬
丁酉	元武、天乙
戊戌	司命、旬空
己亥	勾陳、天乙、日合、旬空

戊辰日（冲甲戌）

時	神煞
壬子	天牢、路空
癸丑	元武、天乙、路空
甲寅	司命、不遇、日馬
乙卯	勾陳、日害
丙辰	青龍、日建、日刑
丁巳	明堂
戊午	天刑
己未	朱雀、天乙
庚申	金匱
辛酉	寶光、日合
壬戌	白虎、日破、旬空
癸亥	玉堂、旬空

庚午日（冲甲子）

時	神煞
丙子	金匱、日破、不遇
丁丑	寶光、天乙、日害
戊寅	白虎
己卯	玉堂
庚辰	天牢
辛巳	元武
壬午	司命、日建、日刑、路空
癸未	勾陳、天乙、日合、路空
甲申	青龍、日馬
乙酉	明堂
丙戌	天刑、旬空
丁亥	朱雀、旬空

壬申日（冲丙寅）

時	神煞
庚子	青龍
辛丑	明堂
壬寅	天刑、日破、日刑、日馬、路空
癸卯	朱雀、天乙、路空
甲辰	金匱
乙巳	寶光、天乙、日合、日刑
丙午	白虎
丁未	玉堂
戊申	天牢、日建、不遇
己酉	元武
庚戌	司命、旬空
辛亥	勾陳、日害、旬空

甲戌日（冲庚辰）

時	神煞
甲子	天牢
乙丑	元武、天乙、日刑
丙寅	司命
丁卯	勾陳、日合
戊辰	青龍、日破
己巳	明堂
庚午	天刑、不遇
辛未	朱雀、天乙、日刑
壬申	金匱、日馬、路空、旬空
癸酉	寶光、日害、路空、旬空
甲戌	白虎、日建
乙亥	玉堂

丙子日（冲壬午）

時	神煞
戊子	金匱、日建
己丑	寶光、日合
庚寅	白虎、日馬
辛卯	玉堂、日刑
壬辰	天牢、不遇、路空
癸巳	元武、路空
甲午	司命、日破
乙未	勾陳、日害
丙申	青龍、旬空
丁酉	明堂、天乙、旬空
戊戌	天刑
己亥	朱雀、天乙

乙丑日（冲辛未）

時	神煞
丙子	天刑、天乙、日合
丁丑	朱雀、日建
戊寅	金匱
己卯	寶光
庚辰	白虎
辛巳	玉堂、不遇
壬午	天牢、日害、路空
癸未	元武、日破、日刑、路空
甲申	司命、天乙
乙酉	勾陳
丙戌	青龍、日刑、旬空
丁亥	明堂、日馬、旬空

丁卯日（冲癸酉）

時	神煞
庚子	司命、日刑
辛丑	勾陳
壬寅	青龍、路空
癸卯	明堂、日建、不遇、路空
甲辰	天刑、日害
乙巳	朱雀、日馬
丙午	金匱
丁未	寶光
戊申	白虎
己酉	玉堂、天乙、日破
庚戌	天牢、日合、旬空
辛亥	元武、天乙、旬空

己巳日（冲乙亥）

時	神煞
甲子	白虎、天乙
乙丑	玉堂、不遇
丙寅	天牢、日害、日刑
丁卯	元武
戊辰	司命
己巳	勾陳、日建
庚午	青龍
辛未	明堂
壬申	天刑、天乙、日合、日刑、路空
癸酉	朱雀、路空
甲戌	金匱、旬空
乙亥	寶光、日破、日馬、旬空

辛未日（冲丁丑）

時	神煞
戊子	天刑、日害
己丑	朱雀、日破、日刑
庚寅	金匱、天乙
辛卯	寶光
壬辰	白虎、路空
癸巳	玉堂、日馬、路空
甲午	天牢、天乙、日合
乙未	元武、日建
丙申	司命
丁酉	勾陳、不遇
戊戌	青龍、日刑、旬空
己亥	明堂、旬空

癸酉日（冲丁卯）

時	神煞
壬子	司命、路空
癸丑	勾陳、路空
甲寅	青龍
乙卯	明堂、日破、天乙
丙辰	天刑、日合
丁巳	朱雀、天乙
戊午	金匱
己未	寶光、不遇
庚申	白虎
辛酉	玉堂、日建、日刑
壬戌	天牢、日害、旬空
癸亥	元武、日馬、旬空

乙亥日（冲己巳）

時	神煞
丙子	白虎、天乙
丁丑	玉堂
戊寅	天牢、日合
己卯	元武
庚辰	司命
辛巳	勾陳、日破、日馬、不遇
壬午	青龍、路空
癸未	明堂、路空
甲申	天刑、天乙、日害、旬空
乙酉	朱雀、旬空
丙戌	金匱
丁亥	寶光、日建、日刑

丁丑日（冲癸未）

時	神煞
庚子	天刑、日合
辛丑	朱雀、日建
壬寅	金匱、路空
癸卯	寶光、不遇、路空
甲辰	白虎
乙巳	玉堂
丙午	天牢、日害
丁未	元武、日破、日刑
戊申	司命、旬空
己酉	勾陳、天乙、旬空
庚戌	青龍、日刑
辛亥	明堂、天乙、日馬

Section 45

THE SIXTY-DAY CYCLE OF HEAVENLY STEMS AND EARTHLY BRANCHES WITH THE GOOD-LUCK AND BAD-LUCK STARS

After the charms (Section 44, see p. 88) comes the last table before the calendar proper (see opposite). This lists the sixty-day cycle of the Heavenly and Earthly characters with their good and evil stars, and the 'hours' of each day in the cycle with their auspicious and inauspicious signs. As with the sixty-year cycle (see Introduction, pp. 31–2), the cycle starts with Chia Tzu (reading from top right down).

This brings us to the calendar itself and, with the tables outlined above, it is now capable of use and interpretation.

Section 46

THE CALENDAR

To try to give a flavour of both the calendar and its use we have taken a few examples which highlight the calendar – which is described below – and its meaning in some of the most common cases in which it is called upon to shape and influence the lives of its users.

The following are specific examples of how to use the last quarter of the book to predict or discover suitable days for special events. The major section, the calendar itself, gives details for every single day in the Chinese year. Each day has eight main subdivisions or blocks within it. Reading from the top (p. 186) they are as follows:

(a) The Western calendar date, including which day of the week it is.

(b) The beneficial stars which are on duty that day. These usually number between two and four stars, although New Year's Day has six (see p. 196).

(c) Details of the 'hours' of the day according to the Chinese system of two-hour blocks. The calendar gives details as

廿三 星期六　｜　廿四 星期日　｜　廿五 星期一　｜　廿六 星期二　｜　芒種 星期三　｜　廿八 星期四　｜　三月一日 星期五　｜　二日 星期六　｜　三日 星期日

廿三　星期六
相日　寶光
申酉中戌亥（吉凶）辰丑寅卯未（子）
忌　詞訟　遠行
初四　癸巳　水　柳　平
宜　平治道塗　修飾垣牆
五虛　天麟神　重日　月害
丫　占房床

廿四　星期日
歲支　時德　天德貴
忌　出財　開倉
寅時福星貴人吉
初五　甲午　金　星　定
宜　平治道塗　修飾垣牆
暗金　歲破　小耗　伏斷　山
白　占碓磨

廿五　星期一
歲德合　月德
忌　除服
初六　乙未　金　張　執
宜　拆卸　掃舍
暗金　月破　小耗　長星　水痕
白　占爐灶（鬼）

廿六　星期二
天德　除神
忌　栽種　蒔插
初七　丙申　火　翼　破
宜　求醫治病　破屋壞垣
月破　暗金　小耗　長星　水痕
白　占廚灶

芒種　星期三
三歲支　天德合　福生
午時日祿　癸卯生人
忌　作灶　安牀
初八　丁酉　火　軫　危
宜　祭祀　祈福　入學　出行　嫁娶　裁衣　納采　移徙　安葬
陽將　五離　天死　致死　元武
人　占門庫

廿八　星期四
天喜　天醫
忌　整甲　田獵
初九　戊戌　木　角　成
宜　開市　補垣塞穴
賞木蘭動　陽　犬日　地火　口　致死　元武
人　占房栖床

三月一日　星期五
歲德合　天馬
忌　買業　置田　取魚
初十　己亥　木　亢　收
宜　祭祀　捕捉　醞釀　栽衣　安牀　開市　交易　嫁娶　牧養
地囊　斑煞　復日　重喪　債不入州
占床門

二日　星期六
歲德　母倉　六合
忌　結網　動土
十一　庚子　土　氐　開
宜　祭祀　入學　出行　嫁娶　栽衣　安牀　開市　交易　會友　牧養
白　占碓磨　復喪　重日
占門碓

三日　星期日
月德合　合日
忌　合醬　造酒
十二　辛丑　土　房　閉
宜　祭祀　結網　搭厠　斷蟻
歸忌　水痕　土符　火星
白　占厠灶

to which 'hour' is fortunate, which average and which inauspicious.

(d)   Activities which should not be undertaken on this day. The title in Chinese means 'Avoid'.

(e)   The Chinese date. This includes the day of the month, the Heavenly Stem and the Earthly Branch, the element, the title of the particular constellation for the day and the descriptive term for the day. Certain special or auspicious days have text running down both sides of this block with details of the most auspicious 'hour' and a warning that this day is inauspicious for people born under certain Heavenly/Earthly signs.

(f)   Activities which can be carried out on this day. The Chinese word means 'Right' or 'Suitable'.

(g)   In nearly all cases there is a seventh division giving details of evil or inauspicious stars. On certain very auspicious days the emphasis on the evil stars is lessened.

(h)   The final category consists of two parts. The first is a title which gives a characteristic to the day constructed from (usually) two characters which must be seen as parallel but not linked. Below this are brief details of building activities which should not be undertaken.

To understand the days, it is necessary to know the two horoscope characters for the day you were born on. These are then used in conjunction with 'Respected Master T'ung's Method of Calculating Days' (Section 42) and the fifth block of the calendar (e). The Earthly Branch and the descriptive term are taken together. On good days the descriptive term is printed in red; on not so good days, in black. It is then necessary to turn to Respected Master T'ung's chart and look up the month you are dealing with. Then find the descriptive term combined with the Earthly Branch and below this will be a detailed analysis of your fortune for the day. This, combined with the information provided in the calendar, gives the answer.

Finally, the calendar sometimes carries an inset at the top of the sixth block (f). This will be either information about one of the Twenty-Four Joints and Breaths of the year (see pp. 64–6), details of a major festival such as Ch'ing Ming (p. 188, in the second column from the right), or details of an eclipse of the sun or moon. In all three cases, the calendar gives appropriate instructions about the time when such events start – or simply states in the case of an eclipse, 'Cannot be seen from Hong Kong.'

◁ *First month, days 4–12 (23 February–3 March)*

十一日	十日	九日	八日	七日	六日	五日	四日
星期四	星期三	星期二	星期一	星期日	星期六	星期五	星期四
歲恩 月恩	歲德 麒麟	陽德 生祿	天德 時陽	不將 四相	天喜 德合 天月	天將 天將 不合	合日 歲德 天馬	三合 歲支

忌 行喪 結網 ｜ 忌 除服 穿井 ｜ 忌 祈福 祭祀 置業 買田 ｜ 忌 合帳 裁衣 整甲 理髮 ｜ 忌 取魚 問卜 作灶 修廚 ｜ 忌 嫁娶 栽種 ｜ 忌 出財 開倉 ｜ 忌 作灶 詞訟

廿二 庚辰金 奎 建 ｜ 廿一 己卯土 壁 閉 ｜ 二十 戊寅土 室 開 ｜ 卯時天官貴人吉 十九 丁丑水 危 收 ｜ 酉時天乙貴人吉 十八 丙子水 虛 成 ｜ 酉時天乙貴人吉 十七 乙亥火 女 危 ｜ 十六 甲戌火 牛 破 ｜ 十五 癸酉金 斗 破

宜 祭祀 會友 穿井 ｜ 宜 入倉 嫁娶 開市 安牀 補塞 伐木 ｜ 宜 作灶 修造 動土 上樑 開市 移徙 納畜 ｜ 宜 入學 會友 出行 訂婚 產室 栽種 牧養 安葬 ｜ 宜 上樑 修倉 安葬 會友 出行 嫁娶 納采 醫病 動土 ｜ 宜 祭祀 祈福 入學 會友 遊禍 重日 水痕 天賊 ｜ 宜 安牀 結網 沐浴 納畜 ｜ 宜 求醫 治病 破屋 壞垣 大耗地火 火星災煞

忌 壬申甲申生人 ｜ 忌 辛未己未生人 ｜ 忌 庚午戊午生人

土府 三喪 無祿 月刑 重喪 山 ｜ 黑花蒼鷺 無祿 月刑 重喪 ｜ 口虎 陰 復日 血忌 ｜ 虛 復日 元武 短星 寡宿 ｜ 五 債不 債不 暗金 伏斷 ｜ 斑煞 歸忌 天瘟 重日 水痕 ｜ 清明 寅正四時十四分 宜屋破 桐始華 月破 四擊 天瘟 ｜ 宜屋破 壞垣 大耗地火 火星災煞

人鬼 碓磨栖 ｜ 人占 大門 ｜ 白 爐床 ｜ 火 房床 ｜ 白 廁庫倉 ｜ 神 倉庫 ｜ 地 碓灶廚 ｜ 白 灶廚 ｜ 丁林門栖碓 ｜ 丁天門栖碓 ｜ 丁州房門床

At the start of each month there is a special block of information (see p. 192, starting at top right):

1. The Western calendar month(s).
2. The list of festivals of sages and deities for the month (mostly Buddhist and not including most major festivals; see pp. 194–9).
3. The Chinese month number and whether it is a big month (thirty days) or a small month (twenty-nine days).
4. Details of the basic geophysical phenomena for the month – e.g. earthquakes, floods, etc. – plus details of the colour of the month and its influence.
5. The final block covers the names of the good or fortune stars of the month, side by side with the bad or evil stars.

The following are examples of how the calendar and Respected Master T'ung's chart are used to provide answers. The details are based upon the calendar for the year of the Ox in the Heavenly Stem Yi Earthly Branch Ch'ou – 1985–86.

Example 1

I wish to get married in the 8th month on the 15th day. Is this a good day? My birth sign for the day is Chia Ch'en.

Turning first to the 15th day of the 8th month, the following is discovered:

(a) It is Sunday, 29 September, in the Western calendar.
(b) There are two lucky stars on duty.
(c) Of the twelve 'hours', four are fortunate, four average and four evil. This is not a good combination.
(d) It is a bad day for making soy sauce and for tilling the soil.
(e) The date is the 15th. It is under the element of Earth and the descriptive term is 'Open'. The Earthly Stem is Wei.
(f) It is Mid-Autumn Festival day (see p. 198). It is good for clearing graves and respecting ancestors. Nothing else. It is under the sign of 'Destroyer Day'. This means that nothing should be started on this day for it will fail.
(g) There are four evil stars listed – another bad sign.
(h) The characteristic of the day is Human and you should not build or renovate the threshing machine or toilet.

This is such an inauspicious day that the fortune-teller will not bother to check Respected Master T'ung's chart. The mere presence of the characters for 'Destroyer Day' puts an end to any plans for that day.

The fortune-teller will now search for an auspicious-looking day nearby. The 12th of the 8th month seems promising. The

◁ *Second month, days 15–22 (4–11 April), showing Ch'ing Ming* first task is to check the main features of the 12th but not in great detail. At this stage, the fortune-teller will look to see if, under the auspicious or proper activities for the day, the sign for weddings appears. It does, and in fact heads the list. There are three good-fortune stars on duty, and although the 'hours' are four fortunate, four average and four evil, the descriptive character is in red. So the day is not inauspicious, although it is only average. The Heavenly Stem is Wu and the Earthly Branch Ch'en.

Taking the descriptive character for 'Danger' and the Earthly sign Ch'en, he turns to Respected Master T'ung's chart. Looking under month 8 for the character representing 'Danger' and the Earthly Branch Ch'en, it is found that:

Ping Ch'en is a day good for digging, building, opening a new business, travelling, starting a new job, working and getting married. But Hsin Ch'en and Keng Ch'en and Chia Ch'en are extremely inauspicious.

There is nothing specific about Wu Ch'en. Therefore another day must be chosen. This time the 9th day of the 8th month; this is the day when autumn starts.

(a) It is Monday, 23 September.
(b) There are four lucky stars on duty.
(c) Of the twelve 'hours' of the day, five are fortunate, four are average and only three are inauspicious.
(d) It is not a good day for planning, planting seedlings, visiting a tailor or honouring the dead.
(e) The Chinese date has a border of red characters. These tell that

3–5 p.m. is the most auspicious 'hour' when good fortune abounds and a nobleman will come. But for those born on Chi Wei or Kuei Wei it is not a good day.

The descriptive character (printed in red because it is an auspicious day) is 'Steady'. The Earthly Branch is Ch'ou and the Heavenly Stem Yi.

From Respected Master Tung's chart we find the following for this month:

Hsin Ch'ou, Kuei Ch'ou, Yi Ch'ou or Ting Ch'ou have only average fortune. Chi Ch'ou is very inauspicious. Yi Ch'ou and Szu Ch'ou are days for marriage or engagement.

Thus, although certain Ch'ou-sign days are inauspicious, others are perfectly satisfactory. Turning back with confidence to the 9th day of the 8th month, we find the remaining details are as follows:

(f)   It is the Beginning of Autumn – one of the Twenty-Four Joints and Breaths of the year (see pp. 64–6). Autumn starts in the Szu 'hour' (9–11 a.m.) at 10.08 a.m.
      It is a good day to go on a journey, hold a meeting, get married, stock up, dig the earth, raise a beam (this refers to the main support beam of a new house upon which the wellbeing of the house, physically and spirit - ually, depends), open a new business and bury the dead. There is an inset which says there will be no more thunder now.
(g)   The names of the four inauspicious stars.
(h)   The signs are Forest/Human. It is best not to work on the threshing machine, grinding stone or toilet.

Thus this is a good day for the inquirer to marry on between 3 and 5 p.m.

Example 2

I wish to open a new shop on the 2nd day of the 3rd month. My day sign is Ting Yin.

The calendar details for the 2nd day of the 3rd month are as follows:

(a)   It is Sunday, 21 April.
(b)   There are four auspicious stars on duty.
(c)   Five of the 'hours' are good, three average and four evil.
(d)   It is best to avoid making fishing nets, constructing a kang (stove-cum-bed), honouring the ancestors and praying to the gods.
(e)   The best 'hour' is from 11 a.m. to 1 p.m. when Heaven's favour shines and a nobleman comes. It is not a good day for people whose day sign is Chia Shen or Hsin Shen. The Heavenly Stem is Keng. The Earthly Branch is Yin. It comes under the element Wood. The descriptive charac- ter (in red – auspicious) means 'Open'.
(f)   It is a proper day for study, travel, meeting a friend, getting engaged, buying livestock, moving, visiting the doctor, making repairs and building, tilling the soil, raising a beam, opening a business, signing a contract, buying property, preparing a bed (this usually means a new bed. It was prepared or 'opened' by inviting a couple with many children to come and sleep in it. This should assist the new couple whose bed it was to have children), opening a gutter, visiting the tailor.

陽曆

十六	十五	十四	十三	十二	十一月二	十二月廿	十一月廿	
星期六	星期五	星期四	星期三	星期二				

| 月合日 | 德月十靈日 | 歲支德日 | 天驛后馬 | 司解命德神 | 歲合德日 | | | |

初一東岳旦初二周
將軍旦初三二茅眞
君旦初五達摩旦
公旦菩諸司旦初十
花花婆婆旦十五初
六天曹神劉使者旦
元旦虛神劉使者下
温娘旦十六虛天
娘娘旦二十巫山
師旦廿七五岳旦
微旦三十周將軍旦

| 忌 | 忌 | 忌 | 忌 | 忌 | 辟卦行坤 | 丁亥尾宿 | 曆十月大建 | 律中應鐘 | 農 |
| 作詞訟竈 | 搭置買廁產田 | 遠行理髮 | 修動作竈土廚 | 栽穿種井 | | | | | 上生嫠賓 |

| 初五己未火女成 | 初四戊午火牛危 | 初三丁巳土斗破 | 初二丙辰土箕執 | 初一乙卯水尾定 | | | | |

| | | | | | 綠碧 | 紫黃 | 黑赤 | 奇奇丁中 | 三奇丙乾 | 立冬兌 |

| 宜 | 宜 | 宜 | 宜 | 見金匱香港地區不見 地始凍 | 星凶 | 神 | 吉 | |

| 拆卸掃舍 | 拆卸修造動土上樑安葬 | 求醫治病破屋壞垣 | 整甲伐木捕提田獵 | 訂婚嫁娶裁衣合帳 | 小建離五黃中六甲床房馬胎 | 大建中月破戌兌煞九良申羊胎溝 | 地官坤月煞戌離寺門牛胎廁 | 天官中頭火乾八座申豬胎壁 | 月恩乙帝尊巽陰貴乾金匱戌修方宜 | 月德甲天道東眞馬巽玉堂丑丁坤乾山 | 天德乙月空庚眞祿震天喜未造塟利 |

| 歲破月忌 丁火星 | 儿上四陰致死祥不 丁 | 月破重日 白州 | 土陰天賊將復喪 白水 | 月破四廢 白人 | 井帥不利 星光門扇神 | 渠灶廁門 占胎神 | 修方宜 十 | 日寅時宮 | 月十一 | 太陽本 |

| 丁占廁門 | 房床確 | 倉庫 | 白廚栖竈 | 水痕確門 | 占竈處 | 逐日 | 入寅宮 | |

(g) Caution. There are two bad stars; do not show off or kill any fowl.

(h) Fire/White. It is best to avoid working on the threshing machine, grinding stone and stove.

Turning to Respected Master T'ung's chart, the following can be seen from the entry under month 3, character 'Open', Earthly Branch Yin:

Hsin Yin is a fortunate day. Jen Yin has two lucky stars blessing it. Any other sign with Yin is only a second-best day.

Thus, although this day is not particularly inauspicious, neither is it particularly auspicious. The inquirer might look for a better day using the methods outlined above, or he might check the suitability by another method (see, for example, Section 29).

Example 3

Our son was born on the 29th day of the 8th month. Thirty days after birth there is the full-month feast to celebrate his birth and survival and to name him. We wish to know what that day will be like. Because both the 8th and 9th months are small months (only twenty-nine days), the full-month feast will fall on the 1st day of the 10th month. The sign for his birthday is Yi Yu.

The reading of the calendar for the 1st day of the 10th month is as follows:

(a) It is Tuesday, 12 November.

(b) There are two lucky stars on duty.

(c) Five of the 'hours' are good, four average and three bad.

(d) It is not a good day for planning or making a well.

(e) The Heavenly Stem is Yi. The Earthly Branch is Mao. It comes under the element Water and its descriptive character is 'Steady'.

(f) There is an eclipse of the sun today, but no times are given, simply the information that it cannot be seen from Hong Kong.

In an inset there is the information that the earth is now starting to turn cold – winter is setting in.

(g) There are two inauspicious stars.

(h) Human/White. Avoid working on the ground, the threshing machine and the door.

Tenth month, days 1–5 (12–16 November)

193

Turning to Respected Master T'ung's chart, the following is recorded under the 10th month for character 'Steady', Earthly Branch Mao:

Yi Mao has the star Heavenly Virtue. Hsin Mao and Chi Mao are good for digging, building foundations, raising a beam, marriage, for family, for travel, for opening a business and so on. There is a good star shining.

Thus this is a good day.

FESTIVALS IN THE CALENDAR

The calendar section of the Almanac carries details of all the major and minor festivals of the Chinese year. The calendar deals with them in two separate ways. At the start of each month it lists all the Buddhist and Taoist deities or festivals for that month. Some of these are very obscure and rarely observed. Others, such as the birthday of Kuan Yin or of Kuan Ti, are occasions of major festivals in certain areas or for certain groups. Similarly, English diaries often carry details of religious events which have true significance for only a few, e.g. Ember Days or Ascension Day. A full list with explanatory details of these minor festivals will be found below.

The major festivals are not, with a couple of exceptions, mentioned in the block of dates at the start of each month. They are featured with the vivid use of red printing and enlarged space on the actual day they occur. The amount of extra detail such a day has to carry often means that that day's column grows to double or even treble the ordinary size. In most cases the calendar assumes that the reason for the festival is known, as well as the appropriate activities. It contents itself with giving details of when and how these activities should take place. Hence, in the subsection below, we have provided basic background details to the festivals.

As we saw in the introduction to the calendar, the majority of festivals, major and minor, are tied into the lunar calendar, thus changing each year. Only two, Ch'ing Ming and the Winter Festival, are tied to the solar year, thus occuring on the same Western date each year.

MAJOR FESTIVALS

Month 1 Day 1 – New Year

The preparations for New Year start two weeks beforehand when the Kitchen God and the God of Wealth are sent up to Heaven to report on the family (see Minor Festivals, Twelfth

Moon, Day 24). On New Year's Eve the family will gather together to eat and to paste up the new good-luck charms and Door Gods ready for the New Year. The children of the family are given small red packets with money inside. This 'lucky money' is also given to children of friends over the fifteen days of the New Year celebration.

New Year's Day is a time for special food and for *not* doing or using certain things. For instance, no one sweeps the house on this day in case they brush away the good fortune. Nor are knives or scissors, or indeed anything sharp, used in case the good luck is cut. In most families, the food on New Year's Day itself is vegetarian out of respect for the animal world, from one of whose number the name of the year comes. The food is carefully chosen using Chinese puns in order to have names which mean good luck, fortune, plenty of money, etc. An example of this is the sticky rice ball with sesame seeds, the name of which in Cantonese puns with 'gold'.

At the turn of the year the new Kitchen and Wealth Gods are instated in their shrines and, in traditional families, incense is offered to Heaven, Earth and the ancestors. Firecrackers are then exploded to scare away the old and the demonic and the doors are thrown open. In many places, not least in the West, the next few days will see Lion, Unicorn and Dragon dances through the streets. Those wishing to be sure of good fortune in their business will hang out a lettuce and red packets of money for the Lion or the Unicorn to 'eat'. The Lion is teased through the streets by a comic figure who is in fact supposed to be Mi Lo Fo, the Future Buddha. When he comes to reign all will be well (he is usually shown with a large belly) and life will be extended. Those families who can afford to buy special potted bushes. If these bloom on New Year's Day, especially good fortune will be theirs.

Traditionally New Year went on for fifteen days until the Feast of the Night of the First Full Moon or Lantern Festival as it is sometimes called. Nowadays three to seven days is the norm, although visiting – a vital part of New Year – continues throughout. The 7th day is called Yan Yat – Everyone's Birthday. On this day everyone is one year older.

Month 1 Day 15 – Feast of the Night of the First Full Moon or Lantern Festival

This marks the end of New Year. Lanterns are strung out (this occurs more in north China than in the south). This is a day for the ancestors when offerings are made and official notification is given to the ancestors of any new sons born during the previous year.

陽曆 二月 三月

廿二 星期五	廿一 星期四	二十 星期三 二月十八 一九五〇年			列聖神誕日期

列聖神誕日期

初一 天臘之辰 初二 車公 地靖上元 三 皇 初八 毅王旦 旦伯旦許 溫 初十 土神旦 廿六 庇佑財神旦 二十招財童子 上元天官旦 招財童子 元許真君旦 十九門官旦 十五 皇旦 初三 孫臏真人 初四 諸葛姑娘 初十 玉旦

農曆 正月小建

律中太簇 下生南呂 辟卦行泰 戊寅星宿

緣碧白 紫黄白 黑赤白 奇三春立 奇丁奇丙奇乙 離艮兌

星凶神吉

小大地天 建建官官 離中具具 五月月月 黄破火頭 中申震煞 六兇八丑 甲煞座九 床離東良 房北北亥 馬羊牛猪 胎胎胎胎 門樋堂身

月恩丙 月合辛 帝尊貴乾 陰貴乾 金匱辰

月德丙 天赦中 陽貴坤 玉堂未 修方宜 戊乾山 辛山 逐日胎神

天德丁 月空壬 天道南 天醫戌 眞馬中 坤庚酉辛 三十日丑 時入亥宮

天喜戊 造葬利 太陽甲子 天祿乾 眞祿乾 艮丙午丁年 十二月 光門扇神 占處

忌
進水新船

忌
開池穿井 造酒

宜
祭祀祈福求嗣會友出行納采嫁娶移徙修造動土安葬

不宜 子戌時出行五鬼正西鶴神正北勿向

初三壬辰水鬼滿 宜 開市動土上樑安葬 三喪 水痕 丁地倉庫栖

初二辛卯木井除 宜 上樑栽種納畜安葬 不債 大敗大時朱雀咸池白門灶廚

初一庚寅木參建 立春節 寅時天乙貴人吉 民間紀夏時 世界行陽曆

貫神東北財神正東炷香用丑時 天乙貴人上吉寅卯時亦吉出行宜用丑時 丑寅卯辰巳時向東北方迎吉貴神正 子戌時五不遇過午未時破未時歲破正

On either side of the date details for New Year are red letters which read (on the right-hand side): 'The world uses the solar Western calendar' and (on the left-hand side): 'The Chinese citizen and farmers use the traditional timing.'

The correct title for New Year is Spring Festival. Details below this are:

The noble star is on the northeast side. The God of Wealth is in the centre of the east. If you wish to worship, burn joss sticks at the 'hour' of Ch'ou [1–3 a.m.]. If you make offerings at this time then a special Tien Yi [lucky star] nobleman will bring good fortune to you. If you offer during the time of Yin [3–5 a.m.] or Mao [5–7 a.m.], then this will also bring you good luck. If you want to travel, then go during Ch'ou [1–3 a.m.], Yin [3–5 a.m.], Mao [5–7 a.m.], Ch'en [7–9 a.m.] or Szu [9–11 a.m.] period and face towards the northeast. There a noble star will shine on you. If you go to the east you will approach the God of Wealth and have very great fortune. Shen [3–5 p.m.] is a 'broken day' [bad luck] and Wei [1–3 p.m.] is a 'broken age' [bad luck]. During Tzu [11–1 a.m.] and Hsu [7–9 p.m.] times, the five auspicious aspects cannot meet and evil will abound. During Wu [11–1 p.m.] and Wei [1–3 p.m.] the road is cut off [bad luck] and all is empty and lost. This is not a good time to travel. There are five ghosts in the west and the bad star in the centre of the north. Do not turn to face them.

Month 2 Day 16 (in 1985) – Ch'ing Ming

Ch'ing Ming means 'Clear and bright' and is in fact one of the Twenty-Four Joints and Breaths of the year. It heralds the changing weather which comes just after the start of spring. This is the major festival of the dead when families go out, sometimes for three consecutive days, to honour the dead. This is done by clearing weeds from the graves, cleaning up the tombs themselves and making offerings. These are of two main kinds. First, the offering of paper goods such as model clothes, cars, etc., as well as Bank of Hell notes; these are burned and it is believed they then go to the credit of the dead on the other side. Secondly, food is offered. Traditional amongst this is a whole roasted pig and various cakes.

As this is one of the Joints and Breaths, the only detail given for this day other than the special name is the exact time of the start of Ch'ing Ming.

Ch'ing Ming. Starts in Yin period [3–5 a.m.] at 4.14 a.m.

◁ *First month, days 1–3 (20–22 February), showing New Year*

Month 5 Day 5 – Dragon Boat Festival

The 5th day of the 5th month is a very dangerous day. This is the Dragon month, when disease is most rampant and threatening. Hence the Dragon Boat Festival to help dispel and ward off evil, as well as marking the start of summer.

The story behind the Dragon Boat is that there was once a corrupt and greedy Emperor who taxed his people until they could hardly survive. One honest official, Ch'u Yuen, protested to the Emperor, but his protest was mocked and scorned. In a last desperate attempt to draw the Emperor's attention to the suffering he was causing, Ch'u Yuen threw himself into a lake and drowned. Local fishermen rushed in boats to save him, but without avail. To ward off the dragons and evil spirits they threw dumplings of rice into the water while they pulled Ch'u Yuen's body out.

Each year Dragon Boat races take place to commemorate this event and dumplings of sticky rice tied in bamboo leaves are eaten. Other than the festival title, the calendar gives no more details apart from surrounding the date with borders inscribed:

Szu 'hour' [9–11 a.m.] is when the Heaven-sent nobleman will bring good fortune. It is not a good day for people born under Ping Hsu or Chia Hsu.

Month 7 Day 7 – The Seventh Evening

See Minor Festivals for the same day (p. 208).

Month 8 Day 15 – Mid-Autumn Festival

A day of offerings to the Moon Goddess, as detailed in the calendar itself. The moon is at its brightest on this day and in south China this is the night for lanterns. Vastly diverse in shape and colour, they are paraded in honour of the moon and its goddess, about whom many stories abound. People also try to see the rabbit on the moon pounding the elixir of eternity. The rabbit was immortalized in the moon by the Buddha, according to legend. One day the Buddha visited a forest. All the animals and birds brought him food they had collected. But the poor rabbit had nothing to bring, so he gave himself. Rushing into the clearing, he threw himself upon the fire. Buddha pulled him out, but was too late to save him. So he was immortalized and given the moon as his home. The lanterns are often rabbit-shaped.

Month 9 Day 9 – Chung Yang or Climbing the Heights

This is another day, to set alongside Ch'ing Ming, for visiting the graves of the ancestors. As this usually involves going to hills or mountains, the requirement of 'Climbing the Heights' is fulfilled. Picnics are held on high points in memory of a scholar who was warned by a fortune-teller that on this particular day, the 9th of the 9th, a terrible disaster would befall his town. He quickly told everyone to flee to the hills with their families and animals. Many scorned him and few climbed up the hills. But when they returned that night all who had stayed behind were dead from an unknown disease. Two requirements for the picnic are chrysanthemum wine, which the scholar took with him, and a special cake. The name of this cake is punned to give a double meaning, one of which is 'top'. Those who eat it on top of the heights hope for advancement at work.

The calendar carries red border inscriptions around the date:

The Yin 'hour' [3–5 p.m.] is when the spirit star blessed nobleman comes bringing good fortune. It is not a good day for those born under Wu Tzu or Jen Tzu.

This is one of the few festivals which is also mentioned in the block of festivals at the start of the month.

Month 11 Day 11 – Winter Festival

This is a major event standing alongside New Year in importance. It always comes on the winter solstice and thus, like Ch'ing Ming, it is one of the Twenty-Four Joints and Breaths of the year and never alters so far as the Western calendar is concerned. The festival is one vast feast at which the entire family gathers. It is a time to honour and respect the living ancestors as well as to enjoy good food. It is purely a domestic festival but is no less important for that. For Western readers, its significance as a family event and meal can be compared to Thanksgiving Day dinner or Christmas dinner.

Month 12 Day 26 – Li Ch'un

Li Ch'un is the start of spring and is also a solar festival, being the very first of the Twenty-Four Joints and Breaths of the year (see pp. 64–6). This is the official start of the year so far as astrology is concerned. It also marks the start of the farmer's year (see Section 1).

MINOR FESTIVALS

In the following section, the details in square brackets are not part of the translation but information provided for the reader. The list of festivals occurs as blocks of text at the start of each month. They do not include many of the best-known festivals. These are given on the specific day(s) upon which they fall (see 'Major Festivals' above). (Buddhists fast every 1st and 15th day of each month.)

SOME HOLY AND GODLY FESTIVALS AND BIRTHDAYS

First Moon

Day 1   Offerings made to Heaven. *[On the first day of the New Year the family makes offerings to all deities and ancestors, who are collectively titled 'Heaven'.]*

Day 2   Birthday of Ch'e Kung. *[A former general who was made an Immortal and is seen as a bringer of good luck, particularly wealth. A wheel is spun before him on this day to give a good spin to the New Year.]*

Day 3   Birthday of Sun. *[Worship is offered to a Taoist deity called Sun and offerings are also made to the sun itself.]*

Day 4   The day for prayers to Chu T'ung, guardian of women.

Day 8   Birthday of the Cereal King *[who grants long life]*.

Day 9   Birthday of the Jade Emperor. *[The Jade Emperor is seen as the supreme god in Heaven. At times a rather vague figure, he is often called upon to decide matters, both on earth and in Heaven. The authority of the emperors came from the Jade Emperor.]*

Day 10   Earth God Festival. *[The Earth God represents Heaven's power and authority on earth. Small shrines can be found in homes, streets and at significant landmarks.]*

Day 13   Birthday of Wen Hsu *[God of Wealth and Fortune]*.

Day 15   Celebration of the Lantern Festival of Superior Principles. *[New Year officially ends with the Lantern Festival. It is known as Superior Principles or Three-Principles Day for it commemorates the Three August Ones who taught humans the first principles of civilization; see Introduction, p. 15.]*

Day 16   Festival of Sui Ching *[a deity who assists farmers]*.

Day 19   Celebration of the Door Gods and the Earth God.
門   *[This ensures protection and success in the coming
宮   year. The Door Gods are colourful posters depicting
土   fierce-looking soldier deities. Legend traces them back
地   to Emperor T'ai Tsung (c. 650 CE). When the
旦   Emperor was unable to sleep at night because of
         ghosts, two loyal soldiers volunteered to guard his
         door. This scared off the demons – until they found a
         third door. So another loyal soldier took up duty
         there. However, the Emperor was concerned for the
         soldiers and ordered paintings of them to be made.
         These replaced the real soldiers and were just as
         effective. The custom of Door Gods spread throughout
         the country.]*

Day 20   Birthday of Shen Tai. *[Shen Tai is the devoted
         follower of Kuan Yin, the goddess of mercy. He is
         worshipped as a dispenser of money.]*

Day 26   Festival of Pi Yu *[god of money]*.

Second Moon

Day 1   Festival of the Sun. *[This is the day the sun visits
         the palace of the Jade Emperor to discuss the coming
         year.]*
         Birthday of the Star God Ch'u-tien.

Day 2   Birthday of the local Earth God. *[In every village
         and house there is a small, ground-level shrine to the
         Earth God.]*
         Birthday of Mencius. *[The Confucian philosopher
         who is most revered after K'ung Fu-tzu himself.
         Mencius lived from 371 to 289 BCE.]*

Day 3   Birthday of the god of literature – Wen-ch'ang.
         *[Highly valued in Confucian and Buddhist thought
         because of the great importance attached to literature
         and literacy, Wen-ch'ang was a historical figure who
         lived either during the Chin (265–317 CE), T'ang
         (618–906 CE) or Sung (960–1126 CE) dynasties. In
         all stories he is a man of outstanding intellectual
         achievements. He was made a god in 1314 CE.]*

Day 6   Birthday of the god of the Eastern Mountain.

Day 8   Birthday of the Ruler of the Third Court of Hell.
         *[This, one of the Ten Hells, is presided over by
         Sung-ti Wang – King Sung-ti. This is the Hell for
         disobedient and unfilial sons, ministers and others.]*

Day 10   Birthday of Earth Spirits. *[Linked and sometimes
         identified with the Earth God, they are more often
         associated with agriculture.]*

Day 13　Birthday of Hung Sheng. [Hung Sheng is a very popular god of fishermen and the sea. Legend tells of his being an official who was killed in foretelling the weather. On this day, fishing communities stage operas and hold great feasts.]

Day 15　Birthday of Lao Tzu. [The founder figure of Taoism, reputed to have lived c. 550 BCE and to have written the T'ao-te Ching.]
　　　　Birthday of General Yo Shuai.

Day 18　Birthday of the Ruler of the Fourth Court of Hell. [Ruled by King Wu Kuan, the fourth Hell is reserved for cheats, frauds and people who let their animals disturb others.]

Day 19　Birthday of Kuan Yin. [The most popular and beloved of all Chinese deities. The goddess of Mercy, she was the daughter of a king who wished to marry her off. She, however, wished to be a Buddhist nun. After terrible trials she was killed on her father's orders. Descending to the Ten Courts of Hell, she transformed them by her merit into places of bliss. She was given life again in order to preserve Hell's role! In her new incarnation she saved her father's life. He was brought to Buddhism by this act. Kuan Yin is much revered by women and comes to those who are ill or in need. For instance, it is she who pulls Monkey out of his greatest difficulties on the journey to India. See also Sixth Moon, Day 19.]

觀
音
旦

Day 20　Birthday of Pu-hsien. [The title of the all-pervading Buddha or Bodhisattva. He sits with Manjushri Buddha on either side of the Buddha.]

Day 25　Birthday of the Ruler of the Whole Heavens. [Celebration of all in the Palace of Heaven.]

Third Moon

Day 1　Birthday of the Ruler of the Second Court of Hell. [King Ch'u Chiang. The second Hell contains a great frozen lake where the damned are tortured.]

Day 3　Birthday of Pak Tai. [Guardian of the north. There are many legends about Pak Tai, the best known of which is that the earth was being ravaged by a giant snake and tortoise. The gods sent Pak Tai to defeat them. A very popular deity in the south.]

Day 4　Birthday of the secretary to the Jade Emperor.

Day 6　Birthday of Ch'ang Lao. [This is a day for remembering the elderly.]

Day 8   *Birthday of the Ruler of the Sixth Court of Hell.*
[King Pien Ch'eng deals with those who challenge or
abuse Heaven, earth or the North Star.]

Day 10   *Birthday of one of the gods of the Five Directions*
[east, west, north, south, centre].

Day 12   *Birthday of Chung Yang, one of the Five-Ways*
Spirits. [The Five Ways refer to fates or destinies.
Each destiny has an aweful spirit attached to it.]

Day 15   *Birthday of the god of medicine.*
Birthday of General Chao [a god of wealth].

Day 16   *Birthday of Ch'un T'i. [Known as the Queen of*
Heaven by Taoists and as Maritchi to Buddhists, she
is shown with eight arms and is seen as a goddess of
light.]

Day 18   *Birthday of the god of the Central Mountain.*
[Believed to have been the General Wen P'ing, who
died in the semi-mythological struggles at the end of
the Yin dynasty, c. 1030 BCE.]

Day 19   *Birthday of the Sun.*

Day 23   *Birthday of the Empress of Heaven. [Also known as*

天   *Queen or Mother of Heaven. T'ien Ha is a very*

后   *popular deity. She is also revered as a goddess of the*
sea and great festivities lasting a number of days take

旦   *place around the 23rd day. Reputedly born in the*
tenth century CE, she had a miraculous birth and her
name was Lin Ma-tzu. A follower of Kuan Yin, she
was very devout. One day she fell into a trance
during which she saw her brothers and father in
danger on the sea. She led her brothers to safety
across the raging seas, but her mother woke her from
her trance – not realizing what was happening –
before her father was rescued. She died aged twenty-
eight, but was seen many times after that, always
helping people in danger on the sea. In 1683, as a
reward for assisting the Chinese fleet in their
recapture of Taiwan, Lin Ma-tzu became Queen or
Empress of Heaven. She is much venerated and
women often simply refer to her as 'Mother'. Great
operas are staged for her benefit along the coastal
areas such as Hong Kong and Macau.]

Day 27   *Birthday of General Ch'e [a famous soldier who*
became an Immortal].

Day 28   *Birthday of the sage Ts'ang-hsieh [reputed inventor*
of writing].

Fourth Moon

Day 1 Birthday of the Ruler of the Eighth Court of Hell. [King Tu Shih rules over the Hell for ungrateful subordinates or sons.]

Day 4 Birthday of Wen Shu Buddha. [This is Maitraya Buddha, the popular Buddha of Wisdom.]

Day 8 Birthday or celebration day for the Three Realms. [In Buddhist philosophy there are three realms of reality. The first is that of sensual desire. The second is that of form or substance. The third is that of the formless, sense-less world of pure spirit. Sometimes celebrated as Buddha's birthday.]
Birthday of the Ruler of the Ninth Court of Hell. [King P'ing Teng. The place for murderers and other committers of terrible crimes. They have to stay until all their victims have been reborn.]

Day 10 Birthday of one of the gods of the Five Directions.

Day 14 Birthday of Lu Tung-pin. [One of the Eight Immortals and thus very popular. Born 798 CE, he was an official who one day, after drinking rice wine, fell asleep. He dreamed that he was promoted. Honour after honour came his way. For fifty years he was top dog. Then he fell. He was exiled and his family wiped out. Lu awoke and realized the transient nature of life. He became a Taoist hermit and was famed for his wisdom. He is usually shown holding a baby boy.]

Day 15 Birthday of Chung Li. [He is another of the Eight Immortals. Born c. 3000 BCE, he was a powerful soldier who became a hermit in old age. He is usually shown holding either a feather fan or a peach of immortality.]

Day 17 Birthday of the goddess of midwifery.

Day 18 Birthday of Hua T'o [celebrated as the first doctor in China].
Birthday of the Ruler of the Pole Star [a favourite deity of fortune-tellers and astrologers].
Birthday of Sung San Sei Ma [a venerated fighter and official from the period of the Three Kingdoms, 221–65 CE].

Day 20 Birthday of Mien-kuang [goddess of eyes and eye diseases].

Day 23 Birthday of the Worthy Virtue [the festival of the literati].

Day 26 Birthday of Chung Shan [a general from the Han period, c. 200 CE].

Day 28 Birthday of Yao Wang. [King of medicine or the
Bodhisattva of medicine, he is one of the most
important Bodhisattvas. His statue is found in most
temples and he is much revered.]

Fifth Moon

Day 1 Birthday of the South Star of Longevity. [The god of
longevity guards the start of what is considered a
dangerous month. One of the most popular of deities,
he is pictured with a high forehead, often riding a
stag, and he holds a peach, staff, gourd and scroll.
Around his head flies a bat. These are all symbols of
longevity. He, along with two other star deities, those
of happiness and wealth, appears in just about every
shop, restaurant or business.]

Day 5 Day for sacrifices to the Earth.

Day 8 Birthday of the Mother of the Sea Dragon. [Seen as
particularly good for preventing disasters to children
and at sea.]

Day 10 Birthday of one of the gods of the Five Directions.

Day 11 Birthday of the City God. [Each city has a guardian
deity who appoints local deities for each area. Many
of these city deities are in fact former officials who
ruled a city or area well.]

Day 12 Birthday of the son of the god Tai-shan.

Day 13 Birthday of Kuan P'ing, son of Kuan Ti. [Kuan Ti
is the god of war and in many places this day is
celebrated as his festival. A historical figure from the
period of the Three Kingdoms, he and his two friends
pledged themselves to fight in defence of the poor and
oppressed. After many battles, betrayals and fights,
Kuan was killed. He was later deified as god of war
and, of course, peace. He is the patron of the martial
arts. Students pray in front of his shrine before
practices, to remind themselves that strength must be
used for justice. A very popular god, his festival day
is one for feasts and displays. See also Sixth Moon,
Day 24.]

Day 16 Festival of the day Heaven and Earth united and
如 天 creation began. [Chinese creation stories picture
来 地 Heaven and Earth being produced from chaos. From
佛 造 Heaven and Earth come forth yin and yang. From
旦 化 these two vital forces come the four seasons, the Five
之 Elements and all creation.]
神 Birthday of Tathagata Buddha. [This refers to the
historical manifestation of Buddha in earthly form
such as Gautama the Prince.]

Day 18   Birthday of the Old Royal Mother. *[Chief goddess of
the Immortals, she cares for the peach orchard where
the peaches of longevity grow. It was her garden that
Monkey desecrated when he ate the 3000-year-old
peaches. She is seen as a dispenser of long life and
thus much revered.]*

Day 20   Birthday of Tan-yang Ma *[a Taoist sage].*

Day 29   Birthday of Hsu-wei Hsien Wang *[a minister during
the T'ang dynasty].*

Sixth Moon

Day 1   Birthday of Wei T'o. *[Guardian Bodhisattva who
helped create the world. He stands with drawn sword
and fierce face outside most Buddhist temples.]*

Day 6   Birthday of Yang Sze Tsiang-kun *[a general
renowned for his filial piety].*
Birthday of Ts'ui-fu. *[An official who was much
loved. He became a city god and then was given the
role of assisting people through the Courts of Hell.]*
Day for remembering T'ai Shan. *[Although this is
actually called a birthday, it is in fact a day to recall
the giving of revelations on T'ai Shan, which
literally means 'large or lofty mountain'. T'ai Shan is
the most important of the Five Sacred Mountains.
Regular pilgrimages are still made there from all
parts of China. Every historical and mythological
figure of any importance went to T'ai Shan. In 1008
CE a magnificent Imperial procession occurred, during
which the Emperor received a revelation from
Heaven. This day commemorates this.]*

Day 10   Birthday of the Immortal Lin-hai. *[A Taoist
Immortal who had two major lives. Once, as a
minister, he was visited by Han Chung-li, one of the
Eight Immortals. Through discussion, Lin realized
the pointless nature of honour. He became an ascetic.
Later, in another life, he was born as a servant.
Various miraculous events showed him to be an
Immortal. He is often pictured as a boy with a string
of cash (Chinese pierced coins) and a frog. He is
popular because he aids financial ventures.]*

Day 12   Birthday of P'eng Cho *[a general who was deified
for his feats].*
Birthday of wells and streams.

Day 13   Birthday of Lu Pan. *[The patron deity of builders,
Lu Pan is reputed to have lived in the sixth century
BCE and to have been a gifted carpenter. In his*

*middle age he became a hermit and learned magic
skills. These he combined with his carpentry to
produce wonderful machines and creations. He is
invoked whenever a new building begins and the
ceremony of raising the beam of a new house (see
p. 191), is dedicated to him.]*

Day 19   Birthday of Kuan Yin. [This is the second date given
          as Kuan Yin's birthday – see Second Moon, Day 19.
          A lesser feast than the earlier one, this day usually
          commemorated the granting of Bodhisattva status
          on Kuan Yin. As a Bodhisattva, she has delayed
          her full Buddhahood in order to save suffering
          humans.]

Day 23   Birthday of Ma Wong [the King of the Horses].

Day 24   Birthday of Kuan Ti. [Kuan Ti is the god of war
關   (see Fifth Moon, Day 13). With his two friends, Lui
          Pei and Chang Fei, he is seen as protector and
帝   model. He is usually shown flanked by Lui and
          Chang and is greatly revered.]
旦   Birthday of the Fire God. [There is a whole
          Ministry of Fire in the Chinese Heaven and many
          legends abound about who the god of fire is and how
          he acts. A feared and yet also respected god.]
          Birthday of Wang Ling-kuan [a Sung-dynasty hero
          now seen as the gatekeeper of Heaven].
          Birthday of the Five Thunder Gods.
          Birthday of Hwo-hoh and the Two Immortals [three
          brothers who became Immortals and are respected as
          deities of peace and harmony].

Day 26   Birthday of Erh-lang. [This famous nephew of the
          Jade Emperor is an immensely powerful fighting god.
          It was he who, through skill in arms and cunning in
          magic, eventually captured Monkey, the Great Sage
          Equal to Heaven, when all the armies of Heaven
          had failed.]

Day 29   Birthday of T'ien Ch'u [the deity of the Great Bear
          constellation].

Seventh Moon

Day 1   Birthday of Tai Shung Lao-chun. [The birthday of
          Lao Tzu, also known as Tai Shung Lao-chun,
          meaning the very Exalted Lord Lao. This is the
          deified Lao Tzu, part of the triad of the Three
          August Ones. In Taoist popular thought Lao Tzu
          was but one incarnation of the supreme force behind
          creation. In his supreme form he is Tai Shung Lao-*

chun and it is this aspect which is particularly worshipped on this day.]

Day 7

康公旦

七宫仙女下降

魁星旦

Note: Double 7th [7th day, 7th moon] is seen as a very dangerous day. This is the month of ghosts and is not a good month for planning weddings or similar events.

Birthday [or festival] of T'ao-kung [a sort of Taoist Mercury or messenger of the gods who achieved immortality and flew away on a dragon].

Meeting day of the Herdsman and the Weaver Girl. [The one day of the year when these two stars meet in the Milky Way. The story behind this tells of the hard-working Weaver Girl, daughter of the Sun. He married her to the Herdsman across the Milky Way. Once married, she was so in love that she forgot her work and her loom. The Sun was so angry he separated the lovers. However, once a year they are permitted to meet. This is very much a festival for lovers.]

Day 12   Birthday of Chang-chun [a Taoist Immortal].

Day 15   Festival of the Three Taoist Principles [The Three August Ones who first taught humanity. See First Moon, Day 15, and Introduction, p. 15].

Birthday of Ling Tsi Chen [a Taoist Immortal].

Day 18   Birthday of the Queen Mother [of Heaven].

Day 19   Birthday of Tang Nien T'ai-sui. [The festival of whichever god happens to be guardian deity of the year and thus in charge of all births and deaths during the year.]

Day 20   Birthday of the god of the Palace of the King. [He helps the poor or needy to approach the royal throne.]

Day 21   Birthday of P'u-nien [one of the Patriarchs of Buddhism of the Sung dynasty, 960–1126 CE].

Day 22   Birthday of the god of riches. [Traditionally associated with T'ai Shan.]

Day 24   Birthday of the local city god. [Usually a more local city god than that revered on Day 11 of the Fifth Moon.]

Birthday of Tsao Sheng [a star deity who guards the Palace of Heaven].

Day 30   Birthday of Ti-tsang Wang. [A Buddhist title of a Bodhisattva who is usually identified with Yama, King of the Dead. Ti-tsang is a saviour figure who aids those in Hell. Yet so in a strange way is Yama, for the paper money burned at funerals carries his picture and his help is thus sought to ease the path of the dead. This day is thus celebrated as the King of the Dead Day, with the expectation of salvation or mitigation.]

Eighth Moon

Day 1　Birthday of Hsu-chen Kun. *[Known as the Dragon Slayer, he lived* c. *239* CE *and was made an Immortal.]*
Birthday of the Gold-Armoured God. *[Chin Chia is a god of scholars. Wearing his gold armour, he defends them from attack. If they are wicked, however, his sword will seek them out. His flag brings great fortune to a family.]*

Day 2　Birthday of the Village God *[subservient to the City God].*

Day 3　Birthday of Kitchen or Store God *[see Twelfth Moon, Day 24].*

Day 5　Birthday of the Thunder God *[a major figure for handing out punishment and restoring order].*

Day 10　Birthday of the Northern Mountain *[one of the Five Mountains and Directions].*

Day 12　Birthday of one of the Five-Ways Spirits *[see Third Moon, Day 12].*

Day 15　Birthday of the Great Yin. *[The Great Yin is the moon, its counterpart being the Great Yang – the sun. This is the day when the moon is brightest of all. See Major Festivals, Mid-Autumn Festival.]*

Day 16　Birthday of Monkey, Great Sage Equal to Heaven. *[This is a popular festival, for Monkey is both a cheerful trickster and a sort of Robin Hood or David-versus-Goliath figure. His miraculous birth from stone and his adventures in Heaven, where he extorts the title Great Sage Equal to Heaven, along with his subsequent fall and redemption by Buddhism are recounted in the great novel* Monkey. *See also Sixth Moon, Day 26, and Fifth Moon, Day 18.]*
Birthday of Chun Yuen Shih *[a general who was deified because of his teaching skills].*

齊天大聖旦

Day 22　Birthday of Jan-teng Buddha. *[One of the Previous Buddhas who came before the most recent incarnate Buddha, Guatama. Guatama Buddha is supposed to have studied under Jan-teng Buddha.]*

Day 24　Birthday of T'ao Yeh *[god of pleasure and wealth].*

Day 25　Birthday of the Great Yang *[the Sun; see Day 15 above].*

Day 27　Birthday of K'ung Fu-tzu. *[Known in the West as Confucius. He was born in 551* BCE *and died in 479* BCE, *having had an odd career as a minister and official, but mostly as a teacher. His writings have profoundly affected all aspects of Chinese life and behaviour. His own thoughts and ideas are best seen in* The Analects, *his collected sayings. He taught duty and responsibility as the Way of Life. He stressed obedience and filial duty as the cornerstones of society. He has constantly been the focus of state attention. Shrines to him were erected before 50* BCE *and honours were heaped upon him over the centuries. It is not without significance that he was a major target during the Cultural Revolution (1966– 75).]*

Ninth Moon

Day 1   *Remembering Nan Tou's Descent. [The god of the south constellation descends to rule over the deaths of humans. A preparatory day for this month much concerned with death and ghosts.]*
From Day 1 to Day 9, the nine spirits of the North Star come to Earth. [This is an official period of fasting.]

Day 9   *Birthday of the Heavenly Queen. [This deity lives in the Dipper constellation.]*

斗
母
旦

Birthday or Festival of Chung Yang. [This is one of the major festivals and it is unusual for it to be listed here, as well as on the appropriate day of the calendar. See Major Festivals, p. 199.]
Festival to commemorate Kuan Ti becoming an Immortal. [Kuan Ti's day of ascension into Heaven to become the god of war. See Fifth Moon, Day 13.]
Birthday of Buddha holding tower.

Day 15   *Birthday of the Sage of the Principles Chu Tai. [The leading light in Chinese philosophy, Chu Hsi, called here Great Chu, lived in the twelfth century* CE *and was a major Confucian thinker and policy maker. His commentaries, such as* T'san T'ung Ch'i K'ao I *and* T'ung Chien Kang Mu, *are still considered standard texts.*

Day 17   *Birthday of King Golden Dragon. [One of the four dragon kings of the four points of the compass. A major force for good.]*
Birthday of Hsien Feng [a general who blesses warriors].

Day 18   *Birthday of the Sage of the Principles Tsang Sheng. [Holy Tsang, a Taoist Immortal who is supposed to have invented writing. This is a good day to seek blessings on grain stores.]*

Day 19	Festival of Kuan Yin's departure from Earth and becoming a Bodhisattva. [See Second Moon, Day 19.]
Day 29	Birthday of Great Ruler Hua-kuang. [He protects from fire.]

Tenth Moon

Day 1	Birthday of the Eastern Ruler. [Festival of the planet Jupiter. A time for remembering the dead.]
Day 2	Birthday of Chou Tsiang Kun [Wise Immortal Chou].
Day 3	Birthday of Erh Mao Chen Chun [a deified general].
Day 5	Birthday of Ta-Mo. [The festival of the great Buddhist teacher and missionary, Bodhidharma, a semi-historical, semi-mythological figure who was preaching and travelling in the sixth century CE. He is the founding patriarch of Ch'en Buddhism, best known through its Japanese development of Zen.]
Day 6	Birthday of the Heavenly Rulers of the Sacred Mountain. [There are five sacred mountains, the most famous of which is T'ai Shan; see Sixth Moon, Day 6. The Heavenly Rulers are linked with these mountains as well as with the Five Elements. They are also associated with the five basic colours – white, black, red, yellow and green. This is a popular collection of deities as they dispel disease.]
Day 10	Birthday of the goddess of smallpox. [Formerly a much feared and revered goddess, on this day she is propitiated and asked not to visit.]
Day 15	Birthday of the Three Principles. [The third such event; see First Moon, Day 15, Seventh Moon, Day 15, and Introduction, p. 15.] Birthday of Ten Shen. [A minor smallpox god, Ten Shen is the one who actually carries the disease.] Birthday of the Sage Wen [a deified general associated with T'ai Shan; see Sixth Moon, Day 6].
Day 16	Birthday of the goddess Wu-shan [a deity specifically to be worshipped by married couples as a thanksgiving for their life together].
Day 20	Birthday of Heavenly Master Hsu-ts'ing. [The thirtieth Heavenly Master or Patriarch of Taoism in line from Chang Tao-ling; See Section 10, pp. 82–3. Hsu was a skilled alchemist and ascended to Heaven.] Birthday of one of the gods of the Five Directions.

達
摩
旦

Day 27   *Festival of the North Pole Star.*
Day 30   *Birthday of General Chau [a general also known as*
           Ma, from the Three Kingdoms period, 221–65 CE].

Eleventh Moon

Day 4   *Festival of the Greatest Sage K'ung Tzu Sheng.*
           [This is Confucius again. His family name was
           K'ung; see Section 32. Here he is given his full
           honorific title.]
Day 6   *Celebration of the Jade Emperor as Supreme Ruler.*
           [See First Moon, Day 9.]
           Birthday of the god of the Western Mountain and
           Direction.
Day 11   *Birthday of Tai-yih Heavenly Being. [This is the*
           Bodhisattva or spirit who relieves suffering.]
Day 17   *Birthday of O-me-t'o-fo. [This is the great Buddha*
           Amitabha. The story of Amitabha is found in one of

阿
彌
陀
佛
旦

           Chinese Buddhism's most popular books – The Pure
           Land Sutra. Amitabha is pictured as a comic
           Buddha whose compassion for humanity is boundless.
           Anyone who calls sincerely on his name will be
           released from some, if not all, of their rebirths. Those
           thus saved go to the Pure Land, a great western
           Paradise ruled over by Amitabha. Amitabha is very
           popular and his birthday is a time for sincerity and
           repentance.]
Day 19   *Birthday or Festival of the Nine Lotus Leaves. [An*
           honorific title given to Kuan Yin; see Second Moon,
           Day 19. The Nine Lotus leaves refer to the nine
           realms of Buddhist philosophy. Kuan Yin is in
           control of all nine.]
           Birthday of Kuang T'ien-tze. [Also known as the
           Festival of the Vision. He is known as Son of
           Heaven.]
Day 23   *Birthday of the Immortal Chang, Giver of Sons.*
           [One of the Eight Immortals, Chang Kuo was a
           hermit living in the eighth century CE. Various
           attempts to draw him into the Imperial Court failed –
           most notably when he died on descending his
           mountain to take up an office, only to reappear alive
           and well back on the mountain. His symbols are his
           white mule, a phoenix feather and a peach of
           immortality. He is a favourite figure above the beds
           of newly married couples.]
           Fast day when the South Pole Star comes to Earth
           and humanity; if you wish for a long life, do not
           harm any living creature and good fortune will
           accrue. [A day of strict vegetarianism.]

Day 27   Birthday of P'u An [the anniversary of the person
          who founded the first nunnery in China].

Twelfth Moon

Day 9   Festival of Ju-Lai Buddha. [This day commemorates
          the historical Buddha Sakyamuni's becoming a
          Buddha – achieving enlightenment.]
          Day of sacrifices offered by kings and princes.[1]
Day 15   Birthday of the Sage Wan. [A high-ranking general
          who was deified. This is a good day for prayers to the
          gods.]
Day 16   Birthday of the South Mountain and Direction.
          Festival of Supreme Ruler Lao Chin.
          Festival of Lao Tzu. [See Second Moon, Day 15.
          On this day certain of the household gods return to
          Lao Tzu to report on the family's behaviour during
          the year.]
Day 20   Birthday of Lu Pan [god of building; see Sixth
          Moon, Day 13].
Day 21   Birthday of the Heavenly Doctrine.
Day 24   Day that the Kitchen God goes to Heaven to report to
          the Jade Emperor. On Day 23 prepare to give
          messages to the Kitchen God and burn joss sticks on
          the 23rd at midnight so he can take messages to
          Heaven.
Day 29   Day the North Star descends to Earth to judge.
          [Preparation for the New Year, and a time to forget
          and forgive wrongs of the past year. A family event
          entirely.]
          Day when the Hua-yen descends. [A Bodhisattva
          closely linked to the historical Buddha. She also
          judges and grants forgiveness.]
Day 30   Day when all the Buddhas come down to judge the
          good and evil actions which have occurred through
          the year.

Section 47

THE SPRING FESTIVAL COW AND THE GEOMANCER'S COMPASS FOR THE NEXT YEAR

The Almanac ends with the picture of next year's Li Ch'un, the Spring Festival Cow and herdsboy, plus the bare details of next year's feng-shui compass (see p. 216). Basic details for the coming year, such as the size of each month, the dates of the Twenty-Four Joints and Breaths and basic forecasts of weather and crops, are also included. Thus the scene is set for next year's Almanac and the pattern and continuity, started so many thousands of years ago, rolls on.

丙寅年春牛交節圖

未得乙丑大有年　丙寅又恐慮魏燕
玄鳥高翔沿江躍　牛羊登垅荒野眼

全期桑葉初殘決　當年豆麻受熬煎
孩兒淚泣牛餐餓　荊楚相應稻花甜

日

正月小	二月大	三月大	四月小	五月大	六月大
十一日卯正雨水	十二日卯正春分	十二日酉初穀雨	十三日申正小滿	十六日子正夏至	初一日酉正小暑
廿六日卯初驚蟄	廿七日巳正清明	廿八日寅初立夏	廿九日辰初芒種		十七日午初大暑

七月小	八月大	九月小	十月大	十一月小	十二月小
初三日寅初立秋	初五日卯正白露	初五日亥正寒露	初七日丑初立冬	初六日酉正大雪	初七日卯初小寒
十八日酉正處暑	二十日申初秋分	廿一日丑初霜降	廿一日亥正小雪	廿一日午正冬至	廿一日亥正大寒

丙寅年流年事歎大利東西不利北方

太歲壓煞主

乙亥癸巳辛亥
甲申壬寅庚申
六生人 下半時
避之吉

亥壬子癸丑申六山忌用其餘各山俱利

是年三柔在北五黃占中宮歲破在申凡利神利

大金小神利 大歲殺煞 大年煞 坐災煞 坐煞煞

土王用事

三月初十日
六月十八日
九月十五日
十二月十八日

分龍 初伏 中伏 末伏
五月廿三日
六月初九日
六月十九日
七月初九日

是年太歲姓沈名興
天干屬火地支屬木
歲德合在辛室火
值年箕宿豹局遇
西日觜宿伏斷八日得
為九龍治水六牛耕
辛為暗金伏斷八日
葉行雷趙元帥值年
地大姑把蚕食七

地母經 地母曰

丙寅為歲首
蟲獸沿林走
疾疫多憂煎
燕子居山巖
牛羊宿高荒
蝦魚入庭隔
燕魏桑麻貴
荊楚禾稻厚

桑葉初賤不成錢
蚕娘無分却相煎
魚行人道豆麻少
晚禾幹枯多不全
貧兒乏糧相對泣
只愁米穀貴當年

春社 秋社
二月十六日
八月十八日

<u>APPENDICES</u>

1
THE TEN HEAVENLY STEMS AND THE TWELVE EARTHLY BRANCHES

THE TEN HEAVENLY STEMS

Stem	Character	Element	Planet	Direction
Chia	甲	Wood	Jupiter	East
Yi	乙	Wood	Jupiter	East
Ping	丙	Fire	Mars	South
Ting	丁	Fire	Mars	South
Wu	戊	Earth	Saturn	Centre
Chi	己	Earth	Saturn	Centre
Keng	庚	Metal	Venus	West
Hsin	辛	Metal	Venus	West
Jen	壬	Water	Mercury	North
Kuei	癸	Water	Mercury	North

THE TWELVE EARTHLY BRANCHES (THE HORARY BRANCHES)

Branch	Character	Animal	'Hour'	Direction
Tzu	子	Rat	23–1	North
Ch'ou	丑	Ox	1–3	East
Yin	寅	Tiger	3–5	North
Mao	卯	Hare	5–7	East
Ch'en	辰	Dragon	7–9	South
Szu	巳	Snake	9–11	East
Wu	午	Horse	11–13	South
Wei	未	Ram	13–15	South
Shen	申	Monkey	15–17	West
Yu	酉	Cock	17–19	West
Hsu	戌	Dog	19–21	North
Hai	亥	Pig	21–23	West

The Heavenly Stems and Earthly Branches combine together to form a cycle of sixty. The Heavenly Stems are repeated six times; the Earthly Branches five times. This cycle always starts with Chia and Tzu and is used to count days as well as years. (See Sections 2, 4 and 43.)

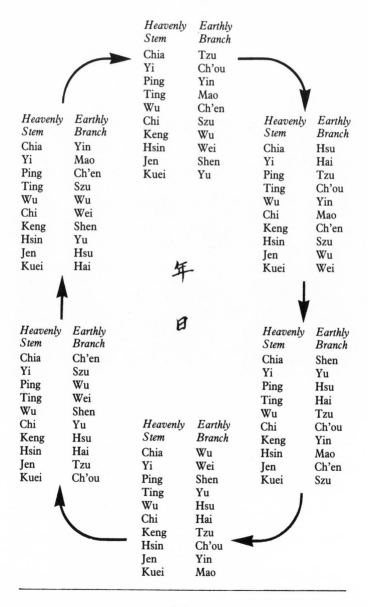

Heavenly Stem	Earthly Branch
Chia	Tzu
Yi	Ch'ou
Ping	Yin
Ting	Mao
Wu	Ch'en
Chi	Szu
Keng	Wu
Hsin	Wei
Jen	Shen
Kuei	Yu

Heavenly Stem	Earthly Branch
Chia	Yin
Yi	Mao
Ping	Ch'en
Ting	Szu
Wu	Wu
Chi	Wei
Keng	Shen
Hsin	Yu
Jen	Hsu
Kuei	Hai

Heavenly Stem	Earthly Branch
Chia	Hsu
Yi	Hai
Ping	Tzu
Ting	Ch'ou
Wu	Yin
Chi	Mao
Keng	Ch'en
Hsin	Szu
Jen	Wu
Kuei	Wei

年

日

Heavenly Stem	Earthly Branch
Chia	Ch'en
Yi	Szu
Ping	Wu
Ting	Wei
Wu	Shen
Chi	Yu
Keng	Hsu
Hsin	Hai
Jen	Tzu
Kuei	Ch'ou

Heavenly Stem	Earthly Branch
Chia	Wu
Yi	Wei
Ping	Shen
Ting	Yu
Wu	Hsu
Chi	Hai
Keng	Tzu
Hsin	Ch'ou
Jen	Yin
Kuei	Mao

Heavenly Stem	Earthly Branch
Chia	Shen
Yi	Yu
Ping	Hsu
Ting	Hai
Wu	Tzu
Chi	Ch'ou
Keng	Yin
Hsin	Mao
Jen	Ch'en
Kuei	Szu

2
THE FIVE CLASSICS AND THE FOUR BOOKS

At various points throughout the book we refer to the Five Classics and the Four Books. The following is a short description of each to assist the general reader, and details of English translations.

THE FIVE CLASSICS

These are often referred to as the Five Ching. Tradition states that they were edited by Confucius.

I Ching – The Book of Changes

Reputedly the oldest book. It contains divination methods based upon the Sixty-Four Hexagrams. The material is probably late Chou (i.e. pre-1000 BCE) with additional sections and general editing dating from 300–200 BCE.

The I Ching or Book of Changes, trans. into German by Richard Wilhelm and rendered into English by Cary F. Baynes, 2 vols., Routledge & Kegan Paul, 1951.

Yi King, trans. James Legge, *The Sacred Books of the East*, Oxford University Press, 1882, vol. XVI.

Shu Ching – The Book of Historical Documents, or Book of History

Much of the material in this book dates before 1000 BCE although there is considerable academic dispute on precisely what. Certainly the major part dates from before Confucius. The *Shu Ching* records episodes in Chinese history from the reign of Emperor Yau (reputedly reigned *c.* 2350–2250 BCE) to the Chou dynasty. A very important source book for the earliest calendrical material.

Shu Ching, trans. James Legge, *The Sacred Books of the East*, Oxford University Press, 1879, vol. III.

Shoo King, trans. James Legge, *The Chinese Classics*, Oxford University Press, 1871, vol. III; reprinted by Southern Materials Center Inc., Taipai, 1983.

Shih Ching – The Book of Odes, or Poetry

This collection of ancient songs or poems dates back to around 900 BCE and was probably in this form by the sixth century BCE. The poems give vivid glimpses into both the philosophical, structural world of that time and also the ordinary lives and emotions of the citizens.

She King, trans. James Legge, *The Chinese Classics*, Oxford University Press, 1871, vol. IV; reprinted by Southern Materials Center Inc., Taipai, 1983.

Shih King, trans. James Legge, *The Sacred Books of the East*, Oxford University Press, 1889, vol. III.

The Book of Songs, trans. Arthur Waley, Allen & Unwin, 1937.

Li Chi – The Record of Rites

This was compiled during the Early Han period (*c.* 207 BCE–9 CE). Some of the material dates back to *c.* 600 BCE. It contains duties, calendars and details of the Court and its officials. Of particular significance for the Almanac is the section entitled *Yueh Ling*, this being a complete copy of the Imperial Calendar dating from *c.* 250 BCE.

Li Ki, trans. James Legge, *The Sacred Books of the East*, Oxford University Press, 1855, vols. XXVII and XXVIII.

Ch'un Ch'iu – Records or Annals of Spring and Autumn

This is a very dry listing of events, from 722 to 481 BCE, which occurred in the state of Lu. Confucius is traditionally ascribed as its author.

Ch'un Ts'ew, trans. James Legge, *The Chinese Classics*, Oxford University Press, 1871, vol. V; reprinted by Southern Materials Center Inc., Taipai, 1983.

Chuang Tzu, trans. Herbert A. Giles, 1889; Allen & Unwin, 1980.

THE FOUR BOOKS

These are often referred to as the Four Shu – The Books of the Four Philosophers.

Lun Yu – The Analects of Confucius

More accurately translated as *Conversations and Discourses*, this famous compilation was made by Confucius's disciples *c.* 450 BCE and contains his sayings. It forms the most accurate and comprehensive account of his teachings.

Lun Yu, trans. James Legge, *The Chinese Classics*, Oxford University Press, 1871, vol. I; reprinted by Southern Materials Center Inc., Taipai, 1983.

The Analects, trans. D. C. Lau, Penguin Books, 1979.

The Analects of Confucius, trans. Arthur Waley, Allen & Unwin, 1949.

Ta Hsueh – The Great Learning, or Study

Written *c.* 250 BCE, it is ascribed to Tseng Shen, a disciple of Confucius, although certain scholars think it was written by a pupil of Mencius.

The Great Learning and the Mean-in-Action, trans. E. R. Hughes, Dent, 1942.

Ta Hsueh, trans. James Legge, *The Chinese Classics*, Oxford University Press, 1871, vol. I; reprinted by Southern Materials Center Inc., Taipai, 1983.

Chung Yung – The Doctrine of the Mean or *The State of Equilibrium and Harmony*

Written in the fourth or third century BCE by Kung Chi, the grandson of Confucius, it develops Confucian thought and philosophy with particular regard to human behaviour.

Chung Yung, trans. James Legge, *The Chinese Classics*, Oxford University Press, 1871, vol. II; reprinted by Southern Materials Center Inc., Taipai, 1983.

The Chung Yung, trans. L. A. Lyall and Ching Chien-chun, Longmans Green, 1927.

The Great Learning and the Mean-in-Action, trans. E. R. Hughes, Dent, 1942.

Meng Tzu – Master Meng – Mencius

The works of Mencius (*c.* fourth century BCE) are the fullest expression and defence of Confucian ideas and virtues. It explores morality at both the public and the personal level.

Meng Tzu, trans. James Legge, *The Chinese Classics*, Oxford University Press, 1871, vol. II; reprinted by Southern Materials Center Inc., Taipai, 1983.

Mencius, trans. L. A. Lyall, Longmans Green, 1932.

Meng Tzu, trans. D. C. Lau, Penguin Books, 1961.

3
DYNASTIES FROM *c.* 2000 BCE TO THE PRESENT DAY

Hsia★	*c.* 2000–1523 BCE
Shang or Yin★	*c.* 1523–1028 BCE
Chou★	*c.* 1028–221 BCE
Early Chou	*c.* 1028–722 BCE
Ch'un Ch'iu	722–480 BCE
Warring States	480–221 BCE
Ch'in★	221–207 BCE
Han★ (Early Han)	207 BCE–9 CE
Hsin	9–23 CE
Han★ (Later Han)	25–220 CE
Three Kingdoms	221–65 CE
Shu (Han)	221–64 CE
Wei	220–64 CE
Wu	222–80 CE
Chin	
Western	265–317 CE
Eastern	317–420 CE
Sung Liu	420–79 CE
Northern and Southern dynasties	
Chi	479–502 CE
Liang	502–57 CE
Ch'en	557–89 CE
Northern Wei	386–535 CE
Western Wei	535–56 CE
Eastern Wei	534–50 CE
Northern Ch'i	550–77 CE
Northern Chou	557–81 CE
Sui★	581–618 CE
T'ang★	618–906 CE
Five Dynasty period	907–60 CE
Liao (Tartars)	960–1125 CE
Hsi Hsia (Tibetan)	968–1227 CE
Sung★	
Northern	960–1126 CE
Southern	1127–1279 CE
Chin (Tartar)	1115–1234 CE
Yuan★ (Mongol)	1260–1368 CE
Ming★	1368–1644 CE
Ch'ing★ (Manchu)	1644–1911 CE
Republic★	1911–49
People's Republic	1949–

★ = Major dynasties.

NOTES

INTRODUCTION

1. Cao Xuequin, *The Story of the Stone*, trans. David Hawkes, 2 vols., Penguin Books, 1973, vol. I, p. 61. The Chinese title of this novel is *Hung Lou Meng – The Dream of the Red Chamber*, the name by which it was first known in English.
2. C. K. Yang, 'Confucian Thought and Chinese Religion', in J. K. Fairbank (ed.), *Chinese Thought and Institutions*, University of Chicago Press, 1957, p. 270.
3. J. G. Cormack, *Chinese Birthday, Wedding, Funeral and Other Customs*, La Librairie Française, Peking, 1923, p. 12.
4. Wolfram Eberhard, *Studies in Chinese Folklore and Related Essays*, Indiana University Research Center, 1970, p. 202.
5. Adapted from *Shu King: The Canon of Yao*, Part 1, Book 2, trans. James Legge, *The Sacred Books of the East*, Oxford University Press, 1879, vol. III, p. 32.
6. *Shu Ching: The Canon of Shun*, Part 2, Book 1, verse 8.
7. See Marcel Granet, *Chinese Civilization*, Kegan Paul, London; Trench, Trubner, New York, 1930, p. 18.
8. *Shu Ching: The Great Plan*, Part 5, Book 4, verse 8.
9. Ssu-ma Ch'ien, *Selections from the Records of the Historian*, trans. Yang Hsien-yi and Gladys Yang, Foreign Languages Press, Peking, 1979, p. 167.
10. Adapted from *Li Ki*, Book 4, section 1, pt 1, trans. James Legge, *The Sacred Books of the East*, Oxford University Press, 1855, vol. XXVII, pp. 249–56.
11. See Ssu-ma Ch'ien, *Records of the Grand Historian of China*, trans. Burton Watson, Columbia University Press, 1961, vol. II, p. 108.
12. ibid., vol. I, p. 263.
13. *Hsun Tzu*, trans. Burton Watson, Columbia University Press, 1963, ch. 17.
14. Quoted by Mark Elvin, *The Pattern of the Chinese Past*, Stanford University Press, 1973, p. 181.
15. *The Travels of Marco Polo*, edited by Manuel Komroff, Boni & Liveright, New York, 1926, ch. 44, p. 82.
16. M. Broomhall, *Islam in China*, China Inland Mission, London, 1910, p. 71.
17. *The Travels and Controversies of Friar Domingo Navarete 1618–1686*, edited by J. S. Cummins, Cambridge University Press, 1962; quoted in J. Spence, *The China Helpers*, Bodley Head, 1969, pp. 20–21.
18. Cormack, op. cit., p. 11.
19. *Selected Works of Mao Tse-tung*, Foreign Languages Press, Peking, 1967, vol. I, pp. 46–7.
20. J. Needham, *Science and Civilization in China*, Cambridge University Press, 1956, vol. II, p. 357.
21. Donald E. MacInnis, *Religious Policy and Practice in Communist China*, Hodder & Stoughton, 1972, p. 38.
22. *Religion in the People's Republic of China*, Documentation no. 6, p. 47.
23. ibid., p. 43.

24. *The Story of the Stone*, vol. I, p. 61.
25. Quoted in Needham, op. cit., vol. II, p. 269.
26. *Hai Nan Tzu*, quoted in Theodore de Bary (ed.), *Sources of Chinese Tradition*, Columbia University Press, 1960, vol. I, pp. 192–3.
27. *Shu King: The Zah Yueh*, trans. James Legge, *The Sacred Books of the East*, Oxford University Press, 1879, vol. III, pp. 433–4.
28. See F. Capra, *The Tao of Physics*, Fontana, 1983, pp. 161 ff.
29. *T'ai-chi-t'u Shou*, quoted in Bary, op. cit., vol. I, pp. 458–9.
30. *Shoo King: The Great Plan*, trans. James Legge, *The Chinese Classics*, Oxford University Press, 1871, vol. III; reprinted by Southern Materials Center Inc., Taipai, 1983.
31. See J. M. Huon de Kermadec, *The Way to Chinese Astrology*, trans. N. D. Poulsen, Allen & Unwin, 1983, p. 44.

SECTIONS 1, 16 AND 24

1. H. C. du Bose, *The Dragon, Image and Demon*, Partridge, London, 1886, p. 431.
2. E. J. Eitel, *Feng-shui*, 1873; Cokaygne, Cambridge, 1973, p. 7.
3. Needham, op. cit., vol. II, p. 42.

SECTION 5

1. Quoted in Granet, op. cit., pp. 376–8.

CHARMS

1. See the writings of the third to fourth century BCE Taoist sage Chuang Tzu, whose book is called *Chuang Tzu*, trans. Herbert A. Giles, 1889; Allen & Unwin, 1980, ch. 7, p. 90.
2. *The Annals of the Bamboo Books*, trans. James Legge, *The Chinese Classics*, Oxford University Press, 1871, vol. III, pp. 112 ff; reprinted by Southern Materials Center Inc., Taipai, 1983.
3. *Wu-shang Pi-yao*, ch. 24, p. 46, line 3, quoted in Michael Saso, *The Teachings of Taoist Master Chuang*, Yale University Press, 1978.

SECTION 18

1. *Shoo King: The Great Declaration*, trans. James Legge, *The Chinese Classics*, Oxford University Press, 1871, vol. III; reprinted by Southern Materials Centre Inc., Taipai, 1983.

SECTION 32

1. See especially *Shoo King*, ch. 5, Parts 25, 27 and 28.
2. See James L. Watson, *Emigration and the Chinese Lineage*, University of California Press, 1975, and Burton Pasternak, *Kinship and Community in Two Chinese Villages*, Stanford University Press, 1972.
3. Maxine Hong Kingston, *China Men*, Picador, 1981.
4. Melford Weiss, *Valley City: A Chinese Community in America*, Schenkman Publishing Co., Cambridge, Mass., 1974.

SECTION 40

1. Quoted in H. Doré, *Researches into Chinese Superstitions*, 15 vols., Walsh, Shanghai, 1914, vol. V, p. 218.

SECTIONS 42–46

1. *Li Ki: Yueh Ling*, trans. James Legge, *The Sacred Books of the East*, Oxford University Press, 1855, vol. XXVII, p. 249–310.

GLOSSARY

Astrolabe

An astronomical instrument used to measure the altitude of the stars and planets.

Bank of Hell

The paper money burned at funerals, during the festival of Ch'ing Ming and on other appropriate occasions is credited to the 'Bank of Hell'. It is believed that the accumulated credit is used by the dead to ease their way through the Ten Hells.

Boxer Uprising

So called after the secret society which, in 1899–1900, staged major rebellions and riots against Westerners and their interests in China. The society was the I-ho Ch'uan, which means Righteous and Harmonious Boxing – a form of martial art. The revolt crumbled after an unsuccessful attack on the foreign legations in Peking in 1900 which led to reprisals against Peking itself by an international force.

Buddhism

Buddhism entered China some time between 65 CE (the date of the famous dream of Emperor Ming who saw a 'golden man from the West') and 100 CE. Chinese Buddhism developed its own styles, schools and hierarchy. It took many centuries before it was finally accepted as part of the overall Chinese religious and cultural scene. It now affects and shapes, and has been itself moulded by, the everyday life of most Chinese.

Calligraphy

The use of writing as a decorative or art form. To be capable of fine calligraphy has always been a highly prized goal in China.

Cathay/Cathians

The European medieval name for China and the Chinese as used by Marco Polo, for example. It derives from the Khitan Mongols who controlled large sections of northern China from 960 to 1125 (Liao dynasty).

Ch'i

The life force, similar to the idea in Judaeo-Christian thought of 'the breath of God'. It is not life itself, but the motivating, sustaining power, which finds one of its major forms of expression through the Five Elements.

Chiang Kai-shek

Leader of the nationalist, republican and ultimately anti-Communist Party, the Kuomingtang (*q.v.*) – the National People's Party. Founded in 1912, it ruled much of China from then until 1949 when it retreated to Taiwan in the face of the Communist victories. The son of Chiang Kai-shek and the Kuomingtang still run Taiwan today.

Chronomancy	Belief in the magical or auspicious powers of time, particularly days. In Chinese thought it finds its clearest expression in the descriptions of each day in the calendar as either lucky or unlucky for certain activities.
Confucians	Followers of K'ung Fu-tzu (*q.v.*) (Latinized as Confucius). Confucians follow a variety of schools but have dominated Chinese social, economic and political thought for over 2000 years. Despite anti-Confucian campaigns in mainland China since the coming to power of the Communists, Confucian attitudes still influence aspects of family life and governmental policy. There is a religious aspect to Confucian practice, but it is not as significant as the moral and ethical dimensions.
Diaspora	A term previously used solely to describe the dispersal of the Jews across Europe and the Middle East, now also applied to the dispersal of Chinese across most of Southeast Asia and to America, Europe and Australasia. This dates from the early nineteenth century. It increased dramatically during the T'ai-ping Rebellion (1850–65). Fresh waves were also created by the fall of the Ch'ing dynasty in 1911, the warlordism of the early Republic, the Japanese invasion from 1931 to 1945, and the coming to power of the Communists in 1949.
Dominicans	Roman Catholic preaching order of monks founded by St Dominic in 1220 CE. Often the instruments of papal authority, they clashed frequently with the vigorous Jesuits who were more adventurous in their theology, particularly in their attitudes towards mission. The Dominicans vigorously opposed the Jesuits in China and were a major cause of the eventual open conflict between Rome and Peking.
Eight Immortals	Among the most popular characters in Chinese folk tales and mythology, they consist of both historical and mythological personages. They represent a range of virtues and attitudes.
Evangelical	Term used to describe a particular expression of fervent Christianity. Its roots lie in the large revivalist movements which took place in Britain and the USA in the late eighteenth and early nineteenth centuries. Firmly Bible-based and fundamentalist, it inspired, through intense personal conversion, many missionaries, especially to China. It was very intolerant of much in traditional Chinese culture and hence had an initial appeal for the founders of the T'ai-ping and others who were disgruntled with traditional society.

Five August Emperors	Legendary early rulers who followed the Three August Ones (*q.v.*). They reputedly were Huang-ti, Chuan-hsu, Kao-hsin, Yao and Shun. They are seen as models of behaviour and learning, upon whom all rulers should base themselves.
Five Sacred Mountains	Those in the centre, the north, the south, the east and the west. The most famous is Tai Shan in the south. They have always been centres of pilgrimage.
Gnomon	An astronomical instrument used to measure, by the casting of a shadow, the meridian altitude of the sun.
Han	The term given to the original ethnic Chinese. It comes from the Han dynasty. It marks out the main bulk of the 'Chinese' from the scores of other ethnic groups which have been absorbed as China has grown over the millennium.
Heaven	This is seen as both a primal force, as in the creation story in which Heaven produces yang and the Earth ying, and as a term describing general transcendent powers. In its latter meaning it has two main roles. First, as an impersonal force which directs, on a purely ethical basis, the workings of the world and of people. Secondly, as the sum total of the various hierarchies of gods which reach their peak in the Emperor of Heaven, the Jade Emperor.
Honoured parent	An honoured parent is one who adopts a child, usually while the actual mother and father are still alive. It is a fairly common practice for grandparents, wealthy friends or colleagues or relatives to adopt a child if they themselves are childless.
Hsun Tzu	Also known as Hsun Ch'ing or Ch'ing-tzu. He was a major Confucian who lived *c.* 312–230 BCE. He developed Confucian thought and policy at a time when China was taking shape at the end of the divisive Warring States period (480–221 BCE). While Confucian philosophy is at the centre of his teaching, he was also able to draw upon other schools of thought and to create a compatible system of philosophy. This ability to hold various streams of thought together came to be the hallmark of Chinese continuity.
Islam	The term 'Islam' means 'submission'. It is the title given to those who submit themselves to the One God as revealed in the Qu'ran. Those who do so are called Moslems or 'those who submit to God'. Islam, one of the major religions of the world, sees its distinctive beginning with the revelation of the Holy

Book, the Qu'ran to the Prophet Mohammed. This dates from the end of the sixth century CE. Within a hundred years Islam had spread from its Middle Eastern home base of Mecca and Medina (now in present-day Saudi Arabia) to much of Arabia, the Middle East in general, North Africa and through Persia to the gates of China itself. In China, Islam has remained a powerful minority faith, with its particular strength being in the Mongol, Turkish and other northern and northwestern areas. China has had Moslem rulers, most notably under the Yuan dynasty. Islam was also the basis of several large rebellions in the nineteenth century. The China Islamic Association today controls and assists Moslems throughout mainland China.

Jesuits

This order, the Society of Jesus, was founded in 1540 by St Ignatius Loyola. It swiftly became the intellectual and strategic spearhead both of the Counter-Reformation (the restructuring and response of Catholicism to the Protestant Reformation) and of the vast new mission fields opening up as a result of European expansionism in Asia and America. The Jesuits sought to combine Christian belief with the best of indigenous culture. The order was suppressed by the Pope in 1773 because of political fears about its power and influence. It was restored in 1814 and continues its role to this day.

Khan

Formal title deriving from the word *chagan*, meaning 'lord' or 'prince'. The title was given to the overall leader of the Mongols (*q.v.*). As such it was the formal title of the great emperors of the Yuan dynasty – the Mongols who captured China along with most of the Middle East, Eastern Europe and Southern Russian between 1240 and 1360.

Kowtow

The symbolic acceptance, particularly by vassal states, of the superiority and authority of the Chinese Emperor. The kowtow consisted of a ritual of 'three kneelings and nine prostrations' in which the supplicant banged the floor with his head to show his utter subservience to the Emperor.

Kublai Khan

Grandson of Genghis Khan, the military leader of the Mongols (*q.v.*) who conquered China and Central Asia between 1205 and 1227. Kublai ruled China from 1279 to 1294 and drew together a powerful intellectual Court. It was to this Court that Marco Polo journeyed.

K'ung Fu-tzu

Known in the West in his Latinized form of Confucius. Born 551 BCE, he died, to all appearances a failure, in 479 BCE. Yet his teachings, captured in *The Analects* and reflected in other works credited to him, came to shape the social and governmental structures of China to a far greater degree than any other person. He taught strict hierarchy and obedience, which was most clearly expressed in filial loyalty – that of the son to the father – and in subject loyalty – that of the subject to the ruler. His followers are known as Confucians (*q.v.*).

Kuomingtang Founded in 1912, the National People's Party arose from the success of the 1911 Revolution which declared China a republic. Originally a left-radical movement with strong links after 1917 with the Communist government of Russia, it soon lost its leftist identity. In 1927 the Communist and leftist members were brutally purged, leaving Chiang Kai-shek (*q.v.*) in control. From then on, the struggle for power in China was between the Kuomintang and the Communist Party led by Mao Tse-tung. In 1949 the Kuomingtang abandoned mainland China and fled to the island of Taiwan. Here they are still the government.

Lamaist Buddhists The form of Buddhism which in Tibet in the eleventh and twelfth centuries CE is known as Lamaism. The title comes from the Tibetan *bla-ma* meaning 'the Superior One' and was a title originally given to the most important teachers. Through the conversion of the Mongol hordes, and in particular the interest of Kublai Khan (*q.v.*), Lamaist Buddhism gained a powerful authority over Chinese Buddhism. Under later dynasties this was modified, but Lamaist Buddhism remained one of the most important schools of Buddhism in China, with strong links to the ruling families, well into the twentieth century.

Lord Khan Quoted in Mao Tse-tung's famous talk on superstitions (see p. 25) above). Almost certainly this refers to Kuan Ti, the god of war (see Section 46, Minor Festivals).

Manchu The name means 'pure' and was the tribal name of the Mongolian group which conquered China in 1644 and ruled until 1911. The Manchu's non-Chinese origin was a major cause of Chinese rebellion throughout the dynasty.

Mao Tse-tung Founder member of the Chinese Communist Party and its main organizer and theoretician from the 1930s onwards. Mao took Chinese Communism on its distinctive path by seeing the revolutionary power base as being amongst the peasantry. Throughout the war against the Japanese and then against the Kuomingtang (*q.v.*), Mao's policy was shown to be successful. In 1949 he formally announced the establishment of the People's Republic of China. From then until his death he was Chairman of the Party – hence his title Chairman Mao. In his last years he depended upon the ultra-left and radical young people in the Cultural Revolution (1967–76). He died in 1976 and by 1985 many of his principal policies had been overturned or allowed to decline under the 'new' leadership of the Communist Party.

Mongols
The collection of tribes based in the areas to the north of the Great Wall, who invaded China in the 1240s and 1250s and took power. The term was also applied to the Manchu (*q.v.*), who came to power in 1644.

Mother(s) of Earth
A dedication on the first page of the Almanac speaks of the 'Mother(s) of Earth'. This is thought to be a very early Chinese belief which pictured Heaven (*q.v.*) as male and earth as female and, between them, to have given birth to all life.

Mohammed
The Prophet Mohammed (*c.* 570–632 CE). Seen by Moslems as the last prophet in a line stretching back through Jesus to Moses and Adam. To Mohammed was revealed the Qu'ran, the Holy Book of Islam, and he founded Islam (*q.v.*) as a religious community.

Moslems
See Islam.

Nestorians
A heretical form of Christianity which nevertheless converted much of Persia and parts of China. Founded by Nestorius, who died *c.* 450 CE, it spread quickly across Central Asia from its home base of Edessa in Persia. By 635 CE, missionaries were active in China under Bishop Alopen, who founded what grew to be a powerful church, although they were mostly confined to the Turko-Mongolian tribes. Marco Polo met many Nestorians in China during his visit and two famous Chinese Nestorians came on pilgrimage to Rome and Jerusalem in the thirteenth century, even celebrating mass before Edward I, King of England. However, the crushing invasion of the Mongols (*q.v.*) seems to have wiped out most traces of Nestorian Christianity in China. The heresy of Nestorius was to teach that there were two separate persons in Christ, the divine and the human, rather than the orthodox teaching that Jesus was both God and man.

Pitch-pipes
It is unclear quite what function the pitch-pipes or pitch-tubes had. Twelve in number, they appear to have had a regulatory role in sacred music. However, there are hints, particularly in the *Li Chi*, that they were also

associated with regulating the calendar and may have been seen as quite literally tuning in to the cosmic forces which controlled the year.

Planchette writing The receiving of messages, apparently written without human assistance. This ghost or spirit writing often carries forecasts of the future and is very popular in China where a pointed stick and a tray of sand is used. The process is known as *fu-chi*, meaning 'to divine with help'.

Saracen The name originates from the Greek word *sarakenos*, meaning the nomads of the desert areas. During the Crusades the Western Christians learned the term from the Greek-speaking Byzantine or Eastern Church and applied it to the Arab conquerors of the Holy Land. Later, Saracen was used as both a general term for all Arabs, all Moslems and even all non-Christians.

Son of Heaven One of the main official titles of the Emperor. It was used to show that he ruled as the obedient son of Heaven, from whom he obtained his mandate to rule.

Ssu-ma Ch'ien Died *c.* 85 BCE. The first great true historian of China, Ssu-ma Ch'ien wrote the *Shih Chi* recording events from the semi-legendary Five August Emperors to his own day. He was both a court astrologer and Recorder or Grand Historian. His book is 130 chapters long and immensely detailed. The work established the pattern for official histories until the start of this century.

Sun Yat-sen Also known as Sun Wen, he was the leading figure in the downfall of the Ch'ing dynasty and the formation of the Republic. He had sought for many years to overthrow the Ch'ing and in 1912 was declared President of the fledgling Republic. However, the early years of the Republic were a period of intense civil war during which the Republican government was unable to hold power over all of China. Sun Yat-sen is claimed as a hero by both the Communist Party of China and the Kuomingtang (*q.v.*).

T'ai-chi The ultimate motivating force within the universe, and is the unity of which yin and yang are the basic manifestations. The roots of T'ai-chi lie back in early myths of chaos and order. In the philosophical thought of Confucians (*q.v.*) such as Chou Tun-yi, it becomes the Ultimate Power. In Taoist thought it is often associated with imminent Tao owing to its having created yin and yang, the Four Seasons and the Five Elements. Sometimes Taoists venerate the Three Heavenly Worthies or Pure Ones – T'ai-chi, yin and yang. The three are captured in the famous Taoist symbol ⑤. T'ai-chi Ch'uan – the meditative exercises drawing upon this power – has become well known in the West.

Taoism/Taoists

The philosophical and structural religious belief system which seeks to follow the Way – Tao. Its founding figure is Lao Tzu (*q.v.*) who lived *c.* sixth century BCE. Its key texts are Lao Tzu's *Tao Te Ching*, Chuang Tzu's writings called *Chuang Tzu* and Lieh Tzu's works, called *Lieh Tzu*. However, these have been interpreted and used in very diverse ways. Taoism split into two forms around the first and second centuries CE: Tao Chia – meaning the School of Tao – the philosophical, ascetic group, and Tao Chiao – Tao religion – being the more magical, structured local religious expression of Tao. Taoism can be seen as either complementing or countering the authoritarian moralism of Confucianism, by stressing the unknown and the unknowable, the mystic and the mysterious. Taoist symbolism, imagery and thought still deeply influence much of rural China, as well as the overseas communities. Since the end of the Cultural Revolution in China (1976) Taoism has begun to reorganize itself both on a local basis and through the China Taoist Association. The old mountain pilgrimage sites such as Tai Shan are being restored and are much frequented. In Taiwan, Singapore and Hong Kong Taoists thrive, and their expertise is increasingly being called upon by communities overseas.

Three August Ones

The earliest named figures in Chinese history. They are mythological figures and come before the Five August Emperors (*q.v.*). The Three August Ones are seen as having been sent by Heaven to teach the fundamentals of wisdom, agriculture and civilization to humanity. The most common list of names for the Three August Ones is Fu-hsi, Nu-kua and Shen-nung. They are reputed to have lived in a period before 3000 BCE.

Town and village gods

Under Tao Chiao thinking (see Taoism) a highly complex hierarchy of gods developed. Believers see this hierarchy as the model by which traditional Chinese society sought to organize itself. Thus, the Jade Emperor is reflected on Earth by the Emperor, the god of war is reflected by the Minister for War, and so on. At the most basic level, the town governor or village elder is the reflection of the town's god or the village's god – one being assigned to each community. The bureaucratic structures of Imperial control are also found in the gods. For a new suburb to open a temple to its own local god, permission must be sought from the town or city god within whose jurisdiction the new suburb is situated. Below these deities come the Earth Gods, literally the deity in charge of the area in which your house, shop or factory is sited.

Yao, Emperor

The Emperor Yao is the fourth of the Five August Emperors (*q.v.*) and is notable with regard to the Almanac because it was he who (according to tradition) established the calendar. He is reputed to have reigned from 2357 to 2255 BCE

Yueh Ling

The chapter or section of the *Li Chi* which contains the full calendar of Imperial activities and observations. This is the earliest (*c.* 300–400 BCE) complete copy of the calendar we possess.

BIBLIOGRAPHY

Hugh Baker, *Chinese Family and Kinship*, Macmillan, 1979.

Theodore de Bary (ed.), *Sources of Chinese Tradition*, 2 vols., Columbia University Press, 1960.

H. C. du Bose, *The Dragon, Image and Demon*, Partridge, London, 1886.

Juliet Bredon and Igor Mitrophanow, *The Moon Year*, 1927; Oxford University Press, 1982.

Marshall Broomhill, *Islam in China*, China Inland Mission, London, 1910.

V. R. Burkhardt, *Chinese Creeds and Customs*, South China Morning Post, Hong Kong, 1982.

Cao Xueqin, *The Story of the Stone*, 2 vols., trans. David Hawkes, Penguin Books, 1973 and 1977.

Paul Carus, *Chinese Astrology*, 1907; Open Court, Illinois, 1974.

Jonathan Chamberlain, *Chinese Gods*, Long Island Publishers, Hong Kong, 1983.

Kenneth Ch'en, *Buddhism in China*, Princeton University Press, 1973.

Chuang Tzu, *Chuang Tzu*, trans. Herbert A. Giles, 1889; Allen & Unwin, 1980.

Louis de Comte, *Journey through the Empire of China*, Tooke, London, 1699.

J. G. Cormack (Mrs), *Chinese Birthday, Wedding, Funeral and Other Customs*, La Librairie Française, Peking, 1922.

Vincent Cronin, *The Wise Man from the West*, Hart-Davis, 1955.

H. Doré, *Researches into Chinese Superstitions*, 15 vols., Walsh, Shanghai, 1914.

E. J. Eitel, *Feng-Shui*, 1873; Cokaygne, Cambridge, 1973.

Mark Elvin, *The Pattern of the Chinese Past*, Stanford University Press, 1978.

John K. Fairbank (ed.), *Chinese Thought and Institutions*, University of Chicago Press, 1957.

John K. Fairbank and Edwin O. Reischauer, *China – Tradition and Transformation*, Allen & Unwin, Sydney, 1979.

Marcel Granet, *Chinese Civilization*, Kegan Paul, London; Trench, Trubner, New York, 1930.

J. J. M. De Groot, *The Religious System of China*, 6 vols., Brill, Leiden, 1892.

James Harrison, *The Communists and Chinese Peasant Rebellions*, Gollancz, 1970.

Tem Horwitz and Susan Kimmelman, with H. H. Liu, *T'ai Chi Ch'uan*, Rider, 1982.

J. M. Houn de Kermadec, *The Way to Chinese Astrology*, trans. N. D. Poulsen, Allen & Unwin, 1983.

Immanuel C. Y. Hsu, *The Rise of Modern China*, Oxford University Press, New York, 1975.

Hsun Tzu, *Hsun Tzu*, trans. Burton Watson, Colombia University Press, 1963.

Max Kattenmark, *Lao Tzu and Taoism*, Stanford University Press, 1969.

Manuel Komroff (ed.), *The Travels of Marco Polo*, Boni & Liveright, New York, 1926.

Lao Tzu, *Tao Te Ching*. The following editions and commentaries were used: D. C. Lau, *Lao Tzu*, Penguin Books, 1963; Cheng Man-jan, *My Words Are Very Easy to Understand*, North Atlantic Books, Richmond, California, 1981; James Legge, *The Sacred Books of the East*, Oxford University Press, 1889, vol. XXXIX.

Marie-Luise Latsch, *Chinese Traditional Festivals*, New World Press, Peking, 1984.

Joan Law and Barbara Ward, *Chinese Festivals, South China Morning Post*, Hong Kong, 1982.

James Legge, (trans.), *The Chinese Classics*, 5 vols., Oxford University Press, 1871; Southern Materials Center Inc., Taipai, 1983.

James Legge, (trans.), *The Texts of Confucianism, The Sacred Books of the East*, Oxford University Press, 1881–95, vols. III, XVI, XXVII and XXVIII.

James Legge, (trans.), *The Texts of Taoism, The Sacred Books of the East*, Oxford University Press, 1881–95, vols. XXXIX and XL.

Evelyn Lip, *Chinese Geomancy*, Times Books International, Singapore, 1979.

Evelyn Lip, *Chinese Temples and Deities*, Times Books International, Singapore, 1981.

Liu Da, *I Ching Coin Prediction*, second edn, Routledge & Kegan Paul, 1984.

Liu Da, *The Tao and Chinese Culture*, Routledge & Kegan Paul, 1981.

Liu Wu-Chi, *A Short History of Confucian Philosophy*, Penguin Books, 1955.

Michael Loewe, *Crisis and Conflict in Han China*, Allen & Unwin, 1974.

Donald E. MacInnis, *Religious Policy and Practice in Communist China*, Hodder & Stoughton, 1972.

Mao Tse-tung, *Selected Works*, 5 vols., Foreign Languages Press, Peking, 1967–77.

A. C. Moule, *Christians in China before the Year 1550*, 1930; Octagon, New York, 1977.

Donald J. Munro, *The Concept of Man in Early China*, Stanford University Press, 1973.

Joseph Needham, *The Grand Titration*, Allen & Unwin, 1979.

Joseph Needham, *Science and Civilization in China*, Cambridge University Press, 1956, vol. II.

Martin Palmer (ed.), *The Chinese Community in Manchester*, Sacred Trinity Centre, Salford, 1982.

Burton Pasternak, *Kingship and Community in Two Chinese Villages*, Stanford University Press, 1972.

Clifford H. Plopper, *Chinese Religion Seen Through the Proverb*, 1935; Paragon Book Reprint Corp., New York, 1969.

Michael Saso, *The Teachings of Taoist Master Chuang*, Yale University Press, 1978.

Joyce Savidge, *This is Hong-Kong – Temples*, Hong Kong Government, Hong Kong, 1977.

Timothy Severin, *The Oriental Adventure*, Angus & Robertson, 1976.

W. E. Soothill, *The Three Religions of China*, Hodder & Stoughton, 1912.

W. E. Soothill and L. Hodous, *A Dictionary of Chinese Buddhist Terms*, 1937; Motilal Barmarsidass, Delhi, 1977.

Jonathan Spence, *Emperor of China*, Penguin Books, 1977.

Jonathan Spence, *The China Helpers*, Bodley Head, 1969.

Ssu-ma Ch'ien, *Selection from the Records of the Historian*, trans. Yang Hsien-yi and Gladys Yang, Peking, 1979.

Robert K. G. Temple, *Conversations with Eternity*, Rider, 1984.

Donald W. Treadgold, *The West in Russia and China, 1582–1949*, Cambridge University Press, 1973.

Arthur Waley, *Three Ways of Thought in Ancient China*, Allen & Unwin, 1946.

Arthur Waley, *Monkey*, Penguin Books, 1979.

Melford Weiss, *Valley City – A Chinese Community in America*, Schenkman Publishing Co., Cambridge, Mass., 1974.

Holmes Welch, *The Parting of the Way*, Methuen, 1957.

Thomas Welch, *The Practice of Chinese Buddhism*, Harvard University Press, 1973.

E. T. C. Werner, *Dictionary of Chinese Mythology*, Kelley Walsh, Shanghai, 1932.

E. T. C. Werner, *Myths and Legends of China*, 1922; Sinclair Browne, London, 1984.

Arthur P. Wolf (ed.), *Religion and Ritual in Chinese Society*, Stanford University Press, 1969.

A. Wylie, *Notes on Chinese Literature*, 1867; Paragon Book Reprint Corp., New York, 1964.

Journals of particular help are:

Ching Feng (quarterly notes on Christianity and Chinese religion and culture), 1974–, Tao Fong Shan, Shatin, Hong Kong.

Religion in the People's Republic of China, 1980–, documentation series, China Study Project, 6 Ashley Gardens, Rusthall, Tunbridge Wells, England.

INDEX